MEHRAB IRANI is a qualified chartered accountant, company secretary and CFA (Level I) with rich experience in investment research, portfolio management and investment banking. He has diversified experience of both equity and fixed income markets, including research, dealing and portfolio management. He has been responsible for managing the portfolios of a third party (mutual fund) and also proprietary money (corporate). He has also experience of investing in different categories of mutual funds including equity, fixed income and cash management. He has worked in Delloitte's audit department and has also done research on US and European financial services sector, including investment banks, money center banks, commercial banks, retail banks, AMCs and investment companies, brokerage houses, insurance companies, independent research service providers, thrifts, etc.

Mehrab is fired by an almost missionary zeal for spreading financial knowledge among investors and is utterly convinced that it is possible for anyone to become financially free. He has written numerous articles for many finance and investment journals and online websites. He also appears on various TV channels in India, like CNBC, ET Now, NDTV Profit, Bloomberg TV, etc. He also writes a widely read blog named www.intelligentmoney.blogspot.com

Mehrab is currently General Manager, Investments with Tata Investment Corporation in Mumbai, India. He may be contacted at mehrabirani10@gmail.com

Advance Praise for *10 Commandment for Financial Freedom*

"Money — a problem or a solution? Mehrab tells you how it is neither and then frees you from most of your money woes."

— F K Kavarana, Director, Tata Sons

~

"Mehrab Irani has done a great service to humanity by explaining the ten financial commandments to permanently free us from our money problems. This book is surely destined to instantly become a bestseller because everybody in the world wants to get free from the shackles of their money problems and this book is the best solution to it. This book will someday become an invaluable treasure."

— H N Sinor, CEO, Association for Mutual Funds in India

~

"Mehrab's first financial planning book seeks to be refreshingly different, where he has used his first hand industry experience to provide insights on how to attain financial independence. With a different way of looking at money, the book attempts to deal with complex financial subjects, and to do so in a manner which everyone can understand."

— Pramit Jhaveri, CEO, Citi India

~

"The book will serve as a refresher course for the professional investment advisor, a reference book for the seasoned investor and a textbook for the part time investor."

— Pradip Shah, Chairman-IndAsia Fund Advisors P Ltd & Founder, MD, CRISIL

~

"This outstanding book has seamlessly blended traditional and behavioral finance into ten unique commandments that serve as an able guide to investors along the path of sustained wealth creation and protection. Mehrab's lucid conversational narration of otherwise intricate topics makes this book a wonderful read and a primer to non-professional investors... a truly remarkable start by Mehrab."

— Dr Rana Kapoor, MD & CEO, Yes Bank

~

"A timely book in the ever changing complex global financial world providing a pragmatic way of understanding money, its intricacies and functioning." — Sanjay Nayar, CEO, KKR India

~

"The author's unconventional way of addressing conventional problems strikes a chord in everyone."

— Gopal Srinivasan, Chairman & MD, TVS Capital Funds Limited

~

"A mesmerizing book. Mehrab simplifies and decodes money while providing the reader his perspective on long term wealth creation."

— F N Subedar, Vice Chairman, Tata Investment Corporation Ltd.

~

"Having been privy to some of Mehrab Irani's previous articles, I have no doubt that this book will provide realistic arguments on financial independence." — Niraj Shah, ET Now

~

"Most people work hard at their jobs. Very few, unfortunately, expect their money to work equally hard for them. Mehrab's book is aimed at helping people do that. He explains how to go about securing your financial independence – something most dream of but only a few plan and achieve." — Prashant R Nair, Editor-Markets, NDTV Profit.

~

"A hard-nosed look at securing, multiplying and retaining money is combined with folksy wisdom on the role of money. There is no secret formula to get rich but the ten commandments enumerated in the book comprise the essential elements of earning, protecting, budgeting, spending, saving, leveraging, investing and insuring money. A distinguishing feature is the writer's belief that money for its own sake has no meaning unless it is utilized for some higher purpose. The simplicity of the book is enriched by anecdotal evidence, historical perspective and scientific rationale." — Ruby Anand, Jt MD, Capital Market

~

"Clear-headed thinking about money matters is hard to find in India. That kind of thinking is the very basis of this book. If you are keen to manage your money smartly, read it and apply the invaluable insights." — Debashis Basu, Founder, Publisher, Editor, *Moneylife*

~

"This book will teach people that wealth, both lack and excess of it, can be a problem if not backed by financial knowledge."

— Milind Barve, Managing Director, HDFC AMC.

~

"One of those books on personal finance that explore the myths of financial planning and admirably tries to unravel them . . . a must read." — Madhusudan Kela, Chief Investment Strategist, Reliance Capital

~

"Mr. Irani brings his expert knowledge to the readers which will be of great value to them in making important decisions."

— Dr Atindra Sen, Director General, Bombay Chamber of Commerce and Industry

~

"A fascinating book that makes you see money in a different way."

— Manish Chokhani, MD & CEO, Enam Securities Pvt. Ltd.

~

"Wise investors often say, . . . most people get interested in stocks when everyone else is. That is a poor choice. The time to get interested in stocks is when no one else is. You can't buy what is popular and still do well. In a similar vein, the time to plan for your retirement is when you are young and not when it is staring at you in the face. Treat this book as a Google map steering you in the right direction and helping take you safely to your destination, which of course is financial freedom." — Ramesh S. Damani, Member, BSE

~

"This book should help you achieve financial independence by making money work for you, rather than you working for money."

— Sandesh Kikire, CEO, Kotak Mahindra AMC

~

"Mehrab Irani has done a commendable job of writing this book which will lead you to the right financial path. This book, unlike many others available in the market, is not a text book and yet explains many important concepts in a simple fashion. If you want to learn about money and its behavior in entirety then this is just the book for you. It opens a totally new gateway in the way we think about our savings, insurance, wealth creation, etc. Not just this; the book also enlightens one on how to protect money from the various financial pitfalls once you earn it. I would call this book a must read for what it can deliver to anyone over the years." — Kailash Kulkarni, CEO, L&T MF.

~

"Mehrab Irani has the ability to demystify complicated financial jargon and turn it into investor friendly tips. This is a book packed with information, advice and suggestions for effective money management."

— Shernaaz Engineer, Editor, *Jame-e-Jamshed*

~

"A book that is a must have in these days of fluctuating markets and a challenging economic scenario."

— Ruzbeh J. S. Mistry, Advocate & Solicitor, Partner, M/s Desai and Diwanji

~

"The author has gone in detail covering various risk areas in the nature of speculation while investing in various asset classes. This in some sense also provide financial security in the form of awareness. And it also provides natural insurance cover as part of the discipline of investing. The book is all about knowing more about each asset class that an investor in India owns. It also goes on to explain the various finer aspects of these asset classes to give a better understanding. Very interesting coverage with length and breadth on various topics. I am sure the readers will find it useful for gaining better insight, knowledge to take informed decisions in their various investment activities. Every investor, rather individual, should have the foresight and discipline to put their money into better and efficient use so that the future is taken care of efficiently. Happy reading."

— Bala Subramanium, CEO, Birla MF

"First of all congratulations on writing an excellent book . . . . I had read a book on similar lines, *Rich Dad Poor Dad*. Not that I am comparing the two, but your book has become the bible of finance for me as it has been written in my context very pragmatically. After reading *Rich Dad Poor Dad* I was inspired to quit my job, get out of the rat race and start a business of my own. However, on the way I seemed to have lost sight of what I had set out to do. It is only after reading *10 Commandments* . . . that I got invigorated about my actual goal, i.e. achieving financial freedom.

— Unsolicited comment from a reader

10 Commandments for Financial Freedom

How to Stop Worrying About Money — Forever!

Mehrab Irani

www.visionbooksindia.com

www.vision**books**india.com

Disclaimer

The author and the publisher disclaim all legal or other responsibilities for any losses which investors may suffer by investing or trading using the methods described in this book. Readers are advised to seek professional guidance before making any specific investments.

A Vision Books Original

First Published 2013
Reprinted 2013, 2014, 2018

ISBN 10: 81-7094-876-2
ISBN 13: 978-81-7094-876-6

Published by
Vision Books Pvt. Ltd.
(Incorporating Orient Paperbacks and CARING imprints)
24 Feroze Gandhi Road, Lajpat Nagar 3
New Delhi 110024, India.
Phone: (+91-11) 2984 0821 / 22
e-mail: visionbooks@gmail.com

Printed at
Thomson Press
B-315, Okhla Industrial Area, Phase 1
New Delhi 110020, India.

Dedication

~

The book is dedicated to Mr. N. A. Soonawala — my mentor who encouraged me on the path to become what I am today.

Contents

Acknowledgements

MY DUE ACKNOWLEDGEMENTS TO ALL THE VARIOUS PEOPLE who have come in my life and left some kind of impact on me. I acknowledge my deepest gratitude to those people who have always been constant support and encouragement in my life. But more than that I acknowledge the irreplaceable help of my greatest critics since it was because of them that I was always pushed to revisit my limits and the more I stretched my limits, the more they expanded. Without them, it would not have been possible for me to advance my mission of gifting you financial freedom. I am deeply grateful for all those who helped me in my attempt to bring you out from the shackles of money slavery. I also acknowledge the help of fellow seekers, those brave people who exercise the courage to leave the crowd and deal with money as it is to be dealt with.

It is most pertinent to express my deepest appreciation to the entire Vision Books team for the support which they have shown towards me and my book. It would be wrong if I did not thank my publisher Kapil Malhotra who encouraged me from the very beginning. His untiring effort, timely advice and relentless service towards his duty in the face of extreme personal adversity is beyond description by words. It has been a great fortune to get associated and work with such extraordinarily people.

I would like to thank my parents with deep gratitude and high respect because if they were not there then I would have not been born, nurtured and grown in this world. They gave me an opportunity to enter this world and be of service to humanity.

My sincere thanks to my 7-year daughter Simone Irani because it is she who reminded me daily of the need for financial education.

As she commenced her schooling few years back, I realized that while we may get degree just by learning literature, science, mathematics, environmental studies, etc., that will not free us from our monetary problems. Looking at her going to school daily reminded me that school education is necessary but certainly not sufficient in this modern age of money and currency. People have to be equipped with a deeper knowledge about money, its intricacies and functioning. Besides school education, our future generations require a stream of knowledge and understanding of money and finance, including earning, protecting, budgeting, saving, spending, leveraging, investing and insuring with the ultimate aim of arming themselves with a complete perspective on sustainable long term wealth creation. It is my daughter who made me realize this urgent need by bringing me face to face with the grave problem.

Last, but certainly not the least, I express my utmost acknowledgement to my better half, my companion, advisor, savior and encourager — my wife Shirin Irani. I used to bore her everyday with my different ideas on money and financial commandments. However, rather than getting frustrated with my ideas she was the one who constantly encouraged me to write a book and do my duty of sharing my ideas with others as I did with her. It was she who consistently showed confidence in me that I would be able to actually write a book giving my message to the world. It was she who constantly brought me to the truth that knowing something and not revealing it is being selfish — it was my duty to share with the world the wisdom which I had acquired, irrespective of whether anybody listens to me or not. I thank her for helping me in leaving my mark in this world.

Chapter 1

Introduction

The Road to Financial Freedom

FIRST OF ALL, CONGRATULATIONS FOR BUYING THIS BOOK. By doing so, you have made the best investment in yourself.

Now, why did you buy this book?

Perhaps you did so because you realize that money is not the solution to your problems. Or, perhaps, because you understand that your financial problems are not going to be solved merely by earning more money. Maybe you did so because you are in constant battle with your finances and you actually want to win this game of money. Or, perhaps, because you want to learn about the behavior of money in its entirety, including how to earn it, how to protect it, how to budget, how to save, how to spend it, how best to leverage it, how to invest and how to insure it. Possibly you purchased this book not only because you want more money but also because you are eager to know the best ways of earning income and protecting it from financial predators, and how to pay yourself *via* budget surplus. Also, perhaps because you want to clearly understand how saving is not investing, learn how to spend in order to earn, how to save when spending, how to recognize the difference between good and bad debt and how to unleash the power of positive leverage, how to invest with proper asset allocation and understand the importance of financial insurance. Hopefully, you bought this book because you want to permanently solve your money problems by achieving financial freedom.

Why You Should Read This Book

So, why should you read this book?

After all, there are so many books available on self help, investment, finance, business and money. Is there really need for a new book on money? What is so unique about this book? Why should you spend your precious time, money and energy over it? What purpose will reading this book serve?

This is not a textbook on finance, investments or money. True, the book often uses some of the terms used in a finance textbook but it defines and uses them totally differently. The meaning and context in which the words are used in this book will probably not be found anywhere else. This book challenges conventional wisdom and thinking about money.

More importantly, you don't need any prior knowledge of any of these subjects in order to profit from this book. The only prerequisite is a burning desire to solve your money problems and start the incredible journey of achieving financial freedom.

I sincerely believe that this book will be equally useful both to a seasoned investor and new investor. I assure you that you will find this to be a refreshing new book on the age old subject of money. After reading this book, it is my sincere dream, hope and belief that you will view money from a totally different plateau.

Purpose of the Book

Moses received the ten commandments of proper living from Jesus Christ. This book gives you ten financial commandments — the ten principles of money which will help you permanently solve your financial problems. The ten commandments of financial freedom given in this book deal with all aspects of money and personal finance, including earning, protecting, budgeting, saving, spending, leveraging, investing, insuring, etc. with the aim of providing you a complete perspective on sustainable long term wealth creation.

This book will not teach you how to earn money — although it will tell you the most efficient ways of doing so. Actually, God has given all of us at least one unique ability or gift. We just have to recognize and harness that unique ability. How much you earn then depends on how much you develop your unique knowledge and ability with which you are gifted — and how you reach your highest potential through dedication, determination, hard work, sincerity, patience and perseverance.

Chiefly, this book deals with what to do once you earn money because earning money is not the complete solution to your financial problems — in fact, in most cases it is the beginning of financial problems.

Without money, you don't have any financial future. The poor spend their daily earnings on the day-to-day necessities of life and have no savings left. Thus, just earning money does not solve financial problems. There are also numerous cases of people getting windfall gains in the form of lottery winnings, inheritance, etc. who lose it all in a short span of time and get back to where they started or, in many cases, ending up in a worse state of affairs, mentally, emotionally and financially. This is because they just spend their new found wealth on wasteful expenses or in acquiring luxury assets thinking them to be assets. This book will show you the correct financial path to follow once you have earned money. It will open a totally new gateway in the way you think about money. It will deal with how to protect your money from legal financial predators, budget for yourself, save, preserve and take care of it, intelligently save while spending, distinguish between different money options and leverage, insure properly and invest in such a way that your money grows to reach a stage where you stop working for money and, instead, your money, as well as other people's money, starts working for you. It will show you what is best for your financial well-being and that of your family. It will break the myth that someone can grow rich and stay wealthy for long just by earning a lot of money.

The book will teach you the different rules of money. It will make you understand the different stages of dealing with money and how you can reach the stage of financial freedom.

This book focuses on how each one of us can achieve financial freedom. It will show you how we recognize money for what it can buy but don't understand money for what it is worth. We fail to appreciate that the worth of money might be different at different times. Then, too, a rupee may not be worth the same for a rich person and a poor person. It tries to explain why totally rational and intelligent people often make completely irrational money decisions. This book will touch upon all these and other areas.

Why Do You Want to Stay Poor?

Let me ask you a question which, on the face of it, may seem fairly stupid. Why do you want to stay poor? Your likely retort may well be, "Who the hell wants to stay poor — but where do I get the money from?"

If that's how you think, then this book is for you. Remember, money is the only thing in this world which is available in abundance. Am I sounding paradoxical? Think again; can anyone increase the supply of, say, gold, silver, oil, iron, steel, copper, sugar, wheat, rice or such real commodities at will? Certainly not. Mother Nature has given us these products which can be grown, mined or explored but in limited and finite quantity over a period of time. What about money? This is the only thing in the world whose supply can be increased at will — the government has just to order its printing presses to print currency notes and the supply of money is greatly increased in no time! Now you see how money is the only thing in the world which is available in abundance, and without any limit. Therefore, I ask you the simple question — when money is available in unlimited quantity, in abundance, then why do you want to stay poor?

Don't panic if you don't have the answer to this question. I am confident that by the time you finish reading this book, you would have found the answer.

What is Stopping You from Earning Money and Growing Wealthy?

If anybody or anything is truly stopping you from earning money and becoming wealthy, it is only you. Yes, this may surprise you but it's true.

If you think that being poor is stopping you from being wealthy, then you are mistaken. People like Gillette, Henry Ford, Thomas Edison, Abraham Lincoln, Mustapha Kemal, Reza Khan, etc. who were born very poor became rich and famous personalities of their time. And that was in the industrial age — when you required factories, machines, mines, etc. to grow rich. In today's fast moving information and technology age, you require nothing but an idea. There is a saying that there is nothing so powerful as an idea whose time has come. Equally, there is nothing so harmful than to keep thinking of old ideas. So just open up your mind and shed the myth that you require initial money to become wealthy. Remember that very few people in this world are born with a billion dollars in their banks and even if they are born that way, they are certainly not capable of taking care of their wealth, nor protecting and growing it.

This book is not about how you can grow rich overnight. Instead, it offers you a systematic plan about earning from the most efficient sources and then to properly protect, budget, save, spend, leverage, invest and insure money so that you always stay rich and wealthy and achieve financial independence.

How to Grow and Stay Rich

There are different methods of becoming rich and wealthy in this world and each one of them comes with a price attached to it.

But there is one — and only one — method which will both help you create wealth and stay wealthy throughout your life, in the process making you truly financially free.

The following are some of the methods of accidentally becoming wealthy:

- **Lucky Gambler:** You can earn money by being a lucky gambler. But very few can remain lucky in gambling long enough to accumulate wealth. And even if a lucky gambler is able to accumulate wealth, it's seldom that he / she will be able to retain that wealth and stay wealthy for long.

- **Lucky Lottery Winner:** Then, too, you could earn lots of money by winning a huge lottery. However, a lucky lottery winner is seldom able to keep that wealth throughout his life.
- **Lucky Marriage Gambler:** You can earn lots of money by marrying someone wealthy. After that, however, you have to spend your entire life with someone you don't love.
- **Lucky Inheritor:** You could become rich by inheriting wealth from your parents, relatives, friends or a well-wisher. Again, it is doubtful whether an inheritor would be able to retain the inherited wealth and stay wealthy forever.
- **Lucky Star:** You can earn money by being a lucky star — a movie star, a rock star, singer, sports star, etc. However, it's highly unlikely that you would be able to remain a star throughout your life. Once you cease to be a star — the probability of your being able to keep that wealth and grow it diminishes significantly.
- **Lucky Cheater:** You can become rich by cheating, robbery, bribery, etc. However, it's likely that your luck will run out one day and you will be caught by the authorities. Freedom from money also means living a worry-free life — what is the use of plentiful wealth if you are constantly leading a fearful life?

Therefore, it is not worth becoming rich by any of the means mentioned above. Neither do any of these methods guarantee that you will be able to always stay wealthy. Don't mis-understand me. Surely if you have some talent like singing or sports, or if you inherit wealth or win a lottery ticket, etc., then that's a start. The second, and the more important part, is to know how to deal with money at different stages — how to protect, preserve and grow your wealth so that you don't just become accidentally rich but stay wealthy throughout and leave a handsome legacy for your future generations or for charity. You have to achieve financial freedom in the true sense. This book is an attempt to help you do that.

Am I Qualified to Write Such a Book?

A moot question which should come to your mind is whether I am qualified to write this book. My educational qualifications include being a chartered accountant, company secretary, and CFA (Level 1). But are these educational qualifications enough for me to write a book on how people can become financially free? Certainly not.

I also have around thirteen years of experience in investment banking, research and fund management, both on the buy and sell side. But that, too, by itself does not make me competent to write such a book.

What, then, is required to write a book on winning the battle against money and attaining financial freedom?

In my view the only quality which is required to write such a book is the ability to understand money and its peculiar behavior because there is nothing as strange in this world as money. Nothing else can be compared to money. It is the only thing which is available in abundance and can be increased at the free will of the governments but it is so scarce that poor people suffer their whole lives for want of it, and the middle class simply becomes its slave. Therefore, the only qualification required to write such a book is an understanding of this most peculiar thing in the world — money — and a burning desire to impart that understanding to people at large. I humbly hope that I possess both these qualities. You, my reader, will decide whether my assumption is correct.

My Mission in Writing This Book

If you think that my reason for writing this book is money — then, yes, one of the reasons is that I want to earn money from it. As I mentioned earlier, God has given everybody a gift and we have to use that gift to our maximum advantage. I have the gift of writing and I am using it to my advantage. However, I would like to add one more point here. We have to use that gift of God not just for the purpose of earning money or pleasure; we must also use it for a higher purpose — for the service of mankind. If we use our gift just for the sake of earning money, wealth or fame then I am sure very soon we might lose our gift and not succeed in our mission. Therefore, while one of the reasons for writing this book is certainly to earn money but there is a higher purpose as well. And, remember, there are easier ways of earning money than writing a book!

The higher purpose which inspired me to write this book was the pain which I feel when I see the way people deal with money. Today, the rich are getting richer while the poor are getting poorer. We see millions of educated, sincere, hardworking people working harder but earning less, paying higher taxes, saving money which is constantly losing its value to the monster of inflation and then falling into a debt trap. We see poor people trying to make both ends meet by living a day-to-day existence. The middle class earn well but acquire liabilities mistaking them to be assets and fall in the debt trap from which they are seldom able to come out. The rich, on the other hand, just "invent" money because they know the rules of money. I want to make these rules of money available to one and all. That has inspired me to write this book. That is my personal mission in writing this book.

A word of caution; if you are in search for some secret formula on how to get rich with some hot investment or stock tips, then I dare say that you would be disappointed. This book is for students of money and investment written by a person who considers himself as a student of money and investing. This book is for a thoughtful, enquiring person who wants to learn and explore money and its mysterious ways. And once you learn that, you would be on the path to achieving financial independence.

No Retirement Planning in This Book

Books on personal finance and money usually contain a long chapter on retirement. Not this book — because this book will help you retire from day one. By learning its principles and rules, you are freed from the prison of money. You no longer have to keep working for money. Instead, your money starts working for you. When you reach that stage then you have attained financial nirvana. And once you attain financial freedom and are master of your own money, do you think you require a retirement plan? You have already retired from the money trap! And your golden years of old age would not be such wherein you would be cutting your expenses or living beyond your means. Rather, you would be focusing on wealth planning and thinking of the best ways of giving away your money to charity and to your next generation.

Money Cannot Solve Your Problems

Before we start on this incredible journey from being a prisoner of money to the attainment of financial freedom, I want to clear one misconception which has taken root deep in most people — that money can solve all our problems. I regret to say that money cannot and will never be able to solve your problems. It is not a lack of money which is the problem — it is the lack of knowledge about money and how it works which is the real problem. If you are poor and believe that sudden riches, say lottery winnings, will solve your problem — then you are grossly mistaken. In fact, that will put you into deeper problems if you don't have the right knowledge about money. You will be hounded by all kinds of legal and other financial predators and it is very likely that not only may you lose all your sudden wealth but even end up in debt — broken mentally, financially and emotionally. Therefore, both lack of money and too much money can be a problem if not backed by right knowledge.

This book is your guide to solving the problem of lack of knowledge about money and the unbelievable journey to financial freedom. If the book serves this purpose, my mission of writing it will be complete. I wish you all the very best on starting this money journey and great luck for achieving financial freedom.

—

Chapter 2

Commandment 1

Thou Shall Make a Proper Asset Allocation Plan

HAVE YOU EVER COME AWAKE IN THE MIDDLE OF THE NIGHT worrying whether the stock market will soon crash? Have you ever woken up in the morning fearing that your favorite mutual fund scheme will lose money? Have you ever been disturbed in the midst of a holiday by a call from your banker asking you to provide additional collateral on your mortgage loan since the value of your house has fallen? Have you ever grown distracted in the middle of a wedding function or a party wondering whether the central bank (in India, the Reserve Bank of India) will raise rates in its next monetary policy review and how that might affect the performance of your favorite bond fund? Has your mind ever wandered in the midst of important business meetings thinking what return you are getting on your liquid funds and how inflation is eating into your finances? If such thoughts distract you from your daily work, family and enjoyment, you are not alone. Most people undergo similar troublesome doubts. The good news is that you need not worry about such matters from now on because the solution is very straightforward and simple.

The solution lies simply in following a correct asset allocation plan.

Importance of Asset Allocation

The vital importance of asset allocation can be understood by just one fact. Ibbotson and Kaplan's research has revealed that 90% of the variability of an investment portfolio's return is due to asset allocation. This means that only 10% of the variability in portfolio performance is due to individual holdings while 90% of it is determined by how the funds have been allocated to different types of assets. Thus, too, only 10% of the return variability is determined by factors such as market timing and actual stock picking.

In other words, asset allocation is nine times more important than market timing or individual stock selection. This goes to show the overwhelming importance of asset allocation. However, most investors spend more than 90% of their resources, whether it be time, money, etc., in market timing and stock selection while less than 10% of time and effort are spent on asset allocation which actually determines 90% of the income variability. I stress this point to drive home the simple reason why a majority of investors derive sub-optimal returns most of the time.

Take Charge of What is in Your Control

Now, let us examine the same idea from a different perspective. As an investor, what exactly is in your control?

First, let us deal with market timing or the so called "top down approach". Are you sure that you will be able to perfectly, or even reasonably, time the market on a consistent basis? Can you say with reasonable conviction that you will be able to buy at the market's bottom, or close to the bottom, and sell at the market's top or close to the top? No? The truth is that it's simply not possible to time the markets on a consistent basis.

Now let us tackle the second question of stock selection or the so called "bottom up approach". Many research analysts and fund managers take pride in claiming that they have superior knowledge in understanding individual businesses and thus have an edge over the common investor in stock selection. The legendary former fund manager of Fidelity, Peter Lynch, has shown beyond doubt in his book *One Up on Wall Street* that a common investor is, in fact, in a much better position than the typical fund manager in spotting successful investment opportunities by just keeping his or her eyes and ears open to what is going on around. The success rate of entrepreneurs who have made it really big in the corporate world is less than

2%. How, then, can a fund manager consistently spot successful companies?

Thirdly, too much hype has been made about stock valuations. Some analysts take pride in doing discounted cash flow (DCF) analysis. For those not familiar with DCF, it simply means estimating the future free cash flows of a company — and then assessing their present value by applying a proper discount rate. This is perfectly right in theory. I also love DCF — but I hardly ever attempt to do so in practice. How can some analysts sitting in the comfort of an air conditioned office in a large city predict the future cash flows of a company producing something many hundreds of miles away for so many years into the future? How can somebody calculate the discount rate when even the best of the economists miserably fail in being able to predict even short term interest rates? If somebody can't predict interest rates six months down the line with reasonable accuracy, how then can it be done for the next five years with reasonable confidence? Again, how can somebody predict the market risk premium and the beta — a stock market measure of risk — with confidence when these things are dynamic and change constantly? How can somebody accurately estimate the "terminal value" of a business many years or decades in future when the management itself might not know it? When somebody can't predict the prices of commodities, which are the raw materials for companies producing steel or copper, and interest rates with reasonable confidence, how can one predict the earnings and cash flows of a company many years down the line? What a majority of the analysts do in real life is that they first decide the target price of a stock and then accordingly change the different variables in the DCF model accordingly to arrive at their target price! Thus it is quite clear that consistent long term success in stock selection is just a myth, a marketing gimmick with a lot of ink and time being wasted on it.

That leads us to the inevitable conclusion that the only thing which is in your control is asset allocation. In other words, you can decide how much of your investment funds you want to allocate to equities, bonds, commodities, real estate, art, etc. And this is what determines 90% of the variability of your portfolio's return. So instead of wasting precious time, money and energy scanning through various finance and investment journals, analyst reports, business news channels, etc., just be wise and by simply concentrate on your asset allocation plan. Remember the golden rule, whether it is life or investments, simple things always work far better than complex theories, algorithms, etc.

Understanding Economic and Business Cycles

Let us now go one step further which will confirm why asset allocation is the most important factor in determining superior long term risk adjusted returns.

Let us consider the economic and business cycles to clinch this point. Around the equilibrium line, the economic cycle moves from extreme contraction to over expansion. This is the same way in which an equity market moves from extreme under valuation to over exuberant valuations. The economy and equity markets behave like a pendulum — they swing from one extreme to another. That is why different commodities like steel, cement, etc. also move in cycles, as also do most agricultural commodities.

Let us now understand how different asset classes perform at different times in the economic cycle and which asset class performs best in each phase of the cycle.

Interest Rates Peak and Bond Prices Bottom — Best Performing Asset Class: Government Securities

An economic cycle begins as bond prices bottom out and, conversely, interest rates peak. This generally occurs after the economy has entered an over-heated or high growth phase. The preferred asset class at this stage should be government securities.

When Demand for Credit Declines — Best Performing Asset Class: Government Securities

Recessionary conditions in the economic cycle reduce the demand for credit as businesses retrench and consumers cut back on their spending. Companies then find themselves in varying degrees of cash squeeze at this stage of the cycle. Sales start dipping sharply and inventories pile up. Companies respond by cutting production and not ordering further raw materials since they are stuck with high inventory. A cash flow deficit results because of falling or dwindling sales which, in turn, results in forced short term borrowings at high costs. This is one reason why interest rates witness a parabolic rise at the end of the economic cycle.

Central Bank Comes into Action — Best Performing Asset Class: Government Securities and Corporate Bonds

The central bank then increases money supply, cuts interest rates, and frames new and easier rules for borrowing and lending. This results in lower short term interest rates at the shorter end and a steeper yield curve. (A yield curve is a pictorial depiction of the term structure of interest rates *via* a chart plotting the interest rate for each time period). If the market feels that inflation will soon return, then the yield curve will remain steep and investors will forego higher but risky long term yields in favor of lower but safer short-term yields. This period is all about expectations of recovery and inflation. The spread, i.e. the difference in yields between equivalent risk-free government securities and other bonds, is generally high at such times.

Equities Bottom Out — Best Performing Asset Class: Equities

Once interest rates have peaked — and bond prices have bottomed out — it's only a matter of time before equities, too, will bottom. This signals the end of the bear market though not necessarily the beginning of a new bull market because that may be some time away. Once the market believes that interest rates have indeed topped out, then stocks will be accumulated in anticipation of a recovery. During recessions, companies are generally more aggressive in cutting costs and lowering their break-even levels. Therefore the recovery in equities is much quicker and the initial rally from lows might be very explosive.

One clue as to whether the initial recovery rally will be above or below average might be the time lag between the low in bond yields and the recovery in stocks. Generally speaking, the longer the lag, the greater is the implied severity and duration of the recession. For example, in 1877, the lag in the US was four years and it was followed by a doubling of stock prices. In 1920 and 1982, the bottom in bonds and stocks was separated by about one year, and both the periods were associated with longer than average bull markets in equities. The 1920 period was followed by the "roaring twenties" which led to the great depression in 1929 while the 1982 bull market lasted almost eighteen years till the year 2000. The year 1981 marked the end of the near 50-year-long "primary" bear market in US bonds during which period long term US Treasury yields had moved up from 2.03% in April 1946 to 15.10% in October 1981.

One thing we have to remember is that the spreads between government securities and corporate bonds have to narrow, i.e. the borrowing costs for businesses have to come down, in order to put down the roots of a new bull market in equities; just a reduction in the yields of government securities by itself is not enough although that is the starting point.

Commodities Bottom Out — Best Performing Asset Class: Cyclical and Commodity Stocks / Commodities

Now bond prices have risen and stocks are rising in the economic cycle but commodities, particularly industrial commodities, might still be in a bear market. Typically, the price low in commodities occurs during the terminal phase of the recession, but commodities usually remain in a wide trading range and only embark on a sustainable advance once the economic recovery is fully under way. The final peak in commodity prices develops under a cloud of speculative froth as both individuals and companies try to cash in on the boom. That is the trigger for the next economic downturn, an increase in interest rates, and so forth. We can turn our clock back to the year 2007 and see how different commodity prices were rising and how companies were announcing expansion plans in various sectors, including cement, steel, construction, real estate, etc. The roots of the economic recession of the subsequent year were getting laid down perhaps at that point of time.

The above paragraphs summarize the different phases of the economic and business cycles and the preferred asset class during each phase. Now, somebody might well argue that it would be wise for an investor to position his investments in the preferred asset class in each phase so as to make the maximum use of the economic cycle.

However, in practice it is very difficult, if not impossible, to accurately predict the timing of each phase of the economic and business cycles. That being so, such an attempt would not only be futile but could also prove dangerous for your finances. What, then, is the solution? The answer is simple — asset allocation.

Some Historical Perspective and Examples

Equities and Bonds

In 1987, the year of the "great correction" in the US, large-cap company stocks delivered a return of just 5.2%, small-cap company stocks actually lost 9.3%, while ex-US stocks gained 24.9%. The opposite happened in 1992 when US small stocks gained 23.4% while ex-US stocks lost 11.9%. Further, during the period 1995-98, there was unprecedented gain in large-cap US stocks which beat other asset classes. In India, equities lost 50% while bonds gained 100% during the years 2000-2003. Thus, an Indian investor fully invested in equities witnessed his or her wealth diminish to half its original value while another investor with full allocation to bonds saw his portfolio double since interest rates — as represented by 10-year benchmark Government of India security yields — came down from around 12% in the year 2000 to 6% by the year 2003.

Gold

Commodities also move in a similar fashion. Let us take the example of gold. The one thing which most Indians love and also believe they understand is gold. A common person may not understand the benefits of investing in stocks for long term wealth creation, or bonds to enhance the purchasing power in a deflationary environment; he may hoard cash to preserve capital in an uncertain economic world but he believes that he knows the value of gold. Indians have traditionally been the largest consumers of gold. Importantly, most Indians believe that gold prices can only go up. Successive generations of Indian parents have taught their children to invest in gold because that is the one thing which "never falls in value"; also, financial advisors recommend gold as a hedge against inflation.

Now let us review whether this is true or simply a myth. Can gold prices also fall or is it some sacred investment which can never go down?

When investors are hungry for gold, the metal has a habit of rising exponentially which has no parallel amongst metals. While base metals still have to adhere to some form of demand-supply analysis, gold has decades of inventory lying in the central banks of countries around the world and so the inventory consideration doesn't enter the equation, unless these banks decide to sell their gold. Gold rose 2,300% — i.e. 23-fold — over the nine year period that ended in 1980, one of the most spectacular runs that any major financial asset class has ever recorded. Correspondingly, during the same period US equities went nowhere; during the first five years of that period, they almost halved and then during the next five years they doubled which meant that the return was practically zero over the 9-year period. Clearly, an investor who did not have gold in his portfolio during that period lost a "golden opportunity" to multiply his or her funds 23-fold even as equities returned practically nothing during the same period. However, does that mean that gold has always given such exceptional returns and that it can't ever lose value? To answer the second question first, after 1980 gold fell by around 70% over the next twenty years, while US equities delivered a return of 1,050%, i.e. they went up more than 10-fold during the same period (*see* Table 2.1).

Gold is, therefore, certainly not a sacred asset which can't ever lose value and did, in fact, lose as much has 70% of its value during the years 1980-2000, thus significantly eroding the wealth of investors who hoarded their wealth only in the form of gold.

Table 2.1

Historical Return Perspective — Gold vs US Equities

Asset Class	*1970-1980*	*1980-2000*
Gold	2,300%	-70%
US Equities	0%	1,050%

(*Source:* Dow Jones, NMA. org)

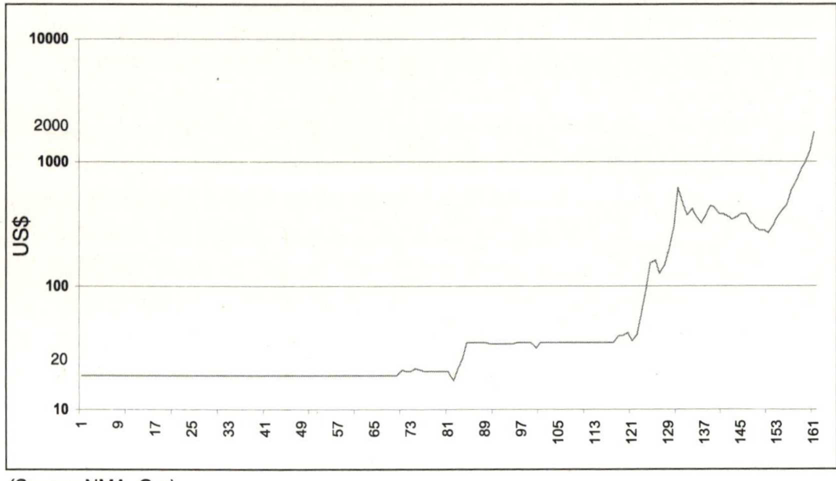

(*Source:* NMA. Org)

Figure 2.1: **160-year history of gold prices: 1 = the year 1850 and 161 = the year 2011.**

Now to tackle the first question, namely, whether gold always provides very high returns. A glance at Figure 2.1 will confirm a big no. Gold rose from US$ 18.93 per ounce in the year 1850 to US$ 1,750 per ounce in 2012, giving a CAGR of just 2.9%. This is hardly impressive.

To conclude, like any other commodity gold also goes up and down in value over time. Since gold does not have any actual industrial use, the value of gold in India depends on the value of the US dollar, real interest rates in US dollar-denominated assets, and the value of the Indian rupee *vis-à-vis* the US dollar. Therefore, an all-gold portfolio is certainly neither sacred nor safe for your financial health. This again brings out the undisputable importance of asset allocation.

Take the First Step — Resolve to Make a Plan

Before starting anything in life, whatever it may be, you have to always plan for it first if you are serious about accomplishing it. If you don't plan to win, then you actually plan to lose. Similarly, you have to make a proper asset allocation plan which will depend on your current income, tax status, your current expenses, future requirements, major expenses, such as your children's education or weddings, etc. You have to estimate how much risk you can tolerate, and then construct a portfolio tailored to produce the highest return for the level of risk you are willing to undertake. You should take all these factors into consideration before making an asset allocation plan. But, you have to make a plan. And, remember, that keeping the plan simple is the best rule for investing and long term wealth creation. Most investors seem to prefer complex rather than simple plans in the mistaken belief that if a formula is not complex and difficult, it can't be a good one. In investments as well as in life, it is the simple things which make us winners. By thinking about too many complicated and impractical solutions, we actually underestimate the power of simple, logical and correct solutions.

Also, many people think that investing is a very exciting process full of a lot of drama, information through print and television media, timing, luck, hot tips, etc. But don't forget that timing is important in family planning and tips are only for waiters! Some realize that they know very little about this mysterious subject of investing and hence they entrust their hard earned money to a so-called investment guru or financial planner hoping and praying that he will do better. However, they little realize that the so-called expert is equally, if not more, susceptible to the same emotional feelings and liable to commit the same mistakes as they are. When you invest on your own, you have to compete only with yourself and do better than what you had done previously. However, when an expert invests, he or she has also to compete with all the other experts and is continuously subjected to critical media review. Accordingly, he or she is much more vulnerable to committing common errors of judgment than you are. Investing and long term wealth creation and maintenance actually rest just on a plan — a dull, boring, mechanical asset allocation plan.

The Different Asset Classes

In making your asset allocation plan, you need to be familiar with the various asset classes. The broad asset classes in which you can invest include equities, debt, commodities, real estate, art and, also, currencies. Just to clear a common misconception, insurance must not be confused with investments because the former is meant for protection while the latter is the means to wealth creation.

The more important thing is to understand the different investment products available within these broad asset classes because finally it is these products you invest in. The main investment products available for an investment within the broad asset classes can be classified as follows:

Equities

- Common stocks
- Preferred stocks
- Large-cap stocks
- Mid- and small-cap stocks
- Warrants
- Convertible stocks
- Equity index funds
- Large-cap equity funds
- Mid- and small-cap funds
- Sector funds
- Balanced funds
- Private equity funds.

Debt

- Bank fixed deposits
- Company fixed deposits
- Income funds
- Gilt funds
- Short term funds
- Liquid / money market funds
- High yield debt.

Real Estate

- Residential real estate
- Commercial office property
- Retail property
- Warehouse
- Industrial property
- Land
- Real estate investment trusts
- Real estate funds.

Commodities

- Precious metals, like gold, silver, platinum, etc.
- Industrial commodities, such as iron, steel, copper, aluminum, zinc, etc.
- Agricultural commodities, like sugar, wheat, rice, chana, etc.
- Commodity funds.

Art

- Art and paintings
- Art funds.

Currencies

- Direct currencies
- Currency futures and options.

Insurance

- Term policy
- Whole life policy
- Endowment policy
- Money back policy
- Unit linked insurance products and as many more imaginative products as the mind can conjure.

Asset Allocation is Successful When You Invest in Non-Correlated Assets

Successful asset allocation is not simply investing in different asset classes. The trick is that the different asset classes you invest in should also not be correlated to one another.

Correlation is a statistical term which in simple language means how two asset classes or financial securities move in relation to each other. Correlation is computed through what is known as the correlation coefficient, which ranges between -1 and +1. Perfect positive correlation (a correlation coefficient of +1) implies that whichever way one security moves, whether up or down, the other security will move in lockstep in the same direction. Conversely, perfect negative correlation means that if one security moves in one direction, the security that is perfectly negatively correlated will move in the opposite direction. If the correlation is zero, the movements of the securities are said to have no correlation with each other; they are completely random variables.

In real life, perfectly correlated assets, whether positive or negative, are very rare and practically non-existent. The aim of successful asset allocation has, therefore, to be to invest in those asset classes and securities which have some significant degree of negative correlation. This would mean that when one of the securities is going down, the other one should go up, thereby protecting your overall asset value and wealth.

For example, as explained earlier Indian equities lost 50% while bonds gained 100% during the period 2002-03. Thus, these two asset classes, namely equities and bonds, were negatively correlated which helped the investor protect his or her wealth.

Determining Your Ideal Asset Allocation Plan

First things first; there is nothing like a universal ideal asset allocation. Every individual is unique, his or her nature and circumstances are different, as is his tolerance for risk and his or her needs and expectations. "Financial experts" might advise you that a young person with high earnings should allocate a very high proportion to highly risky equities, etc., which in my view is as stupid as standing on a mountain cliff and saying since I am young and strong I should take the risk of jumping off. As a young person, you may be able to afford a financially risky investment but are you emotionally prepared for the consequences? Simply because you are young or earning well does not mean that you just squander away your money on wrong investments. Being young, you may still be able to earn more money in the future but if you keep making wrong investments you won't be able to create long term wealth. Your focus should always be on long term wealth creation and, then, its sustenance. Just because you are young and earning well does not mean you can take unwarranted risks.

Later in the chapter, when considering the ideal asset allocation plan for different investors, we will be using the broad asset categories comprising equities, debt, real estate and commodities — art and currencies being the other ones.

Market Related and Non-Market Related Asset Classes

Broadly speaking, there are two kinds of returns which you derive from investments — accruals and capital gains.

Accrual is nothing but the reward for the time value of money — incomes like interest on fixed deposit or dividend on shares.

Capital gain is the reward for buying and selling investments with reasonably correct timing after holding them in the interim period. Examples of capital gains would be the profit derived from sale of shares, real estate, commodities or any other asset whose prices are determined by market forces.

All investments whose price changes are based on market fluctuations would be called market related investments. All market related investments have the potential of giving capital gains and, equally, capital losses.

On the other hand, an investment whose price is not determined by market forces would be called an accrual investment product. For example, a fixed deposit would be an accrual investment product where the interest "accrues" literally every day — though it might be paid monthly, quarterly, yearly, on maturity, or whatever. The price of an accrual product does not vary with the market.

Determining Your Basic Allocation Towards Market and Non-Market Related Asset Classes

Now that we know the difference between market and non-market related asset classes, the next step is to allocate funds to each category. This is the basic building block of asset allocation.

Generally speaking, I would advise an allocation wherein your entire wealth does not ever erode by more than 20% on a three-year rolling basis.

The reasoning behind this is quite simple — nobody likes to lose substantial money in a reasonable investment period of three years and your wealth should ideally not ever erode more than 20% in a three-year period. Otherwise, it will take really long for it to again grow because of the negative effects of compounding. Thus, suppose you lose 50% on ₹ 100, you are left with ₹ 50. For that ₹ 50 to grow back up to ₹ 100 would need 100% return on ₹ 50. Hence, due to base effect and the power of negative compounding, a 100% return is required to recoup a 50% loss.

I would, therefore advise that the maximum allocation towards market related investments should not be more than 75% of your total wealth. In other words, at least 25% should be invested in non-market related accrual products. The ₹ 25 invested in non-market related assets would become almost ₹ 32.4 at 9% compounding (accrual) while the ₹ 75 if properly invested in an intelligent and rational manner in the right market related assets would normally not fall more than 35% on a 3-year basis in the worst case scenario, i.e. to no lower than ₹ 48.8. Thus, the total would be ₹ 81.2, i.e. slightly above our threshold of 80%. Therefore, we come to the conclusion that a successful asset allocator would not invest more than 75% to market related investments. Within this broad parameter, Table 2.2 gives the amount of corpus permitted to be invested in market related investment options as per your tolerance level for losses.

As highlighted by Table 2.2, suppose you can tolerate a 50% mark-to-market loss on your market related investments, you may allocate upto 75% of your wealth to such investments. On the other

Table 2.2
The Asset Allocation Quiz — Tolerance to Risk vs Returns

Tolerance for loss	*In Market Related Investments*
50%	75%
45%	70%
40%	65%
35%	60%
30%	55%
25%	50%
20%	45%
15%	35%
10%	25%
5%	20%
0%	12%

hand, if your tolerance to mark-to-market loss is, say, only 10% then you shouldn't invest more than 25% in market related investments. Kindly note; even if your tolerance for loss is zero percent, i.e. you don't have any tolerance whatsoever for loss, I still recommend and encourage you to allocate around 12% to market related investments simply because addition of some market related investments, like equities or real estate, actually increases your return while reducing your risk. Therefore, even the most conservative investor should have roughly 12% of his / her wealth in market related investments to actually reduce risk and increase return!

You must also know how much time, energy and thought you can spend on managing your wealth. Ideally, this should be one of the most important objectives of your life and you should make ample time and energy for it. But the good news is that even if you are not too inclined to give too much time to managing your wealth, with an asset allocation plan in place, it's really simple for you to actually plan and implement it.

Model Asset Allocation Plans

I have made three kinds of broad asset allocation for three different categories of investors — ignorant, informed and enterprising. Obviously, these are indicative and very broad portfolios to help an investor to take his / her own decision.

Model Asset Allocation for the Ignorant Risk Tolerant Investor

Since this is the portfolio for an ignorant investor, I have tried to keep it as simple as possible without compromising on portfolio risk or return (*see* Table 2.3).

I have assumed 25% each allocation to large cap index fund and mid and small cap index funds. Then I have allocated 15% towards foreign equities for diversification on different markets, economies, geographies and currencies. Since this portfolio is for an ignorant investor, I would advise sticking to the largest market — the US. I have assumed 10% for commodities which could be precious metals, like gold and silver, and even certain agro commodities. Even an ignorant investor would have his / her niche area of knowledge; you can just concentrate on the commodity which fascinates you the most. Finally, I have allocated 25% towards medium term bond funds for portfolio stability and asset allocation. You would have observed that since the portfolio as meant for is a risk tolerant ignorant investor, the allocation towards market based returns is 75%. If your tolerance to risk is lower as indicated in Table 2.2 then you should adjust the market based investments accordingly.

Table 2.3

Asset Allocation for the Ignorant Risk Tolerant Investor

Investment Type	*Allocation*
Large cap index funds	25%
Mid & small cap funds	25%
Foreign (US) large cap index funds	15%
Commodities	10%
Medium term bond funds	25%
Total	100%

Model Asset Allocation for the Informed Risk Tolerant Investor

For a risk tolerant informed investor, I have allocated 20% towards index or large cap funds / stocks (kindly note the introduction of direct stocks in this portfolio). The allocation to mid and small cap funds / stocks has been reduced to 20%. The allocation towards foreign (US) large cap index fund stands at 15% while commodities is at 10%. I have introduced 10% allocation towards rental real estate. Remember, however, that a self-occupied house property is not an investment asset. It is an asset but it's not an investment asset because its does not yield you any return. You may need to buy a house to live in to save yourself unnecessary living expenses but that does not mean that it becomes your asset — for that, it has to put regular income into your pocket which a self-occupied house does not do.

Medium term bonds get an allocation of 15% while longer duration bonds are introduced with an allocation of 10% (*see* Table 2.4). In my view, this would be a simple asset allocation for a risk tolerant informed investor.

Table 2.4

Asset Allocation for the Informed Risk Tolerant Investor

Investment Type	*Allocation*
Index or large cap funds / stocks	20%
Mid & small cap funds / stocks	20%
Foreign (US) large cap index funds	15%
Commodities	10%
Rental real estate	10%
Medium term bond funds	15%
Long term bonds	10%
Total	100%

Model Asset Allocation for the Enterprising Risk Tolerant Investor

Table 2.5
Asset Allocation for the Enterprising Risk Tolerant Investor

Investment Type	*Allocation*
Index or large cap funds / stocks	15%
Mid & small cap funds / stocks	20%
Foreign (US) large cap index funds	10%
Foreign (emerging market) large cap index funds	5%
Commodities	10%
Rental real estate	10%
Collectibles / art funds	5%
Medium term bond funds	15%
Long term bonds	10%
Total	100%

For an enterprising risk tolerant investor, I have allocated 15% towards index or large cap funds / stocks. The allocation towards mid and small cap stocks / funds has been reduced to 20%. For an enterprising investor, foreign large cap index funds has been divided into two parts, with 10% for the US markets and 5% for emerging markets. Rental real estate and commodities have been kept constant at 10% each. I have further introduced collectibles / art funds with 5% portfolio allocation. The allocations towards medium term and long term bonds stay unaltered at 15% and 10%, respectively (*see* Table 2.5).

Some Other Considerations in Asset Allocation

Keep It Simple

If you notice, the model asset allocations suggested above are quite simple. Whether it is life or investments, simple things actually work better over the longer term than do complex and difficult ones. So, it's best to keep things simple as far as possible.

A test of whether your plan is simple or not would be whether in your absence your office assistant is able to understand and implement it. If he is not able to do so, then perhaps you have to review your plan to make it simpler. The other important thing is that asset allocation is not just a theoretical plan — it is something which you have to practically execute. Hence, it has to be kept simple so that you not only understand it but also easily execute it.

Allocate to Investment Assets

You have to allocate your money towards investment assets. I define investment asset as one which either yields income and / or has the potential to yield capital gains which you are in a position to book at a reasonable time and price. Hence, for an asset to qualify as an investment asset, it must satisfy the following conditions:

1. It should yield some kind of income for you. For example, a share will give dividend, a bond or bank fixed deposit will give interest, while a rental real estate will reward you with rent. A self occupied house property does not give you any income. So although it might be an asset but it does not qualify as an investment asset.
2. It should have the potential to give future capital gains. For example, an equity share, bond or real estate all have the potential to appreciate in value and hence the potential to give you capital gains. However, a bank fixed deposit will never appreciate in value and so can't provide you with capital gains. Despite that, a bank fixed deposit would be classified as an investment asset because it yields income in the form of interest.
3. The last but a very important point is that you should be in a position to book the gains at a reasonable time and price. For example, an equity share would give you income in the form of dividend, potential capital gains when the price of the stock appreciates beyond your purchase cost and the ability for you to book the gains. The third point is very important because even if the asset appreciates but you are not able to book the gains for any reason, then it would not be an investment asset. For example, while the price of your self-occupied house property might

increase but you will not be able to realize the gains since you are staying in the house.

Therefore, your asset allocation has always to be in investment assets and not just any security or, worse still, in a liability which you mistake as an asset.

Self Occupied House Property is Not An Investment Asset

All of us have a dream of owning our own house — a roof above our head which is our own. The dream is perfectly legitimate because we require a place to retire to after a full day's hard work. Also, it is important to buy a house for your self occupation since a rented house entails avoidable unnecessary expense. However, the problem is that most of us confuse a self occupied house property with an investment asset. A house property might be an asset but it's not an investment asset because you are not in a position to book your gains on it without losing the roof over your head. So, be clear: while you need a house to live in, but a self occupied house property is not an investment asset.

Beware of Liabilities Disguised as Assets

It's vital to learn to distinguish between a liability and an asset. Many of us actually mistake liabilities as assets. For example, a luxury car or a vacation home which take away money from your pocket are not assets but liabilities. An investment asset is something which puts money into your pocket (income) and also offers scope for future capital appreciation, e.g. rental property which earns rent, and shares which earn (tax free) dividends. Investment assets also have potential for future capital appreciation. On the other hand, a liability — like a luxury car or vacation home which may appear to be an asset will not only take away money from your pocket in the form of interest payments but also require recurring maintenance expenditure in the form of petrol, repairs, property taxes, etc.

Reviewing and Rebalancing Your Asset Allocation

One of the important reasons why most of us don't reach our goals in life — whether they be related to education, relationships, love, religion and spirituality or personal finance — is because once we implement our original plan we just sit back and completely forget about it. However, we have to remember that the world is dynamic and not static. Information flows at the speed of light and things change quicker than we can imagine. Something which may have been good yesterday might not be so good today; a person whom we respected yesterday might not command the same respect today; a friendship which we treasured yesterday may not be the same today; or a love which we thought was ours may, in fact, never have been true. Therefore, we have to keep reviewing and assessing the continuously changing situation.

Over time, your original asset mix will shift, your market related investments may outperform or underperform your non-market related investments. This will disturb your original asset allocation. Therefore, once in a while you will have to do what is called a rebalancing of your portfolio to regain your original asset allocation. I will put it in another perspective. Let's say you own a car. It runs well, gives great mileage and is your most comfortable home away from home. However, you have to constantly keep refueling it so that it can run. Also, once in a while you have to get it serviced for any damaged parts, refilling of oils, etc. Reviewing and rebalancing the portfolio is somewhat similar so that it retains its original efficiency.

Having said that, I do not mean that you have to constantly monitor your asset allocation on a day-to-day basis. If you start doing that, it will turn out to be very injurious to your financial health because then all your emotions will come into play. Remember that we humans are emotional creatures and hence we require well laid plans, else we will surrender to our whims and fancies.

What, then, should be the time interval for reviewing your portfolio? There is no hard and fast rule but it should normally be done once in a year unless some major changes in market conditions significantly alter your allocation between market and non-market related investments by more than 25%. For example, suppose you had originally allocated 75% to market related investments and 25% for non-market related investments. Now, suppose that the value of market related investments has appreciated by 50% so that it has become almost 82% of your portfolio. This goes against your original asset allocation plan and therefore needs a rebalancing of your portfolio. You would now have to sell around 9% of your market related investments and shift to non-market related investments so as to come to your original asset allocation ratio of 75:25.

The correct response to a fall in an asset's price is to buy a bit more of it; the correct response to a rising price is to lighten up a bit. Rebalancing is merely a disciplined way of accomplishing this. Prolonged market declines will make rebalancing seem a frustrating waste of money; in the end, however, asset prices almost always turn around, and you will usually be handsomely rewarded for your patience. However, a clarification is in order: the word, rebalancing here means in respect of asset classes like equities, debt, real estate, etc. and not in respect of individual investments within an asset class like stocks or bonds, etc.

Lessons From This Commandment

1. Almost 90% of the variability of a portfolio's return is due to asset allocation while only 10% of the variability in portfolio performance is due to market timing and stock selection.
2. The only thing in your control is asset allocation and the good news is that 90% of portfolio variability is due to asset allocation.
3. All assets move in business and economic cycles of their own and while one asset might be in a bear market another asset class might simultaneously be in a big bull market. Hence, increase your financial literacy by learning thoroughly about the different asset classes available for investment.
4. The broader asset groups of equities, bonds, commodities and real estate (others being art and currencies) will lead you to the gateway of long term wealth creation and sustenance.

5. Risk and return are inextricably entwined. As a general rule, do not expect higher return from safe investments. However, superior long term wealth creation results from optimal asset allocation in investment assets. A portfolio's combined risk is much lower than the risk of the individual investments which make it up. Therefore, acquaint yourself with the principles of constructing a well diversified portfolio of non-correlated assets.
6. Portfolios behave differently from their individual constituents. The aim of an optimal asset allocation is not to invest only in safe assets but to invest in a combination of safe and risky assets whose combined risk is much less than that of the individual constituents and at the same time which offers higher degree of return. Therefore, focus on the behavior of your portfolio and not its constituents. Small portions of your portfolio will often sustain serious losses but will cause only minor damage to the whole portfolio.
7. An all-bond portfolio is not the least risky portfolio; in fact, addition of a small amount of stock to an all-bond portfolio actually reduces the risk slightly while considerably improving the return.
8. The corollary to the above lesson is that the addition of a small amount of bonds to an all-stock portfolio would significantly reduce risk while only marginally bringing down the return.
9. Long term bonds are riskier than short term bonds. Therefore, it would not be advisable to completely diversify you portfolio with long term bonds. Use more of short term bonds and only opportunistically use long term bonds when the intra market spreads widen beyond long term historical averages.
10. Generally speaking, mid and small cap stocks are riskier than large cap stocks. Therefore, small cap stocks might need more dilution from bonds than large cap stocks.
11. You need not invest directly in stocks, bonds, etc. if your knowledge, time, resources or money do not permit it. An investor can very well attain almost the same returns by purchasing mutual funds. The key to long term wealth creation is to build a correct portfolio of assets — the individual stocks and bonds then lose their individuality in it.

12. Keep periodically rebalancing, reviewing, changing and refining your portfolio allocation with time and your financial goals and circumstances.

Self-Understanding Questionnaire

This commandment teaches us the great importance of asset allocation for your long term wealth creation and achieving financial freedom. Now, honestly answer the following questions in yes or no to check out your understanding of the principles explained in this commandment. The more the number of "yes" answers, the better is your understanding of this commandment.

1. Do you realize that the only thing in your control is asset allocation and that it is the main factor determining 90% of your portfolio variability? Yes/No?
2. Do you believe that wealth creation is not a complex and difficult subject but rather an easy and boring asset allocation plan? Yes/No?
3. Do you believe that long term wealth is created by following a well laid down asset allocation plan rather than just investing in the next hot asset class? Yes/No?
4. Do you understand that the behavior of a diversified portfolio can be very different from that of its individual components? Yes/No?
5. Do you accept that an all-bond portfolio is not the least risky portfolio; that, in fact, the addition of a small amount of stock to an all-bond portfolio actually reduces the risk slightly while improving the return considerably? Yes/No?

—

Chapter 3

Commandment 2

Thou Shall Earn the Right Category of Income and Protect Your Money from Predators

THIS BOOK IS ABOUT HELPING YOU ACHIEVE FINANCIAL FREEDOM. The extent to which you can change your habits and thinking about the way you deal with money will determine whether you are able to achieve this goal.

You have to develop the right attitudes and thinking about money at three different levels:

- Level 1: Your income earning category.
- Level 2: Your income earning vehicle.
- Level 3: Your financial knowledge about protecting, budgeting, saving, spending, leveraging, investing, insuring and all other matters dealing with money.

This second commandment deals with Level 1 and Level 2 listed above.

Income Earning Categories: All Incomes Are Not Equal

Making money from the right income category is the next most important step after proper asset allocation. While the latter is the key to long term wealth creation, the second most important thing is to enhance your net income, i.e. the income you are left with after paying tax. There are lots of financial predators around and the biggest among them is the income tax department which legally takes away money from your pocket. That leads us to the important discovery that all incomes are not equal. There are different categories of income depending on how they arise. In fact, the income tax department also stipulates different categories of incomes, such as salary, rent, income from business and profession, capital gains, interest, dividends, etc., and they are taxed on different principles and also at different rates.

There are some incomes, such as salary and professional income for which you work but on which you pay the highest tax while there are other incomes, like capital gains, rent, dividends, etc., where your money works for you and you pay the minimum or, sometimes, nil rate of tax. Thus, the government makes a big discrimination while taxing your income — you pay high taxes on the income you work hard for but when you let your money work harder for you, you pay lower, or zero, tax. Accordingly, while working hard might increase your current income by a few percentage points, it will generally not help you create long term wealth unless you learn how to make your money work for you.

The following are the four major categories of income.

1. Earned Income

This is the income for which you work the hardest, such as salary, professional income, etc. If your time and energy are being consumed in earning an income, then it will come under this category. Examples of this would be salaried employees, all self-employed professionals like doctors, lawyers, chartered accountants, etc, and small business owners whose full time and energy are taken up by their business. Since you are working hard for your income, it is clearly visible to the eyes of the taxman and hence earned income is taxed at the highest marginal rate of taxation.

2. Guaranteed Income

This is the income where your money works for you through an investment asset and you get a guaranteed income from it. This is the income which a lender to a business receives. Prominent examples under this category would be interest earned on deposits and loans. Since the income here is guaranteed and certain to be received (unless your borrower defaults), therefore the taxman has decided to tax it at the highest marginal rate of tax.

3. Passive Income

This is the income for which your money works as an investment asset but there is no guarantee either of realizing a return or of the extent of the return. This is the income which an owner of a business receives. Examples under this category would be business income, rent from property, dividend on shares, royalty, etc. Note that the demarcation between passive and earned income is very thin. Just because you are into some business does not mean that you are deriving passive income. The moot point is that your time and energy should not be spent on earning that income. If your entire time is spent on business, then clearly it is not business income but a kind of salary for doing your own work — you don't own a business but rather own a job. For business income to graduate to passive income it should be something which does not engage your full time and energy; once the business is set up, the systems are in place and assets deployed, it should be capable of earning income for you on its own. For example, McDonald's gives franchises all around the world. The owner of McDonald's does not go to each outlet and look after the production and sales of burgers; the franchisees do that while the owner keeps on receiving commission on it for life, i.e. till the stores are operative, which may sometimes run into years, decades, or even forever. That is the income which a wealth creator has to aim to achieve. All of us have limited time and energy and therefore if you have to work for money you cannot create unlimited wealth. Another example of passive income would be writing a book. When you write a book, it's only a one time effort but the royalty for it keeps flowing year after year so long as your book keeps getting sold. Since you are not working for your money but your money is working for you in such cases, the taxman gives lot of deductions and the actual rate of tax is lower in the case of business income, rent, etc. In certain other cases, like dividends, there is no tax at all.

4. Portfolio Income

An investment asset not only gives income throughout its life and your holding period but it also makes money for you when you dispose it off. That is the beauty of an investment asset. The money derived from disposing off an investment asset would be termed as portfolio income. For example, the profit derived from sale of a real estate property, equity shares or bonds is portfolio income. There is a trade off between passive and portfolio incomes. Generally, if you try to increase one, the other reduces. You have therefore to be smart enough to know when to extract passive income and when to take portfolio income from an earning asset. The trick would be to move on from one highly valued, lower yielding investment asset to another lower valued, higher yielding investment asset. In the process, this would give you immediate portfolio income and long term sustainable passive income. Again, since you don't work for your portfolio income but your investment asset works for it, the taxman eyes it with relative leniency and many types of portfolio incomes are totally tax free, such as long term capital gains on equity shares and equity mutual funds, and long term capital gains on sale of real estate (subject to fulfillment of certain conditions). Certain other items, like short term capital gains on equity shares, are subject to a much lower rate of taxation as compared to earned income.

Thus, remember that income tax reduces your gross income; interest on any loans taken to buy liabilities diminishes your net income; and inflation nibbles into your remaining income. So earn more money and aim to increase your after tax income.

Legal Financial Predators

Have you ever heard the term legal financial predators before? Well, you would acknowledge that people in this world are generally after your money, whether it be the thief, the government, your child's school, doctor, lawyer, utility company, milkman, fireman, your father, mother, husband, your spouse and children, etc. You may give money to some people, like your father, mother, husband, wife, son, daughter, etc. due to your love and affection for them or to the children's school, doctor, lawyer, milkman because you require their services. Others, such as the thief or the government, forcibly take away money from you.

There is another category, and probably the biggest one of all, which comprises legal financial predators. They are people or entities who legally take away money from your pocket — and it is not small change but big money. In fact, they take away a hefty percentage of your income. So, who are these legal financial predators? Well, they come in many forms; let's find out.

Legal Financial Predator 1: The Government

The government is the biggest financial predator of all. It legally takes away money from your pocket at all stages of your dealing with money. Just consider the following:

- On income earned — the government levies income tax.
- On income saved — the government levies income tax on interest.
- On income invested — the government levies income tax on capital gains.
- On income spent — the government levies indirect taxation, like excise, customs, sales tax, service tax, etc.
- On income insured — the government levies indirect taxation, such as service tax.

Clearly, the government is the largest of all financial predators. It legally and systematically takes away money from your pocket at every stage — whether it be earning, saving, investing, spending, or even taking insurance.

Why the Government Taxes You

Like everyone, you also probably hate to see tax being deducted from your salary month after month, and wonder why the government needs to tax people. It does so for the following two main reasons:

1. The government needs money to govern. Just like an individual or a company, the government has to defray a lot of work such as building infrastructure, providing free or subsidized education and medical assistance to the poor, paying salaries to government employees, ministers, etc.

2. The second — and the more important — reason is that the government itself does not "earn" any money. That's why it taxes you in order to "legally" take away your money. And the bureaucrats and politicians are very clever at it as they find newer and ever more innovative methods for taxing you and legally taking money away from your pocket.

Having said all this, tax is also the price you pay for living in a civilized society. Therefore, I would advise everybody to honestly pay taxes that are legally due. However, just as the government has the right to legally collect taxes from you so, too, you have the right to save taxes — legally. That is one of the tenets of this commandment.

Legal Financial Predator 2: Bankers

You may think that bankers are there to help you make money. Regretfully, that's not the case. Instead, they are in the business of making money for themselves. And the irony is that you yourself go to the bank and hand over your hard earned savings to them!

Have you ever noticed banks advertising that they have become "one stop financial institutions" and wondered why? That's because they can then legally take away money from your pocket at every stage of the money chain — saving, spending, investing and insuring. Here is how.

Stage 1: At the Time of Saving

Bankers are the ones who help inflation rob your savings of their purchasing power. For this, their offer of banking convenience and the modern definition of money — i.e. "currency" — come in particular handy. They keep your money with themselves for free in the form of demand deposits. And then in the name of savings they lure you into locking your hard earned money with them in the form of time deposits which in the long run deplete the value of your money thanks to the ravages of inflation.

Stage 2: At the Time of Spending

Bankers give you high cost debt when you purchase liabilities, whether it be a car, a holiday home, or for incurring expenses like costly vacations, expensive clothes, gift items, imported furniture and such like through credit cards, personal loans, etc. They also offer you loans when you purchase necessary but bad capital assets like house property for self occupation. All such loans that banks give you earn them exorbitant money in the form of interest, processing fees, late payment fees, rentals, etc. This is how banks legally take away money from your pocket at the time of spending.

Stage 3: At the Time of Investing

Banks nowadays also offer investment advice and sell different kinds of investment products, such as mutual funds, equities, bonds, etc. And most of the time, unless it is a specialized bank, they offer little value to their customers. Typically, they charge higher fees for sub-standard services and thus legally take away money from your pocket at the time of investing.

Stage 4: At the Time of Insuring

As a part of their "one shop" service banks also offer and sell insurance products. I want to stress that, as a general rule, they are not the best insurance advisors — they are only good sellers. Therefore, they again prey on your money when you buy insurance through a bank.

How Banks Deplete the Value of Your Money by Money Multiplier

The name of the game is money multiplier; mind you it is multiplication of money for the banks while depletion in the real value of your money.

For example, say you deposit ₹ 100 in a bank savings account which gives you 4% interest. Now, as per RBI regulation, your deposit of ₹ 100 enables the bank to lend out around ₹ 1,000 and charge 15% to 35% rate of interest depending on the type of loan, e.g. personal loan, credit card loan or some other form. In essence, the bank pays you 4% on ₹ 100 and earns around 20% on ₹ 1,000 — pure money multiplication for the bank while you are just robbed of your money without your knowledge.

Cross Selling You Products You Don't Need

Often, banks cross sell you products which you don't actually require. For example, for opening a saving account the bank may push on you an unwanted and inferior insurance product; for allotting you a safety locker, it may influence you to subscribe to an underperforming mutual fund scheme, and so on. The bank makes a double killing with such deals — for example, it earns rent (money) on the locker and then it gets commission (money) on the mutual fund scheme it sells you.

Banks are Undercover Predators

The trouble with banks as compared to government is that in the case of government at least you are aware that they are taking away money from your pocket and you pay it reluctantly, trying to save till the last penny. In the case of a bank, you happily and willingly go about paying them money from your pocket! And the bank will lure you into a debt trap promising that you will get "tax deduction on your mortgage payments." Remember that government gives you a tax break only for getting into debt and to buy liabilities which the bank will very cleverly market to you — a case of two financials predators working together to rob you off your money.

Key Points in Selecting a Good Banker

Keep in mind the following key points when selecting a banker:

- The banker should sell you what you want to buy without attaching any covenants. For example, if you want to open a savings deposit account then the banker should show you the process and not try and sell you insurance.
- The banker should provide you with timely information which is for your benefit and not for the banker's benefit. For example, the banker should tell you when the interest rates on deposits have been raised or those on loans reduced.

Legal Financial Predator 3: Brokers

Brokers constitute the third category of legal financial predators. A broker comes into the picture in acquiring any asset — a house for self occupation or an investment asset, rental real estate, equity shares, bonds, or for taking on a liability such as a mortgage loan, loan for car, spending or even while subscribing to an insurance policy. However, in this category, I would classify the legal financial predators under three classes — the good, the bad and the ugly.

Good Brokers

Brokers who help you buy investment assets could be termed as good brokers because they facilitate you in buying good investment assets which are the very base of a proper asset allocation for the ultimate goal of achieving financial freedom. But the key here is a good broker. Remember a good broker would always be a "student of his / her profession". Beware of people who claim to be experts or gurus — these are probably highly rated individuals who get paid heftily to under-perform the benchmark market indices!

The trick to find a good broker would be to see whether he is a student of his profession and interested in educating you or whether he is just interested in selling something to you. Education gives knowledge and knowledge leads to money by increasing your financial intelligence. So before you shop for stocks, bonds, rental real estate or any other investment asset, first shop for a good broker because the broker will be the bridge between you and that investment asset. And, remember, always properly pay your broker whatever he deserves because you are not going to become wealthy by cutting out a good broker but, in fact, by acquiring investment assets which your good broker will lead you to.

Bad Brokers

Brokers who tempt you into unnecessary expenses are bad brokers. Unnecessary expenses would include a foreign vacation, costly five star dinners, etc. Therefore, beware of these financial predators as they will rob you of your money without creating any investment asset in your balance sheet.

Ugly Brokers

Brokers who make you incur bad capital expenditure would be termed as ugly brokers. As explained earlier, bad capital expenditure would mean buying assets which produce negative income or take away money from your pocket, such as a luxury car, a vacation home, etc. These are the worst kind of brokers because they not only make you buy liabilities disguised as assets, they also lead you into the vicious cycle of incurring continuous unnecessary expenses in order to maintain those bad assets.

Key Points in Selecting a Good Broker

The following are the key points in selecting a good broker:

- The broker should be a student of investing and not claim to be an expert or a guru.
- The broker should also himself be an investor and generally invest in the same scheme which he is recommending to you.
- The broker should sell you what you want to buy and not make you buy what he wants to sell.

Legal Financial Predator 4: Corporate Retailers

All businesses are corporate retailers; whether they actually have a retail outlet or not is immaterial. Whatever may be the business, whether manufacture of cars, air conditioners, television sets, computers or chocolates, corporates have to sell their products to earn money. In that sense, all corporates are retailers. However, all of them are not financial predators because some of them sell us products which we need while others sell us products which make us rich.

Necessary Corporate Retailers

These are corporates which sell us necessary items for our existence, like bread, milk, eggs, normal clothes, etc. Being mortal, human beings cannot survive in this world without certain basic items and corporates which sell these basic items would fall under this category.

Opportunistic Corporate Retailers

These are the corporate retailers who take advantage of our weak emotional behavior and lack of financial knowledge by selling us products held out as being necessary but which actually are not. Retailers selling fashion clothes, luxury cars, expensive foreign vacations, etc. would fall under this category. We have to beware of them because they lead us into incurring unnecessary expenses or into buying bad assets.

Parasitic Corporate Retailers

These are the worst types of corporate retailers. Just as parasites suck blood out of our body, these parasitic corporate retailers keep sucking money out of your pocket. They will sell you products which you don't need — and then keep earning from their sale to you for life or for a very long period of time. One example of this is the retailer's credit card. Nowadays, retailers give credit cards to shop in their stores. First of all, the credit card and the rogue point system will induce you into buying something which you don't require at all and then it will make you pay for it for a very long period of time. For example, a retailer's credit card might tempt you into buying something which you were otherwise not going to buy, like, say, an air conditioner (please see "cash fallacy' and "buyer's remorse" in Commandment 6). This makes you incur higher electricity bills and maintenance for life. And, further, it makes you pay very high interest rates on financing through that retailer's credit card. These types of corporates would, therefore, be termed as parasitic corporate retailers.

Legal Financial Predator 5: Residual Category

The residual category of legal financial predators include those who don't necessarily deal with your money but who are certainly after your money and out to rob you of it. Some illustrative examples are given below.

Death Predators

There are predators who are after your money not only when you are alive but even after your death. "Funeral relatives", i.e. those relatives who never met you when you were alive but come to cry at your funeral, are death predators who come to prey on your assets after your death. A very simple way of protecting your assets from death predators is to prepare a Will during your lifetime in order to bequeath your assets as per your wishes.

Beauty Predators

Outwardly beautiful but ugly from within — beauty predators love and marry for money. Their love for you increases in direct proportion to the increase in your wealth; the more money you have, the more love they have — not for you but for your money. Beware of these predators because they can drain you not only of your wealth and money but also physically, mentally, emotionally and psychologically.

Blackmail Predators

These are predators who know how to take advantage of the system to blackmail you and loot your money. They may come in different forms, like union leaders, lawyers, corporate annual general body meeting blackmailers, etc. You have to know how and where to properly hold your investment and other assets so as to protect yourself (for details, *see* Commandment 9 — Thou Shall Take Proper Financial Insurance).

To conclude this section, remember that not only are there robbers and thieves who want to rob you of your money but there are also financial predators who legally take away money from your pocket. Remember that adage that ignorance is happiness? Well, your ignorance makes the financial predators happily rich — and that, too, legally!

As mentioned at the beginning of this commandment, you require a dual level of protection against legal financial predators.

Level 1 Protection: Your Income Earning Category

Level 1 deals with your income earning category. As explained earlier in this commandment, there are four categories of income:

1. Earned income;
2. Guaranteed income;
3. Passive income; and
4. Portfolio income.

The protection which you get at Level 1 depends on which category of income you earn. And the category of income which you earn determines how much of the income you actually get to retain.

The Income You Get to Retain

As far as income is concerned, people typically ask only one question — how much do you earn? Although this is an important question but it only reveals half the truth and does not give the full picture. That is because the income you earn is not what you get to retain.

For example, take the example of four people — A, B, C and D. They all earn ₹ 10 lakh p.a. Now, refer to Table 3.1 to know the difference between the amount of income a person earns and the amount of income he retains.

Table 3.1
Difference Between Income Earned and Income Retained

Person	*Type of Income*	*Income Earned (₹)*	*Income Tax (₹)*	*Interest on Bank Loan (₹)*	*Income Retained (₹)*
A	Salary	10,00,000	3,00,000	2,00,000	5,00,000
B	Bank interest (guaranteed income)	10,00,000	3,00,000		7,00,000
C	Dividend on shares (passive income)	10,00,000			10,00,000
D	Capital gains on real estate (portfolio income)	10,00,000		1,50,000	8,50,000

As revealed by Table 3.1, while all four earn the same amount of income, namely ₹ 10 lakh p.a., there is a vast difference between what they finally get to keep, ranging from ₹ 5 lakh to ₹ 10 lakh. In other words, there is a 100% difference between the share of income different people get to retain even though they earn the same amount. You will wonder how that is possible.

As you can observe, while A earns ₹ 10 lakh, he pays ₹ 3 lakh as income tax, ₹ 2 lakh as interest on bank loan and is thus left with just ₹ 5 lakh.

B earns the same ₹ 10 lakh and pays income tax of ₹ 3 lakh but does not have bank interest payment and hence keeps ₹ 7 lakh.

Now, C earns ₹ 10 lakh and keeps the entire ₹ 10 lakh. Is this magic? No. It's only that C is financially the smartest among the four with the highest financial intelligence.

In the case of D, the earning remains the same, i.e. ₹ 10 lakh, but he has to cough up ₹ 1.5 lakh as bank interest, leaving ₹ 8.5 lakh in his hand.

From this example it is very clear that C has the best financial knowledge while A has the least. And the great difference between the incomes earned and the money retained in their cases is because of the role played by financial predators — the government (taxes) and banks (interest).

Since you have now understood that it is the money you keep which is important and not what you earn, let us move ahead to understand how you can get to keep more money from what you earn. For answering this we need to consider another question — what category of income earner are you?

This is a very pertinent question because there are two ways of avoiding financial predators — at Level 1, i.e. at the time of earning money, and at Level 2, i.e. at the time of protecting your money. This point deals with Level 2.

As explained earlier in this commandment, there are four different kinds of incomes — earned income, guaranteed income, passive income and portfolio income. World over, the tax structure is regressive and penalizes people for working hard. Thus, earned income, i.e. the income for which you work hard — like your salary — is taxed at the maximum marginal rate of taxation. Similarly, guaranteed income, i.e. the income which is guaranteed and there is no supposed uncertainty about its receipt is also taxed at the maximum marginal rate of taxation. However, passive and portfolio incomes, i.e. incomes for which your money works for you, are either totally tax free or taxed at a lower rate because there are lots of deductions available on them.

Your Income Earning Category Determines the Amount of Money You Retain

Simply put, your income earning category determines the amount of money you get to retain. Table 3.2 depicts the different categories of income and the amount of money you actually get to keep in each case.

In the earned income category, 30% of the gross income goes towards income tax while another 25% goes into other deductions, mainly to fund your retirement account like provident fund (employer's and employee's contributions, superannuation fund, profession tax, etc.). The amount and percentage may wary depending on which country you live in, but the principle is generally the same. I have included both employer's and employee's contribution to provident fund simply because if the employer did not deduct this then it would come to you. Now, somebody may argue that this is for their own retirement and therefore it's not an expense but simply put it's a deduction from your income and you don't get that money in hand immediately. The funds will be put in some instrument on which the interest earned will again be taxed. Hence, there will be tax on income from the income which has already been taxed. Over

Table 3.2
The Money You Retain on Different Incomes

	Earned Income	*Guaranteed Income*	*Passive Income*	*Portfolio Income*
Gross income	100	100	100	100
Less: Income tax	30	30	0	0
Net income	70	70	100	100
Less: Deductions	25	0	0	0
Money you retain	45	70	100	100

Table 3.3
The Regressive Effect of Earning the Wrong Category of Income

	Year 1	*Year 2*	*Year 3*	*Year 4*	*Year 5*
Gross income	100.0	100+46 = 146.0	100+90.6 = 190.6	100+133.9 = 233.9	100+175.9 = 275.9
Less: Income tax and deductions	54.0	55.4	56.7	58.0	59.3
Money you keep in fixed deposit	46.0	90.6	133.9	175.9	216.6

the long term, this considerably reduces your corpus because of compounding. Let's understand this through a simple example.

Table 3.3 shows you how a gross salary of ₹ 100 earned every year for five years gets compounded to only ₹ 217 at the end of the 5-year period, assuming that the amount left after tax and deductions is fully invested in a bank fixed deposit at 10% rate of interest p.a. Kindly note that the total gross salary earned over a 5-year period is ₹ 500 but the money, even after adding the interest on the bank fixed deposit, grows to only ₹ 217. This is because you pay high tax on salary, deductions from salary and tax on interest which eat into your money and then the negative effects of compounding leaves you with only a paltry sum.

Now let us examine the accumulated income of an investor who invests in equity shares, which is an investment asset, and earns just 2% dividend yield every year which is totally exempt from tax (*see* Table 3.4). Let us assume that he invests ₹ 5,000 each year in equities on which he thus earns an annual dividend of ₹ 100 at 2% dividend yield. For those of you who are not familiar with the term, dividend yield is computed by dividing the absolute per share dividend amount by the equity share price. Let us see how such an investor compounds his / her money over a 5-year period. Table 3.4 shows all the computations.

The investor earns ₹ 100 dividend in Year 1. Then in Year 2 he / she earns ₹ 202, i.e. ₹ 100 on the original investment of ₹ 5,000, another ₹ 100 on the additional investment of ₹ 5,000, plus ₹ 2 on the re-investment of the ₹ 100 dividend received in Year 1. Kindly

Table 3.4
The Positive Effect of Earning the Right Category of Income

	Year 1	Year 2	Year 3	Year 4	Year 5
Gross dividend on income	100	102	106	112	120
Gross dividend on additional income	0	100	200	300	400
Less: Income tax and deductions	0	0	0	0	0
Money you keep and re-invest in stock	100	202	306	412	520

note that the assumption here is that the investor invests an additional investment in equities of ₹ 5,000 every year. The investor then accumulates ₹ 520 at the end of five years as compared to ₹ 217 for the salary earner. Further, this investor has also smartly accumulated ₹ 25,000 in equities (an investment asset) over the 5-year period.

This also brings out the importance of Commandment 3 which teaches that you must budget for yourself and create investment assets. Also note that so far we have reckoned returns only from dividends, but equity also appreciates in value giving portfolio return as well in the form of capital gain. This is again tax free. So, the income (dividend) is tax free, profit (capital gain) is tax free and the asset (equity share) itself is free from wealth tax. This is, therefore, the peerless triple combination at play — no tax at the time of earning, no tax at the time of holding the asset and no tax at the time of selling the asset. This is an example of the highest level of financial intelligence using a combination of different commandments explained in this book.

Aim to Earn Your Income in the Proper Category

You should always aim to earn income in the proper category in order to save yourself from the biggest financial predator of all — the taxman, who legally takes away money from your pocket. If you still don't appreciate the importance of this statement, let me make another attempt to prove its truth to you.

Table 3.5

Comparison of Four People Earning Their Income from Different Sources

Income Type	*Salary*	*Bank Interest*	*Rent*	*LTCG Property / Shares*
Income category	Earned income	Guaranteed income	Passive income	Portfolio income
Gross income	100	100	100	100
Less: Deductions	0	0	0	0
Net Income	100	100	100	100
Less: Income tax	30	30	21	0
Income after tax	70	70	79	100

Table 3.5 shows a comparison of four people who earn their incomes from different sources.

As you can see from Table 3.5, people in the earned income and guaranteed income categories retain the least portion of their income after paying tax — on salary and bank interest respectively — while people earning long term capital gains in the portfolio income category retain the maximum income after tax. This is simply because people earning salary and interest get hardly any tax deductions and practically their entire income is taxed, while a person earning passive income in the form of rent from real estate gets deductions because of which his income after tax is higher. A person earning long term capital gain, whether from property or shares, is in a tax haven as his incomes are totally tax free though in the case of property it is so only after satisfying certain conditions of reinvestment. Rules of taxation are generally the same in most countries — the highest tax is levied on earned and guaranteed incomes, while there are exemptions, deductions and tax free status for passive and portfolio earners. On the face of it, then, it would seem that the government does not want you to work hard and that is why it encourages you to convert your earned income into passive and portfolio incomes!

Level 2 Protection: Your Income Earning Vehicle

Now, let us move forward to Level 2 protection, i.e. protection based on your income earning vehicle. Your income earning vehicle simply means the type of legal entity you earn your income as.

There are basically two kinds of entities as which you can earn your income:

1. **Individual:** This is the legal entity which the poor and middle class generally use to earn, hold and invest their income. As an individual entity, you earn your income as an individual, i.e. salary, profession, small business, etc. You also invest as an individual, i.e. you buy stocks or real estate in your individual name. Further, you hold all your investments in your individual or joint names. Thus, all decisions in regard to money, whether it be earning, investing and holding of assets are done as an individual.
2. **Institutional (Corporate / LLP):** The rich generally earn, hold and invest their money in an institutional capacity. The institution could be a company or a limited liability partnership (LLP).

   You may think that it makes little difference whichever route is used — finally, money is money. That is, however, not the case.

Institutional (Corporate / LLP) Structure *versus* An Individual

Let us examine the advantages of earning, investing and holding through an institutional structure as compared to an individual status. An institutional structure could be corporate or LLP but since most probably it is a company, I will limit my discussion to a company though most of the benefits discussed herein would be enjoyed by both corporates and LLPs.

Let us examine one by one the three different stages at which the corporate structure scores over the individual.

At the Time of Earning Money

This is the most important phase at which the corporate structure wins over the individual, primarily because of taxes. As mentioned earlier, the tax laws are regressive and discriminatory — they punish the hard working person who "earns money by his or her labor" and reward those who relax and let their own and other people's money work for them. This discrimination is even more glaring at the time of earning money if you are not using the right vehicle to earn it as. The person earning salary (earned income) in any case does not have a choice as to the vehicle while a person earning the other three categories of money — guaranteed, passive or portfolio — has the choice of either using the individual or the institutional vehicle. Now let us understand the difference and the inequitable tax structure for both the vehicles. To make it simple even for those readers with non-accounting background, I have drawn simple income statements to bring home my point (*see* Table 3.6 and Table 3.7).

Table 3.6 illustrates the income statement of an individual while Table 3.7 depicts the income statement of an institutional vehicle. I

Table 3.6
Income Statement — Individual

Expenses (%)		*Income (%)*	
Income tax	30	Earned income	25
Necessary living expenses	25	Guaranteed income	25
Necessary capital expenditure	20	Passive income	25
Luxury expenses	15	Portfolio income	25
Bad capital expenditure	10		
Surplus for investment assets	0		
Total	100		100

Table 3.7
Income Statement — Institutional Vehicle Corporate

Expenses (%)		*Income (%)*	
Necessary living expenses	25	Earned Income	25
Necessary capital expenditure	20	Guaranteed Income	25
Luxury expenses	15	Passive Income	25
Bad capital expenditure	10	Portfolio Income	25
Income tax	9		
Surplus for investment assets	21		
Total	100		100

have listed all kinds of incomes and expenses which a person can earn or spend in both the categories. I have also deliberately kept the figures the same for all items in both the cases so as to make the point very clear. In the case of an individual, after meeting all the different types of expenses, there is no surplus left for acquiring any investment assets. However, with the same incomes and expenses, the institutional status leads to a surplus of ₹ 21 for purchasing investment assets.

The figures were exactly the same in both the cases then why is there surplus in one case and not in the other? Is there any magic? Yes, it's the magic of the institutional status, it's the magic of the discriminatory tax laws, it's the magic of behaving like a rich man — earning, investing and holding through a "rich man's vehicle".

What is the Magic?

The magic is that in the case of the individual, you first pay tax to the government and only then do you get to keep the remaining money for yourself. In the case of an institution, on the other hand, you first pay yourself *via* all the different types of revenue and capital expenditure (depreciation is a tax deductible non cash expense) and then pay tax only on the remaining profit, if any! It's as simple as that. In the first case, your tax comes to ₹ 30 (30% of ₹ 100). In the second case it amounts to just ₹ 9 [30% of (₹ 100-70)]. Thus, as an individual you pay more than three times additional tax than you would as an institution! Even the salary which you pay to yourself, i.e. your company paying you salary as an individual for managing its business, is tax deductible for the company while you may get the benefit of minimum exemption, deductions and less marginal rate of taxation. So you save money even while paying yourself!

There are lots of other tax planning techniques as shown by Table 3.8. Your tax consultant should be able to help you with these since going into such details is not the purpose of this book. The point which I want to drive home is that if you don't know this simple rule about which vehicle to use while earning money then you are unnecessarily paying more than your normal share of income tax.

Table 3.8
Tax Planning Techniques for Saving Money

Personal Expense	*Business Expense*	*Justification*
Telephone bills	Business equipment	Use your phone to make business calls also.
Printing, postage, xerox	Business expense	Use these machines for business use also.
Computer / TV set / refrigerator / microwave	Business equipment	Mention that all of this are for your office and business use equipments.
Restaurant bills	Business expense	Client acquisition and entertainment expenses.
Medical expense	Business expense	Adopt a proper medical reimbursement plan.
Home costs	Home office expenditure	Track all home expenses used for business and reimburse.

At the Time of Investing Money

There are innumerable benefits of investing your money through an institutional vehicle as compared to investing as an individual. For one, lots of investment opportunities are simply not available to individuals and are available only to institutions. This is because the government believes that these investments are too risky for individuals and so they debar individual investors from lots of good, and comparatively safer, investments. Many a time issuing companies believe that certain investments are not suitable for individual investors, or that they may not be able to fulfill its requirements and so they don't allow investments by individual. Further, banks generally have special offers, schemes and rates for individuals and institutions which mostly favor the institutions. Thus, there are many instances in which there is discrimination against the individual as compared to institutional investors as far as investing your money is concerned.

At the Time of Holding Money

This is another level at which individuals are discriminated against. An institution is allowed to hold lots of investments which an individual is not allowed to hold. There are many "legal eagles" looking at how to take away your assets and money from you. It's easier to take money away from an individual than from an institution. And then there is the matter of passing on your wealth to your next generation when you finally say *adieu* to this world. Succession planning is much easier with an institutional or corporate structure than it is for an individual. This is simply because the assets are held in the corporate and not in your name. You may stay or depart but your company always survives; unless you legally wind it up, it has a separate legal identity with a common seal and perpetual succession. Thus, while you are the owner of your company controlling all its assets, it is legally distinct from you insofar as tax and other benefits are concerned.

So why be an individual and be at the receiving end of the government, issuers, bankers, etc? Instead, use the corporate status and take command of your money and assets at the time of earning, investing and holding.

How to Convert Yourself from an Individual to an Institution

Don't worry, you don't have to be physically converted. You remain the same individual who you are today! It's only that your income, expenses, assets, liabilities and how you deal with money gets converted. Many people have the misconception that a company means a large institution with big factories, plants, machinery, land, assets, etc. Nothing could be farther from truth. In today's information age, a company means nothing but a legal document prepared by your chartered accountant and filed in the appropriate government office. That's all. It's just a legal document. It's as easy to create a company as it is to buy any asset. Therefore, it is in your interest to convert yourself from an individual to an institution so that you open up a totally new window of opportunities while earning, investing and holding your money and assets.

Grow Your Financial and Legal Knowledge

In school we are taught how to read and write, draw, paint and many different languages and literature. However, despite learning different languages in school, we are not educated in the language of money. Of course, somebody with an accounting background will be taught about income statement, balance sheet, assets, liabilities, etc. However, in reality, s/he would not know the difference between a true investment asset as defined in this book and an asset which is actually a liability. Therefore it's very important to increase your financial knowledge — the way you think about money while earning, protecting, budgeting, saving, spending, leveraging, investing, insuring, etc. This book is an endeavor in that direction. If you want to fully explore the power of money then it would make sense to acquaint yourself and get a working knowledge of accountancy and corporate, taxation and securities laws. Being familiar with these laws would certainly not be a substitute for appointing a well-qualified legal and tax advisor but it will make you smarter in dealing with them, always asking them the right questions and seeking the correct answers from them. There are lots of benefits available in the world through adopting a proper financial and legal structure. So increase your financial and legal literacy to take advantage, legally, of all the benefits available to you under the law.

Mutual Funds: Protections from All Investment Robbers

This commandment on protection against financial predators would not be complete without commenting on mutual fund investing — and so this last section. As a fund investor, your life is even more complicated when you have to select from among a plethora of different funds offered by various fund houses. You have an option of investing in open ended or closed end funds, equity, debt or commodity funds, and many different categories within each of them. So, which is the best category of fund for you? Rather than looking at the positives of each type of fund, I will look at the different investment robbers and how well different funds protect and guard you against each one of them. The fund which protects you best against all the investment robbers is the right fund for you.

Protection from Investment Robber 1: Inflation

Inflation is one of the biggest and stealthiest enemies for any investor. In fact, it is that monster which many investors don't recognize. Many people believe in "saving money" and mistake this for investment. But saving is not investing. Never mistake saving for investment otherwise you will be in for a rude shock because you don't understand the rules of money.

The rules of money were permanently altered in the year 1971 when the then US President Richard Nixon took his country off the gold standard and the country granted itself the license to print money. Since then the US dollar and other world currencies have depreciated while the price of all commodities measured against these currencies — be it precious metals like gold or silver, or industrial metals like steel, copper, aluminum or agricultural commodities — have gone up and will continue to go up over the long term. Inflation, then, is Investment Robber Number 1 against which the fund has to protect your investments.

Debt funds don't offer any protection against inflation. Bonds and money market instruments primarily invest for coupon interest, or accrual, which is not capable of protecting your money against deprecation in the value of money due to inflation. These kinds of investments only offer current income and do not provide growth income which can shield your investments against the monster of inflation. Equity funds certainly offer you protection from inflation as they are invested in companies whose earnings are supposed to grow. Also, gold funds would offer you such protection because gold is an inflation hedge. But, then, do equity and gold funds protect you from the other investment robbers? Read on.

Protection from Investment Robber 2: Income Tax

The government is the biggest investment robber of all. It systematically and legally takes away money from your pocket at all stages, whether be it saving, spending, investing or insuring. Most of you are aware of the taxman's robbery but do not know how to actually protect your money against it. Government puts one of the biggest dents in your pocket when you earn a return on your investment. For example, interest on a bond is fully taxable in your hands at the marginal rate of taxation. As far as mutual funds are concerned, all the debt oriented products are taxed and hence pure debt funds will not protect you from this investment robber. Equity funds offer you that protection in the form of tax free dividends and long term capital gain which is exempt from the purview of the taxman. But, then, do they protect you from the other investment robbers? Read on.

Protection from Investment Robber 3: Interest Rates

Another big enemy of your investments are interest rates. In fact, interest rates are such a big enemy that they affect both debt and equity investments.

When interest rates rise, bonds prices fall and so does the NAV of your bond fund.

Again, when interest rates rise, equities as a general rule fall because the earnings of companies drop due to higher finance and interest cost. Equity valuations contract due to a rise in the discount rate. High interest rates also result in reduced fund availability for equities as debt competes with them for the same investor's wallet.

Therefore, neither debt nor equity funds would be able to protect you against rising interest rates. Gold would in all likelihood be able to protect you from the fluctuation in interest rates but would it be equally effective against the other investment robbers? Read on.

Protection from Investment Robber 4: Market Volatility

Prices of all market determined products, be it equities, bonds or gold, fluctuate and remain volatile with day-to-day price movements. The price of an accrual product, like a liquid fund would certainly protect you against market volatility but then it would not protect you against the other investment robbers — inflation, income tax, or Investment Robber Number 5 which is to follow. So which kind of investment has the wherewithal to protect you against market volatility as well? Read on.

Protection from Investment Robber 5: Poor Asset Allocation

The importance of asset allocation can be understood by only one statistical fact. Ibbotson and Kaplan have shown that 90% of the variability of a portfolio's return is due to asset allocation. This means that only 10% of the variability in portfolio performance is on account of individual holdings while 90% of it is determined by how the funds have been allocated. William Bernstein has said in

The Intelligent Asset Allocator that "there are two kinds of investors: those who don't know where the market is headed, and those who don't know that they don't know. Then, again, there is a third type of investor — the investment professional who indeed knows that he or she doesn't know, but whose livelihood depends upon appearing to know."

Therefore, a cardinal principle of investment, which may seem bad news to many, is that the only thing which is in your control is asset allocation. However, equity, bond or gold funds don't offer you protection against poor asset allocation. Then, what does? Read on.

The Fund that Protects You from All Investment Robbers

The fund that protects you from all the investment robbers is — any guesses? — the simple, age old fund called the balanced fund. Don't believe it? Confused? Let us see how a balanced fund indeed protects you from all the different investment robbers:

Protection from Investment Robber 1: Inflation — A balanced fund invests both in equities and debt. The equity component in the balanced fund protects your money from the big, silent monster of inflation.

Protection from Investment Robber 2: Income Tax — A balanced fund is treated as an equity fund as far as taxation is concerned. Accordingly, on the one hand its dividends are tax free and on the other it is outside the purview of long term capital gains tax. The beauty of it is that even the debt portion of the balanced fund becomes tax free in the same manner as equity which never ever happens in any other case.

Protection from Investment Robber 3: Interest Rates — A balanced fund invests in both equities and debt. The equity component in the balanced fund protects your money and investment from that dangerous killer called interest rates.

Protection from Investment Robber 4: Market Volatility — A balanced fund invests in both equity and debt. As explained earlier, when one asset class is in a bear market, most probably there is some other asset class which is in a bull market. A balanced fund, therefore, as the name suggests, helps balance and even out market volatility by providing you with the best risk adjusted returns with minimal market volatility.

Protection from Investment Robber 5: Poor Asset Allocation — This is perhaps the most important protection offered by a balanced fund. As explained earlier, the key to long term superior investment performance is asset allocation and what can be better than a balanced fund which has allocation to both equities and debt. Further, by definition it always buys the cheaper asset and sells the costlier one when one asset class out-performs the other so as to bring the fund back to its optimal asset allocation. A balanced fund, therefore, automatically follows the most important principle of investment — buy cheap and sell dear.

To conclude, the balanced fund protects and shields your money from all the five investment robbers. So the next time you see a balanced fund, don't just brush it aside — remember, whether it is investments or life, a simple and balanced approach always works.

Lessons From This Commandment

1. Income tax reduces your gross income; interest on loans (whether for expenses or bad assets) diminishes your net income and inflation nibbles away at what remains. So, use whatever talent you possess to earn more money and aim to increase your after tax income. Then budget properly for your money, don't make unnecessary expenses or wasteful capital expenditure. Finally, learn how to use other people's money to work for you *via* creating positive leverage (debt) to create income generating investment assets. Work towards achieving financial independence by creating a proper allocation of income earning investment assets.
2. If you truly aspire to achieve financial freedom then you have to develop the right attitude towards money, not only at the time of saving, spending, investing or insuring but also at the time of earning and protecting your money and assets.
3. Financial predators are those who legally take away money from your pocket — and it's not small change but big money.

4. Government is the biggest financial predator of all. It legally takes away money from your pocket in the form of taxes — not only when you earn money but even at the time of saving, spending, investing or taking insurance.
5. Bankers are financial predators who take away money from your pocket in the form of interest and inflation, reducing the purchasing power of your money simply by increasing its supply through the multiplier effect.
6. Brokers are financial predators who not only take money from your pocket, but a bad broker also leaves you holding a bad investment, whether it be a house, insurance policy or a liability.
7. Corporate retailers are parasitic financial predators who legally take away money from your pocket by selling you goods which you probably don't require and by charging the highest rate of interest on those corporate credit cards which you never needed in the first place.
8. There are other financial predators in the form of death predators, beauty predators, blackmail predators, etc. who legally — and many a time inhumanly — take away money from your pocket.
9. You need dual protection against these legal financial predators — at the time of earning money and by adopting the right vehicle through which to earn it.
10. Recognize the four different categories of income and always remember that the amount of money which you retain is the most important figure and not the amount of money which you earn. Your income earning category determines the amount of money which you get to keep.
11. Appreciate the fact that the legal vehicle — individual or institutional — through which you earn money is of primary importance in determining your tax status, as also your investment status and your asset holding cum succession planning. The taxman treats expenses under each vehicle quite differently. As an individual, you incur all expenses from post tax money while as an institution all the expenses are incurred through pre-tax money. Thus as an individual you first pay tax to the govern-

ment and are then left with money for yourself while as an institution you first pay to yourself and then to the government *via* taxes from the money left, if any. Therefore, increase your financial and legal knowledge by learning about accountancy and corporate, taxation and securities laws so as to be on the right side of the earning, investing, holding and succession planning vehicle.

12. The fund that protects you from all the investment robbers is a balanced fund.

Self-Understanding Questionnaire

This commandment introduced you to financial predators who legally rob you of your money. It then showed how you require dual level of protection from them — at the time of earning your money and by way of using the correct vehicle. Now honestly answer the following questions in yes or no to test your understanding of the principles explained in this commandment. The more the number of "yes" answers, the better is your understanding of this commandment.

1. Do you believe that there are legal financial predators who can legally take money out of your pocket? Yes/No?
2. Do you recognize the fact that government taxes are discriminatory and regressive as they tax the working person the highest while leaving alone the person whose money works for him / her? Yes/No?
3. Do you realize that the category through which you earn income can dramatically change your tax status and the taxing power of the government? Yes/No?
4. Do you realize that bankers, brokers and corporate retailers can deprive you of your money through high interest rates and induced inflation? Yes/No?

5. Do you believe that the money you retain is more important than the money you earn? Yes/No?
6. Have you ever thought that your income earning status — individual or institutional — can dramatically alter the amount of taxes you pay and the manner in which you may be able to invest, hold and plan your succession? Yes/No?
7. Do you accept that increasing your financial and legal knowledge will help you in saving your money from financial predators and help you to intelligently deal with your tax accountant and lawyer? Yes/No?

Chapter 4

Commandment 3

Thou Shall Do Proper Budgeting

What Exactly is Budgeting?

A budget is planned allocation of available resources and can mean different things for government, businesses and an individual. This book is about helping you achieve financial freedom, so I will concentrate on budgeting from an individual's point of view.

The importance of budgeting cannot be underestimated. Budgeting is one of the most important skills that you can have. Planning and budgeting are crucial when it comes to preserving and growing your wealth.

Surplus and Deficit Budgets

In accounting terms, budget simply means "income *minus* expenses". Therefore, when one is reduced from the other, arithmetically the answer can either be in the positive or negative.

Deficit Budget

Barron's Finance and Investment Handbook defines a deficit budget as "excess of spending over income, for a government, corporation, or individual". Pay attention to the words "excess of spending over income." Today we see that most governments and companies land up in budget deficits. This is simply because they spend more than they earn. A government will finance its deficit budget either by printing notes or taxing more, both of which hurt you as an individual in the form of inflation or higher tax, as the case may be. A company would try to bridge its budget deficit by either firing some employees, increasing the prices of its products, reducing their quality, or by a combination of these and other factors. Again, all these factors are going to affect you adversely. Individuals who consistently spend more than what they earn accumulate huge debts which result in budget deficits which if not controlled would one day lead them to bankruptcy. Why individuals fall into budget deficits and how to come out of it is the main thrust of this commandment.

People always complain that they don't have money to save, invest or spend. For this reason, this is a very important commandment for helping you attain financial freedom by converting your budget deficit into surplus.

Surplus Budget

Barron's says that "A budget surplus is an excess of income over spending for a government, corporation, or individual over a particular period of time." Give importance to the words "excess of income over spending". Now a budget surplus does not necessarily mean living below your means — it simply means expanding your means beyond your expenses and having a surplus. This commandment will show how it is possible to do so.

Achieving Budget Surplus

There are two ways of achieving budget surplus — either by increasing your income, or by spending less, or both. This book is not about to tell you to cut down all your expenses and live in a miserly manner in order to achieve budget surplus. Neither am I telling you to keep spending lavishly on unnecessary expenses or bad capital assets. I am simply telling you to expand your income and manage your finances in such a manner that you achieve a budget surplus. This might sound too simple and almost like a fairy tale to you. Wait, let us understand how to do so in practice and achieve financial freedom.

Grow Your Income

The first and foremost thing is income. We all have to learn to increase our incomes. We all have some talent — we have to identify that talent, hone our skills, gain experience, improve our net income and increase our knowledge because that is the key in the current technology and information era. We all have to try to consolidate our strengths and minimize our weaknesses and aim to earn as much as possible because income is the first item of your Profit and Loss Account.

Increase Your Net (After Tax) Income

Earning more is just the beginning and will not in any way solve your financial problems unless you follow the other rules.

The second most important thing is to enhance your net income, i.e. your income after tax. There are lots of financial predators and the biggest amongst them is income tax which legally takes away money from your pocket. As explained in Commandment 2, there are four different kinds of income:

- Earned income, such as salary, where the person actually works to earn money;
- Guaranteed income — income from an investment / asset where the return is guaranteed, such as from bank FDs, and hence there is negligible risk; and
- Passive and portfolio incomes where neither the principal nor the return is guaranteed, e.g. dividend from shares, rent from real estate, capital gains, etc.

Typically, the tax structure is discriminating. As a general rule, there is maximum tax on earned income. It would almost seem as if the government wants to punish you for working hard to earn your income. Equally, there is maximum tax on guaranteed income, perhaps because the government thinks you are not innovative enough with your money! However, there is a lower rate of taxation — or even no taxes in some cases like dividends on equities, long term capital gains on equity shares — on passive and portfolio incomes. Thus, rather than working hard for your money and paying higher taxes, you have to be smart and let your money work for you and thus pay low or no taxes.

Avoid Expenses on Luxuries and Bad Assets

Unnecessary expenses include a foreign trip, costly five star dinners, etc. Bad capital expenditure means spending on assets which produce negative income or take away money from your pocket, such as a luxury car, a vacation home, etc. Bad capital expenditure would also include those assets which do not give you any income, such as a self-occupied house. But we all have to live in this world and incur some expenses for food, clothing, medical, etc. for our existence — therefore we have to learn to budget for these expenses and make a judicious use of our finances. Now, just as you would budget for food, clothing, etc., in the same way you must budget for some fixed amount for savings. Then, too, what is the use of money if we can't enjoy life? So everybody has to incur some unnecessary expenses on luxuries or bad capital expenditure as well. But, at least, don't pay for them from your earned income — let your assets pay for them. And, remember, treat all money the same way, whether it be the money you get from, say, a lottery, or from the estate of some deceased relative, or any windfall gain. Treat them all with the same respect as the money you have earned by your hard work. Exercise the same caution in utilizing the money, whatever may be its source — just because it is free money or windfall gain shouldn't lead you to squander it away.

Liability Side — Good Debt, Bad Debt and the Power of Leverage

You need to distinguish between good debt and bad debt. Bad debt would be debt which is used for acquiring bad assets, such as a luxury car or a vacation home which take away money from your pocket, or even a self-occupied house which does not put any money in your pocket. Good debt, on the other hand, would be that which helps you in creating an asset which then puts money in your pocket (income) as well as scope for future capital appreciation, e.g. rental property which earns rent, shares which earn (tax free) dividends — and both also have the potential for future capital appreciation. Never borrow to incur luxury expenses, say, on a foreign trip or for buying a bad capital asset like a luxury car or vacation home because they will not only take away money from your pocket in the form of interest payments but also entail recurring expenditure in the form of petrol, repairs, property taxes, etc.

Assets Side — Create Good Investment Assets

Your aim must always be to create good assets, i.e. investment assets which will provide you income; for example, equities which give you tax free dividends, rental real estate which will give you rent, etc. There are multiple advantages of investment assets. They are either tax free (e.g., dividends) or subject to lower rate of taxation after exemptions (e.g., rent) as compared to earned income (e.g., salary). Learn to use the power of leverage to create investment assets — and let the income from such assets pay interest on your loan. And once the loan installments are over — the future income from the investment asset, which is taxed at lower rate, as well as the asset itself are yours for life. The trick of enjoying life as well as securing your financial future is to ensure that the passive and portfolio incomes from your investment assets pay both for your living expenses and your bad assets. Once you reach that stage, you are close to achieving financial freedom.

Don't forget that income tax reduces your gross income; interest on loans, whether for living expenses or bad assets, diminishes your net income; and inflation constantly nibbles away at your remaining income. So you must earn more money, increase your after tax income, budget properly, and don't pay for your luxury expenses or bad assets from your earned or guaranteed incomes. Instead, let your investment assets pay for these. Use leverage (debt) to create good income generating investment assets.

If you follow the simple rules stated above, you will be working successfully towards achieving financial freedom.

Reviewing Your Financial Status

Generally we believe that our financial status in society depends on the amount of money we earn. This is only partly true. Our financial status is actually determined by the amount of wealth which we accumulate and this can be totally different from the amount of money we actually earn. To understand this concept clearly, check out for yourself which of the categories described below you belong to and what your financial status is.

Category 1: Spending More Money Than You Earn

This is the category of a reckless person who earns a lot of money but still has negative net worth. While such a person understands the concept of earning money, he does not know how to build wealth. Such a person might have a big salary but with it goes a huge house mortgage, a posh vacation home and costly cars bought with high interest bank loans, and imported furniture, jewellery, foreign vacations, etc. financed by high cost credit card or personal loans. Such a person can never build wealth. No doubt, he earns a lot of money but most of his money goes in paying interest on unnecessary luxury expenses like foreign vacations or bad assets like a luxury car or a vacation home which take away money from his pocket. He then uses the wealth effect, i.e. he borrows more against his existing assets to finance further wasteful expenses and luxuries. Things go well so long as his assets can keep financing his recklessness. The day asset prices start falling, his net worth becomes negative and his financial edifice tumbles like a pack of cards.

People in this category are those who earn a lot of money but have no wealth. Such people do not understand the difference between an asset and a liability — they accumulate liabilities, mistaking them to be assets.

Category 2: The Money Savers

This category comprises perhaps the most financially ignorant people of all. No doubt these people have more wealth than those in the first category. They also have a positive net worth but the amount of sacrifice they make for that wealth is much more than what they get in return.

People in this category do not realize that after US President Nixon removed the US dollar from the gold standard in 1971, money is no longer money but merely a "currency". In essence, the US can, and actually does, literally print paper money backed by no tangible asset like gold. Hence, money is bound to lose value over a period of time as more and more currency chases fewer and fewer real assets. A person in this category does not understand this basic principle of money. Also, while he may earn handsome income but he then "saves" all the money in an instrument such as a bank fixed deposit. Thus, although he earns a "safe" return on his capital but he is at a big risk to the financial monsters of inflation and income tax. He also pays the highest amount of income tax based on his tax bracket as there are no specific deductions for interest income; which is fully taxable. At the same time, the inflation monster eats into his real return and, over a period of time, makes him poorer and reduces his standard of living.

A person in this category saves but does not invest and hence subjects himself to the financial monsters of inflation and income tax which legally take away money from his pocket and diminish the value of his wealth.

Category 3: Investing One's Own Money

The third category comprises people who invest their own money in productive assets such as equities and rental real estate or in inflation hedges like gold and silver. This is a category of smart investors who convert their income into wealth. Such people are educated about the principles of finance and investments, know how to save taxes (dividends from equities are tax free, rentals from real estate are subject to lower rate of taxation after deductions, long term capital gains from equities and real estate — after satisfying certain conditions — are tax free), enhance their real income by investing in natural inflation hedges like gold and silver and build wealth over time. This category of investor does allocate some portion of his wealth towards fixed income but that is more for generating current income and providing some stability to the overall portfolio and not as a means of generating long term wealth. This category knows that wasteful expenses on foreign vacations or bad assets such as an expensive luxury car or a vacation home should not be made from one's earned income but should be financed by one's portfolio income, i.e. the income from investment assets.

Category 4: Investing One's Own and Other People's Money

People in this category are the most financially savvy. They invest not only their own earned money in productive assets but also invest borrowed funds, i.e. other people's money, to buy productive assets. They understand the basic principles of how to use money to create money. They realize the fact that the cash flow from productive assets has to be sufficient to repay the interest on the loan. They thus know how to create a productive investment asset out of thin air. This is the category which literally prints its own money.

For example, let's assume you have ₹ 25 lakh. You then borrow (leverage) ₹ 25 lakh from the bank and invest ₹ 50 lakh in a rental real estate at 8% yield, i.e. ₹ 4 lakh p.a. Let's assume that the equated monthly installment (EMI) on the housing loan is ₹ 25,000 per month or ₹ 3 lakh p.a. You therefore make ₹ 1 lakh p.a. (₹ 4 lakh less ₹ 3 lakh) which is 4% yield on your original money of ₹ 25 lakh, i.e. savings bank rate. Further, once the loan gets repaid after a few years, the property becomes fully your own and the rentals keep flowing in making your return on investment infinite. This is called creating assets out of thin air.

To conclude, earning money is the first foundation of being wealthy but nobody can become wealthy just by earning money without understanding the principles of how money works in this modern information and currency age. And then you have to make yours and other people's money work for you. Remember, you have only limited time and energy at your disposal to earn money by working and unless you make your own and other people's money work for you, you cannot become wealthy. Once money starts working for you, there is no time limit, no boundary to which it is subjected — it can just keep creating and multiplying wealth and you can legally print money for yourself!

Budget Deficit or Surplus — The Choice is Yours

This commandment of budgeting is not a commandment of thrift. It's in fact about playing by the rules of money in a smart manner.

And whether it's a budget deficit or surplus — the choice is completely yours.

Barron's states that "an individual with a budget surplus may choose to pay down debt or increase spending or investment." Thus, *Barron's* offers you three choices:

1. Reduce your debt;
2. Increase spending; or
3. Increase investment.

The reason most people have so much financial problem is because they either reduce their debt and / or increase spending. Reducing your debt at least helps you in saving future interest payments but the second option of just increasing spending is suicidal. Imagine a person who keeps getting promoted with increased salary every year but then keeps increasing his wasteful expenses or bad assets which take money away from his pocket. Such a person earns more but he does not grow richer. The people who grow rich are the government (through increased taxes), bankers (through interest on loans and credit cards), car manufacturers and dealers, travel agents, and so on. In other words, such a person works hard so that other people can become rich!

It's for you to decide whether you want to create a budget deficit or surplus. Creating a budget surplus by paying yourself first is the hardest but the best thing to do which, if done consistently, persistently and patiently will help you achieve financial independence in life. Budget surplus must be a priority, paying yourself first must be a compulsory expense the same way as you pay tax to the government or loan installment to the bank. Never spend more than you earn and also learn the difference between mere saving and real investing. You need patience. You need to build wealth slowly, one rupee at a time. As much as you would want to become rich overnight, this is not the way our world works. Once you opt to create a budget surplus, it will help you create investment assets which will then start putting money into your pocket. I'm not saying that you don't deserve to enjoy life — but first you must reach that stage when money from your investment assets pays the bills for your luxury expenses and bad and extravagant assets.

The secret is who pays for what and budgeting helps you in unraveling the key to that secret.

Rules for Creating a Budget Surplus

1. Use Income from Investment Assets to Pay for Extravagant Unnecessary Expenses and Luxury Assets

This is the first rule: earned income should never be used to pay for your luxury expenses and bad assets; income from your investment assets should do that. The biggest mistake people make is that they pay for their unnecessary expenses and bad assets with their earned income. Always remember that investment assets are what make you wealthy. Now, if you keep paying for those unwarranted expenses from your earned income then how would you build your investment assets. Therefore you have to allow your investment assets to grow and reach a level where they start paying for your wasteful expenses and luxury assets. There is nothing wrong in living it up so long as you understand this golden rule of wealth creation.

2. Increase Current Income to Acquire Investment Assets

The question now is how to get investment assets which will generate income to pay for those extravagant expenses and luxury assets. The answer is very simple — increase your current income! As noted earlier in the book, God has sent all of us, His children, to this world with some kind of special talent, skill, gift, etc. Try to recognize your special talent and you will surely be able to increase your income. For example, I would think about writing a book because that is a talent I have and use the income generated from the book to create investment assets which will pay for my future extravagant expenses and luxury assets.

3. Unleash the Power of Positive Leverage — Use Good Debt to Create Investment Assets

Many people don't understand the real power of leverage. They are afraid of debt and think that it is always a bad thing.

I would define leverage as something which helps you in compounding or multiplying — now whether you compound good things or bad ones is completely your choice. Thus, there is both good debt and bad debt. When you borrow money to create an investment asset, then I would term it as good debt. However, when you borrow money to buy a luxury asset or incur extravagant expense, then I would term it as a bad debt. Also, you must always remember that the total income generated from the investment asset should be higher than the total cost of the debt. You are then creating positive return on investment for yourself. Slowly, the higher income from the investment asset will pay off the interest and principal of your debt, leaving you with a fully-owned investment asset. The income subsequently generated from the investment asset would be totally yours and your return on investment would become infinite!

4. Take Stock of Your Bad Debt and Unnecessary Expenses

The only method of getting out of a money trap is to take stock of your bad debts and your unnecessary expenses — whether capital or revenue in nature. Check your outstanding credit card balances, personal loans, etc. and try to repay them as soon as possible. Remember, using revolving credit on credit cards or borrowing through personal loans is financial suicide. Just consider what happens when you take a car loan — and, remember, a luxury car is a bad asset:

- You pay very high interest rates on your car loan;
- You pay for petrol, maintenance, etc., on your car; and
- The bad capital asset — in this case the luxury car — immediately loses almost 30% of its value the moment you drive it out of the showroom.

Which is why it's a financial suicide to fund extravagant expenses and luxury assets through debt.

5. Always Budget for Yourself First

We budget for everybody, be it the government (taxes), bankers (EMI), spouse, children — and even for those expensive cars, costly vacations, etc. But we fail to budget for ourselves. We pay everybody but usually fail to pay ourselves. This is one of the biggest financial mistakes and one which will keep you always poor. There is a mental attitude at play here. The cardinal rule of budgeting is: always budget for yourself first. You decide what kind of a life you want to live, what things you would need in future, then make a fair estimate of all those extravagant expenses and luxury assets. You should then create sufficient investment assets whose income will pay for them. Remember, the budget for yourself is an expense the same way as are payments for income tax, mortgage EMI, medical bills, electricity bills, telephone bills, etc. Just as you treat income tax as an expense which you cannot dispense with, treat paying yourself also as an expense which cannot be dispensed with.

6. Budget to be Wealthy

The point of budgeting is not just to cut spending and necessary expenses. First of all, that won't make you rich. And even if you do become rich, it will not allow you to stay rich for long because for that you must know how to create investment assets which give you income rather than staying focused only on reducing spending. I don't believe you can become rich merely through thrift. You may accumulate some money but you will certainly neither become nor remain rich. A cut in necessary expenses creates some cash but only investment assets create true, long term, sustainable wealth.

7. Expand Your Balance Sheet the Right Way

Whether you are a student of accounting or not, I am sure you must have heard the term "Balance Sheet". In simple terms, a balance sheet is a statement which shows your assets and liabilities. For those on the road to financial freedom, we need to define these two terms differently. An asset is something which puts money into your pocket while a liability is something which takes away money from your pocket. And, at all times, your assets are equal to your liabilities and since both are equal therefore it is termed as a balance sheet.

My version of a financial freedom fighter's balance sheet is shown by Table 4.1.

Table: 4.1
Financial Freedom Fighter's Balance Sheet

Liabilities	*Assets*
Your own money	Physical investment assets
Borrowed money	Paper investment assets

The purpose of budgeting is to help you expand your balance sheet the right way. You would have noticed that you can expand your balance sheet either by expanding your assets or by expanding your liabilities since one must always match the other. Obviously, this is not the typical balance sheet which is taught in an accounting class. This is a much simplified version of it. The more important point is that there are lots of items in the traditional text book balance sheet which are classified differently. For example, in a traditional balance sheet a car will be shown as a fixed asset. For a financial freedom fighter, it's just a liability since it removes money from your pocket in terms of petrol bills, maintenance, insurance costs, etc. For a financial freedom fighter, an asset is one which puts money into your pocket. As explained earlier, only investment assets do that. As such, I have included only investment assets as your true assets. Further, an investment asset can either be in physical form, like rental real estate and gold, or in paper form, such as shares, bonds, gold exchange traded fund (ETF), etc.

You have to fund all the assets through liabilities which are broadly of two types — your own money and borrowed money (other people's money). To pay for your extravagant expenses and luxury assets you have to create investment assets. To achieve ultimate financial freedom, you should be in a position to create investment assets out of borrowed money (good debt or positive leverage) in such a manner that the return from the investment assets is more than the interest on your debt so as to give you positive return on investment.

8. Fund Your Income Statement Correctly

In order for you to take charge of your balance sheet, you must know how to budget your income statement properly. For those

Table: 4.2
Financial Freedom Fighter's Income Statement

Expenses	*Income*
Necessary living expenses	Earned income
Necessary capital expenditure	Guaranteed income
Extravagant expenses	Passive income
Bad capital expenditure on luxury assets	Portfolio income
Surplus going to investment assets in balance sheet	

with non-accounting background, an income statement, also called a profit and loss account, is nothing but a statement which shows your income and your expenses. The difference between the two is either your surplus — if the income is higher than the expenses — or deficit, if expenses are higher than the income.

A financial freedom fighter's income statement is shown in Table 4.2. Before analyzing the income statement further, let's recapitulate the essentials of income categories:

- Earned income is the money that you earn from whatever activity which keeps you busy the whole day, day after day, such as a job, a profession, your business, etc. Such earned income takes your full time and energy but in itself is not able to make you wealthy unless you channelize it in a proper manner.
- Guaranteed income is the income derived from investment assets where there is certainty about the return, such as bank fixed deposits.
- Passive income is the money earned from investment assets where the return is not guaranteed, like dividend, rent, etc.
- Portfolio income is the money realized from disposing of an investment asset, like capital gains on sale of equity shares, bonds, real estate, etc.

Coming back to the income statement, let's first look at the expense side. Necessary living expenses are those which are needed for your daily life, like food, clothing, education, medical expenses, etc. Necessary capital expenditure comprises expenditure which you need to incur in order to avoid unnecessary expenses in the future like the mortgage loan EMI on a house for self occupation. I have already explained the next two items appearing on your expense column, i.e. extravagant expenses and capital expenditure on luxury assets. The financial freedom rule is that these must not come out of your earned income but from guaranteed, passive and portfolio incomes.

The other important rule is that the entire portfolio income and capital gains from investment assets must not to be "wasted" on extravagant expenses or luxury assets. Some of it has to be ploughed back to add to your investment assets. The quantum and absolute amount of the add back would depend on your stage of wealth creation but the sum should be ambitious though to curb the temptation to spend too much on extravagant expenses and luxury assets. Once you achieve this, there will always be a surplus (income *minus* expenses) in your income statement. Upon reaching this stage, your investment assets would keep growing and expanding and will produce more and more guaranteed, passive and portfolio incomes and thus increase your capacity for incurring luxury expenses and acquiring luxury assets. You would then have achieved financial independence. And budgeting helps you reach this stage.

Some Other Points for Consideration

Saving Is Not Investing

When I say you must budget for yourself, it means that first you must save money from your current income and invest it in investment assets.

Many times, however, we confuse saving with investing. Traditionally, saving means you save money and keep it in a safe bank fixed deposit. This is called saving as there are no price and interest rate risks on your investment. However, this leaves you exposed to considerable opportunity loss plus the ravages of inflation. Merely by saving, therefore, you forgo the opportunity of potential capital appreciation. At the same time, you expose yourself to the vagaries of inflation which eats into your income. I will give a real example to make this point clear.

Table: 4.3

Saving *versus* Investing

	X	Y
Total investments (₹ 1 lakh * 31 years)	31,00,000	31,00,000
Gross total return	1,50,94,342	7,43,46,288
	(10% p. a)	(17.1% p. a.)
Income tax	45,28,303	0
Net total return	1,05,66,040	7,43,46,288
Retirement corpus	1,36,66,040	7,74,46,288

Assume two individuals, X and Y are each able to save ₹ 1 lakh per annum. Now, X invests his entire ₹ 1 lakh into a nationalized bank fixed deposit at 10% p.a. rate of interest. On the other hand, Y invests his entire savings of ₹ 1 lakh p.a. in equities. Assume that they were both 28-year old when they started and did this till they became 60, i.e. for a period of 32 years. For simplicity, we will also assume the fixed deposit rate remains constant at 10%. On the other hand, the BSE Sensex returned a compounded rate of 17.1% over the past 32 years, rising from the level of 100 in 1979 to 15,500 by the end of the year 2011. Kindly note, I have ignored dividend yield of around 1.5%, otherwise the return from equities would be even higher. Table 4.3 brings out the results for both X who saves and Y who invests.

The difference is simply startling. X collected a total wealth of ₹ 1.37 crore while Y amassed a total wealth of ₹ 7.74 crore. This is a massive difference between the two. The two main reasons for this are as follows:

1. X compounds his money at a gross rate of 10% while Y does it at 17.1%. The power of compounding is perhaps the most powerful principle of financial mathematics and is clearly brought out in this example.
2. X pays 30% tax on his interest income while Y does not pay any tax because his investment keep compounding at the growth rate of the Sensex. Since his gains have become long term capital gains — gains from equity shares held for more than one year are long terms capital gains — they are totally tax free in his hands.

Thus, while X "saved" and earned guaranteed income from his bank fixed deposit, Y invested and earned passive and portfolio income from his investments in equities — and that, too, tax free. Mind you, I am not suggesting that you invest all your money in equities because that would be against the principles of Commandment 1 on proper asset allocation but this example shows how investing is dramatically different from saving and the two concepts should not be used interchangeably.

Budget Surplus Must Be a Priority

You must make budget surplus a priority. The most efficient way of doing so is to re-prioritize your earning, saving, spending and investing decisions. I am not suggesting you be miserly — you can save some money by being miserly but cannot accumulate wealth and become rich in that fashion. You cannot achieve financial independence by being a miser. I am just saying that most of us don't give due importance to creating a budget surplus which, in the long run, prevents us from becoming rich and wealthy. If you work hard at creating a budget surplus, your financial life will reach a different level altogether. That is what budgeting is all about — saving what you can, however small and little it might be, and then channeling it in the right direction to create life-long wealth for your financial independence. Which is why you must make budget surplus your utmost priority.

Measure Saving as Percentage and Expense in Absolute Rupee Terms

Remember to always measure saving figures in percentage and not absolute terms. This is because the amount saved might look good in absolute terms but in percentage terms it might be very small compared to your income. There is no fixed rule for what percentage of your income should be saved but you must remember that you have to create a positive budget surplus and it has to be at least 50% of the income for a middle class person. The golden rule is that higher your income, higher the percentage of your saving.

The other important point to note is that expenses should always be measured in absolute rupee terms. If you start measuring expenses in percentage terms, your expenses will increase by the same percentage as would your income — and that would be extremely harmful for your long term wealth creation. Just think; simply because your income has increased by, say, 25% it does not mean that your needs also go up by 25% and therefore you should increase your expense by 25%. In fact, if your expenses are reasonable, they may not rise much with an enhancement in your income level. And even if expenses have to increase, they should do so at a lower rate than the increase in your income. Concentrate, therefore, more on the absolute level of expenses and many a time you may actually not need to increase them at all with higher income levels.

To conclude, always measure budget in percentage terms and expenses in absolute terms so that you have simultaneous control over both.

Spending Your Way to Riches

You will find this statement paradoxical but it is true. You must recognize when to spend to get rich. I will explain how.

For example, when there is a recession and the company for which you work is thinking of laying off people, who would they pack off first? Obviously the ones with least qualifications or experience. Therefore, if during bad times you spend money and learn some new skill or attend some training course which enhances your job skills, you may stand a better chance of saving your job. Or, take the example of a stock investor. During bull markets it's very easy to make money in stocks simply because most stocks are going up. But during bear markets the knowledge, experience, skills, temperament, patience, emotional intelligence and all other qualities of a successful investor are put to tremendous test. Now, during a bear market would you just sell off all your stocks and simply stay out of the market? Or, would you spend money on learning some new techniques of stock investing, be it derivatives, futures, options, shorting, hedging, or whatever, so that you can make money during bear markets as well? Remember, investing is that which helps you in making money both during good and bad times otherwise it's only sheer good luck. Therefore, you must know when to spend to get rich.

Lessons From This Commandment

1. Simply put, a budget is planned allocation of available resources. There can be two types of budget — surplus and deficit — and the choice is entirely yours as to which one you opt for. Income more than expense is surplus budget while expense more than income is deficit budget.
2. Saving must be a priority. You must think of it as a compulsory "expense" which you have to incur for yourself the same way as you pay tax to the government and loan EMIs to the bank.
3. Measure saving in percentage terms and expenses in absolute rupee terms.
4. Remember that income tax reduces your gross income; interest on loans (for wasteful expenses / bad or luxury assets) diminishes your net income, and inflation eats out your remaining income. So unless you budget properly to create investment assets, your dream of achieving financial freedom might remain just a pipedream.
5. Always aim to earn more money by using your special gift or talent, increase your after tax income, budget properly for your money, don't pay for wasteful expenses or luxury capital expenditure from your earned income but let your investment assets pay for it and use leverage (debt) to create good income generating investment assets.
6. Earning money is the first premise for being wealthy but you can't become wealthy just by earning money unless you understand how the principles of money work in today's information and currency age — and budgeting is an integral part of it.
7. Income from investment assets has to pay for luxury expenses and bad assets. Therefore, you must increase your current income to acquire investment assets.

8. Once, you budget your own money, then use the power of positive leverage (good debt), i.e. other people's money, to create investment assets.
9. Take stock of your negative leverage and wasteful expenses. Work towards reducing your bad debts, i.e. loans taken to finance liabilities.
10. Learn to correctly fund your income statement and expand your balance sheet in the right way through investment assets.
11. Saving is not necessarily investing. Learn the difference between mere saving and real investing.
12. Recognize when to spend to get rich.

Self-Understanding Questionnaire

This commandment primarily deals with the basic principles and rules of budgeting and the importance of budgeting for yourself *via* creation of a surplus budget. Now honestly answer the following questions in yes or no to assess your understanding of the principles explained in this commandment. The more the number of "yes" answers, the better is your understanding of this commandment.

1. Do you believe in budgeting for yourself and creating a budget surplus? Yes/No?
2. Do you believe in paying yourself at the same time as you pay the government, the bank, the utility company, etc.? Yes/No?
3. Do you recognize the difference between saving and investing? Yes/No?
4. Do you know how to correctly fund your income statement and expand your balance sheet? Yes/No?
5. Do you recognize the importance of budgeting in the entire wealth creation and preservation process and its inevitability in your achieving financial independence? Yes/No?

Chapter 5

Commandment 4

Thou Shall Not Commit These Common Financial Mistakes

YOUR FINANCIAL FREEDOM IS DETERMINED BY YOUR HABITS concerning saving, spending, investing and insurance. We all believe that we are very clever and smart while dealing with money. The truth is we are actually very careless while dealing with money. There are lots of elementary financial mistakes which we commit on a regular basis. This commandment deals with such common financial mistakes, common, yes — but also lethal for your finances.

Just ponder over the following to figure out if have you ever faced similar issues while dealing with money:

- Why do most investors buy a stock after it has already advanced substantially when, in fact, they should actually be selling it?
- Why do most investors sell stocks after a substantial decline when, in fact, they should ideally be buying them?
- Why do so many investors buy a stock just because their friends or neighbors have purchased it without investigating it themselves?
- Why do investors do so much more research when buying stocks than they do when selling them?
- Why do most people more easily buy unnecessary items through credit card as opposed to when they have to actually buy them through cash?

- Why do professional fund managers launch schemes, sector funds or other "new concept" funds when most of the money on that concept has already been made?
- Why do we tend to overeat at a party where we don't have to pay the bill as compared to when we dine in a hotel where we have to foot the bill ourselves?
- Why do we tip a hotel waiter whose service we did not like at all while bargaining to the last penny for the service of a lowly shoe polish boy who really did a good job?
- Why do we keep our money in the bank even at negative real interest rates knowing that we are actually losing purchasing power?
- Why are most workers happy with a 12% salary rise when the inflation rate is 15% and not happy with a 5% rise when the inflation rate is 3% though in the first case they are losing purchasing power while in the latter case they are getting a real gain?
- Why so many investors simply don't invest in stocks when they know that stocks create more wealth over the long term?
- Why do so many people go for, say, money back insurance policies where the costs are much higher just because they will get some money back as opposed to traditional term policies which are the cheapest and truest form of life insurance?
- Why do consumers prefer to buy, say, a dress with a price tag of ₹ 1,500 being sold at ₹ 1,000, i.e. at 33% discount, as compared to the same dress priced at ₹ 1,000 without any discount.

The answer to many of the pervasive and puzzling questions is rooted in behavior economics. I believe that by identifying the psychological causes behind many types of financial decisions, you can effectively change your behavior in a manner which will either put money into your pocket or will allow less money to flow out of your pocket. (In this connection, you might find it interesting to read Appendix 5.1 at the end of this chapter which tells you briefly about how the human brain works).

Now, let us dig deeper into human psychology and behavior economics to understand some of the most common financial mistakes which people commit while dealing with money. This will help you avoid making such common financial mistakes.

Common Financial Mistake 1: Sunk Cost Fallacy — Throwing Good Money After Bad

Imagine that somebody has given you a free ticket for a play in which your favorite star is acting. Hours before the play is going to commence you come to know that your favorite star may not be able to act that day. Also, that there is a major weather problem and going to the theatre and returning home might be difficult.

What would you do?

Now, imagine that you had actually purchased a ticket with your own money. What would you do then?

The likely answer is that in the first instance you might not go for the play while in the latter instance you would go even though your favorite star is not acting in it and there is also the risk of inclement weather. This illustrates the sunk cost fallacy. Since you have not paid for the ticket in the first instance you don't mind skipping the event but in the second instance you don't want to waste the money which you have already spent, i.e. sunk. Similarly, many a time we buy a certain stock of a bad company at a certain price, which then halves. In the name of "averaging", we then invest even more money in the stock, thus throwing good money after bad.

Let me tell you here about Weber's Law which is named after the German physiologist, Ernst Weber. It simply states that the impact of a change in the intensity of a stimulus is proportional to the absolute level of the original stimulus.

In the financial world it suggests that the difference between earning ₹ 100 and ₹ 200 for a certain job will have a larger effect on how happy you feel than the difference between earning ₹ 10,100 and ₹ 10,200. In both cases the difference is the same, i.e. ₹ 100. However, because, ₹ 200 is double of ₹ 100 while ₹ 10,200 is hardly 1% higher than ₹ 10,100, the importance given to earning the additional ₹ 100 in the two cases is vastly different. Therefore, a very common financial mistake which people make while dealing with money is that they see the big picture while forgetting the smaller one. This is not right thinking. We have to remember that ₹ 100 is, in fact, ₹ 100, and will be able to buy us the same amount of goods or services, whether it is a part of ₹ 200 or of ₹ 10,200.

How to Recognize Whether You are a Victim of Sunk Cost Fallacy

When you see the following tendencies in yourself while saving, spending, investing or taking insurance, it is very likely that you are suffering from the sunk cost fallacy:

- Money already spent is more important and dear to you than money in the pocket. In the hope of recovering the money already spent, you are ready to throw in fresh money fully knowing and recognizing the fact that the money already spent was a wrong decision.
- You prefer to sell a good investment only because it's making a profit for you while holding on to bad investments since you will lose money in doing so.
- You sell your good stocks during market downturns after substantial price damage has already been done.
- You continue with a bad insurance policy and pay further premiums just to protect the premiums which you have already paid in the past.
- You continue with something to which you have already financially committed even though, in hindsight, you would not have started it at all.
- Your future money decisions are based on your past money decisions.
- You sit through a boring movie just because you bought the ticket or read through a bad book just because you have already started reading it.

Steps to Rectify this Mistake

- Always make your decisions keeping in mind the future and not the past. The simplest thing to do here is to just mentally think as follows: Would I be ready to commit any time and / or money to this if I had not started the thing at all — be it reading a book, watching a movie, buying a stock, or taking an insurance policy, etc. Don't throw good money after bad money — money lost is gone; forget about it. Start fresh and don't ever base your future financial decisions on the basis of the past. Take a fresh and new look at things, totally forgetting the past.

- Make up your mind that money is money and you don't need to throw good money after bad. Just because you invested in a stock which is now in loss, don't put more money after it. You must accept that you have already lost what you put into it in the past. Are you ready to lose further money?
- Convert losses into profit, first mentally and then in reality. Here is an example. Suppose you've invested in a stock which is down not due to market conditions but due to fundamental deterioration in the future prospects of the company. If you sell the stock within one year you can offset the loss on it against any other short term capital gains on any of your other stocks. Therefore by selling the stock at loss, you are in fact "saving on tax" and hence converting at least some of the loss into profit.
- Consider losses as an opportunity cost. By holding on to a loss-making investment, and making the criminal mistake of adding on to the loss making investment in the hope of its revival, you are in fact paying a big "opportunity cost". You can instead invest that same money into a profitable investment.
- Always adhere to Commandment 1 and make a proper asset allocation plan. Once you have the right asset allocation plan, you simply have to follow it — you don't need to buy a loss making investment in the name of averaging. When you plan for things, then it becomes mechanical, routine and boring and that is what dealing with money has to be as opposed to the general belief that it has to be risky and exciting. This book is about teaching you to deal with your money and investments in a mechanical, boring and routine manner.

Common Financial Mistake 2: Dealing Differently With Profits and Losses

Prospect Theory explains why people behave differently when dealing with profits and losses. For example, you might have noticed that you are willing to hold on to a loss making investment in the "hope" that you might recover your cost although you know very well know that the chances of that are minimal. On the other hand, you might be more willing to "lock" into gains on a winning investment although you may have good reasons to believe that the price can go up still higher. This is called Prospect Theory — locking into a gain too quickly fearing that it might turn into a loss, and holding on to a loss making investment in the hope that it would turn into a profit. This kind of mental thinking is one of the main reasons why gamblers often increase their bets when luck is not going their way; they're willing to take a bigger tick to avoid finishing in the negative.

For example, the difference between gaining nothing or gaining ₹ 1,000 is greater than the difference between gaining ₹ 1,000 and ₹ 2,000, although in both cases the gain is ₹ 1,000. But in the first instance if you don't gain ₹ 1,000 you don't have anything while in the second instance even if you don't gain ₹ 1,000, you still end up with ₹ 1,000. Thus the pain of ending up with nothing — or with a lower amount — might influence your decision although the end result in both cases is the same.

Now let's consider the example of losing nothing or losing ₹ 1,000. Which would be more painful? Again, in both cases it is a question of losing ₹ 1,000 but in the first instance after losing ₹ 1,000 you are left with nothing while in the second case even after losing ₹ 1,000 you are still left with ₹ 1,000. Therefore even in the case of loss, the pain of ending up with nothing, or with a lower amount, might influence your decision although the end result is the same.

Prospect Theory seeks to explain why people choose the way they do.

Now let us take one more example. Assume that there are two individuals, A and B. A earns ₹ 1 lakh p.a. while B earns ₹ 10 lakh p.a. Let us further assume that both A and B lose ₹ 10,000 in gambling. For A, this is a substantial amount as it is 10% of his yearly income while for B it is a comparatively small amount as it is only 1% of his annual income. However, it's likely that both A and B would place the same importance to the loss of ₹ 10,000 simply because they had ₹ 10,000 in the pocket which they now don't have. Therefore, it is the actual gain or loss, rather than what those gains or losses leave us with in terms of our overall financial positions, which matters the most to us.

How to Recognize Whether You are a Victim of Prospect Theory

When you see the following tendencies in yourself while saving, spending, investing or taking insurance, it is very likely that you are indeed a victim of prospect theory:

- When you value loss more than profit.
- When you segregate money based on individual transactions disregarding the big financial picture.

Steps to Rectify this Mistake

- Remember that the pain of losing a given amount of money should always be equal to the pleasure of gaining the same amount of money.
- Always code gains and losses in the same way.

Common Financial Mistake 3: Loss Avoidance

Moving forward from where we left the prospect theory, another grave financial mistake which many people make is called loss avoidance. This simply means that people are loss averse. In fact, being loss averse is one of the main tenets of behavioral economics. The pain people feel from losing ₹ 100 is more than the pleasure they get from gaining ₹ 100. This explains why people behave inconsistently while taking risks.

For example, the same person may act conservatively when protecting gains, say by selling successful investments to lock in the profits, but act recklessly when seeking to avoid losses, e.g. by holding on to losing investments in the hope that they'll become profitable. Loss avoidance also causes investors to sell all their investments during periods of unusual market turmoil. For example, if you sold most of your stock during the market bottom in 2008 then you are probably suffering from loss avoidance.

If you want to understand this more clearly, just answer the following question honestly. Suppose you had invested ₹ 50,000 and ₹ 2,00,000, respectively, in two stocks, A and B. The current market value of Stock A has doubled from ₹ 50,000 to ₹ 1,00,000 while that of Stock B has halved from ₹ 2,00,000 to ₹ 1,00,000. Now, suppose that you suddenly require ₹ 1 lakh for your mother's medical emergency. What would you do? Would you sell A or B? Remember, also, that you now realize that Stock A is a good company and while it has already doubled in value, its future prospects are equally bright. You have also understood that Stock B was a bad investment and neither is its future looking good. In such a circumstance, if you choose to sell Stock A then you suffer from loss avoidance. That's because you are unable to realize, or accept, the loss which you have already suffered because of your bad investment decision. Therefore, when you take financial decisions based on avoiding losses rather than future prospects then you are most likely suffering from loss avoidance.

Another symptom of loss avoidance is that you are likely to abandon the bus at the first instance of trouble. For example, suppose after full research and due diligence you invested in Stock X at ₹ 100 believing that its fair valuation was ₹ 150. All the fundamentals of Company X and its future prospects remain as rosy as before but because of generally weak stock market conditions, the price of Stock X falls to ₹ 75. What would you do in such a situation? Would you panic and sell X just because it has fallen in value? Or, would you stay put knowing that these are temporary market fluctuations and the long term value, and thus the profit target of the stock, is intact at ₹ 150. Or, better still, would you buy more of it because what was good at ₹ 100, is excellent at ₹ 75 without any real changes in prospects? If you panic and sell X at ₹ 75 then in all likelihood you are suffering from loss avoidance.

The best way to combat loss avoidance is to diversify. While individual investments in the portfolio might perform badly at any given time but their influence on the overall portfolio would be minimal. That again takes us back to Commandment 1, namely "Thou Shall Make a Proper Asset Allocation Plan". The importance of this commandment is such that I end up mentioning it again and again. Once you have a proper asset allocation plan, and stick to it, then at least 90% of your money problems would be solved.

How to Recognize Whether You are a Victim of Loss Avoidance

When you see the following tendencies in yourself, it is very likely that you are suffering from loss avoidance:

- You panic at the sight of a notional loss even when you know that it is a short term market phenomenon while the long term prospects of the investment are fully intact.
- When you exit out of good, profit making investments only because you don't want to sell bad, loss making investments.

Steps to Rectify this Mistake

- Always remember Commandment 1. If you have a proper asset allocation plan and stick to it then at least 90% of your money problems are solved, including the psychological mistake of loss avoidance.
- Don't sell winning investments more readily than the losing ones and don't take money out of the equities simply because markets have fallen.
- Whether it is life, relationships or investments, if you cling to the past then you will most probably miss a glorious future. Therefore, don't think too much about the past but look instead into the future.
- Don't spend too much time and thought on your investments. Once you follow a proper asset allocation plan, then your investments should become mechanical, routine and boring and only require a periodic review. Never get stampeded by the market's day-to-day fluctuations.

Common Financial Mistake 4: Mental Accounting

The term mental accounting refers to the phenomenon of treating money differently depending upon the source from which it has been received. For example, a person may treat salary (earned money) as precious and be over cautious with it while treating gifts, unexpected bonus, unanticipated tax refunds, or huge inheritance as "free money" and be careless with it. The "preciousness" of earned money may lead a person to let the money just remain idle in a savings account, thus getting beaten down by inflation. On the other hand, carelessness about "free money" may lead a person to casually spend the money or invest in risky ventures resulting in eventual loss. Thus by assigning relative values to different moneys that in absolute terms have the same buying power, you run the risk of being too quick to spend, too slow to save, too conservative to invest, or too reluctant to take insurance — all of which can cost you dearly. Another possibility is that you may be ready to take risk with your short term funds but may be too conservative with your long term retirement money labeling it as "sacred money". This would, in effect, lead you to put all your retirement funds in conservative bank deposits which, in turn, would expose you to the bigger monster of inflation which will eat into your real returns over the long term. Therefore, while your money might be safe in the bank but on retirement you will realize that your actual purchasing power has significantly diminished because of the ravages of inflation.

An example of mental accounting in regard to spending would be that you also end up buying unnecessary small things when you are buying a bigger thing. For example, your car stereo is working fine. But because you are doing some major repairs to your car which cost, say, ₹ 1.5 lakh, you "waste" an extra ₹ 10,000 for a new stereo, mentally "clubbing" it with the larger expense of ₹ 1.5 lakh. This is a kind of mental accounting when it comes to spending — clubbing unwarranted small expenses with necessary large expenses. You incur those small expenses which you would not have otherwise incurred only because they seem a small and insignificant part of the total larger expense.

How to Recognize Whether You are a Victim of Mental Accounting

When you see the following tendencies in yourself, it is very likely that you are suffering from mental accounting:

- You consider your retirement funds as different from your normal funds.
- Unnecessary spending comes naturally to you while saving money seems to be a curse.
- You set up a special "kitty box" to fund your vacation while simultaneously carrying credit card debt.
- You are more likely to waste windfall gains than your salary income.
- You are more comfortable spending through a credit card than with hard cash.

Steps to Rectify this Mistake

- Whenever you receive any unexpected windfall gain, like a lottery win, tax refund, free gift, inheritance, etc., don't put it into your normal savings account. Instead, immediately lock it into some kind of long term instrument, such as a long term bond, fixed deposit, or equity stock. This will ensure that the windfall gain goes into a long term instrument and is not available for you to squander. And once you are locked into a long term investment, your mind will then automatically think of it as your own money and not as a windfall or unexpected gain. However, while applying this solution in practice, do take care to lock the windfall gain in one-off investment, like a bank fixed deposit or a fully paid up equity share, and not in a recurring investment like a recurring bank deposit or partly paid up share because the money you are using to buy that investment is one-off money.
- When spending, consider each item individually. Don't combine two items. Just because you are revamping your kitchen set does not mean that you buy a new pressure cooker if your current one is working fine and you wouldn't otherwise have purchased it.
- Imagine that all bills which you are paying are through cash rather than credit card or cheque. You may finally pay it *via* a credit card or cheque but first "mentally" imagine that you have

to pay by cash — that you have to actually go to the bank, withdraw the money, count the money and then hand it over by cash. The pain of withdrawing money from the bank, counting it, knowing that you have to give it to someone and then actually handing it out is psychologically much more painful than swiping a credit card or just writing a cheque. Once you train your mind in this manner, then you would actually start using mental accounting to your advantage.

- Remove the concept of "free money" from your mind because in reality there is neither a free lunch nor free money. Tell yourself that all money is actually hard earned income — the reason we recklessly spend one form of income rather than another is because of the mental belief that we have not worked hard for the "free" money. However, explain to your mind that all money is actually earned income. For example, if you have got a tax refund then imagine the pain which you went to while filing your return, the discussion which you had with your tax consultant, the risk you took of not getting the refund and then you will realize that it was not actually "free money". Similarly, if you win a lottery ticket think back to how many times you bought tickets and did not win anything, and how much money you actually spent over the past so many years on lottery tickets till you finally won a prize and then you will realize that it is not actually "free money". Further, if you have received a "free gift" from some friend or relative, then think of the time you have spent with that friend or relative and also of any gifts that you might have given that friend or relative. He / she may now just be returning that past favor. Therefore, a "free gift" might, in fact, not in reality be a free gift.

Common Financial Mistake 5: Decision Paralysis

Whether it is protecting, budgeting, saving, spending, investing, insuring or any other money matter, many a time we are not able to make a decision and just maintain *status quo*. However, we don't realize that not making a decision is also a decision in itself — the decision being that we have confidence in the way we are doing things. Not being able to take decision under uncertainty leads to decision paralysis. Because we are not able to take the right decision, many a time we continue with the wrong decisions. This leads us to a very important principle — that in the world of money, there are not only decisions of commission but also decisions of omission. In reality, some very costly financial mistakes which people commit are because they are not able to take action at the right time.

For example, say you purchased a stock at ₹ 100 thinking that its true worth was ₹ 150 — a level the price is likely to achieve in one year. However, the stock price reaches ₹ 150 in just six months. Now that your price target has been achieved in half the time, you get confused since you had two objectives — hold the stock for one year, and after one year sell it for ₹ 150. Now your price target, which is your final goal, has been achieved in only six months, i.e. in a far shorter time frame. Therefore, other things remaining constant, ideally you must sell the stock at ₹ 150 unless of course the prospects of the stock have changed on a long term basis and it's likely to go up even higher. In such a situation you may experience total decision paralysis. You may decide not to take any action and keep wondering what to do little realizing that by not doing anything you have decided to hold onto the stock.

Decision paralysis is more likely when there is "decision under conflict". The inability to take a decision increases when we are presented with a plethora of problems. For example, today there are so many competing mutual fund products available in the market. This can lead to decision paralysis as you may not know which scheme to select or invest in. Let us take another example. You might have decided to buy your dream home. However, you are unable to decide upon its timing. In the meantime, the price goes up further and this makes your decision making process even more difficult.

How to Recognize Whether You are a Victim of Decision Paralysis

When you see the following tendencies in yourself while saving, spending, investing or taking insurance, it is very likely that you are suffering from decision paralysis:

- You delay, or avoid, taking spending or investment decisions.

- You find it difficult to select between different investment or insurance products.
- You come down very hard on yourself for making mistakes, however genuine they might have been.

Steps to Rectify this Mistake

- Don't give yourself the option that not taking a decision is an option. In other words, make it very clear to yourself that you have to select and decide from one of the possible alternatives, and that you don't have the option of just sitting put and not deciding anything.
- Make a plan and stick to it. Again, remember Commandment 1 — Thou Shall Make a Proper Asset Allocation Plan. Once you have made a plan; you are on auto pilot — then you don't need to take decisions time after time. And when you don't need to take recurrent decisions, there is no question of suffering from decision paralysis! This once again shows the importance of Commandment 1.
- All of us are making decisions all the time — whether we want to or not and whether we realize it or not. To eat is a decision about not remaining hungry, to drink water is a decision about not being thirsty, to have friends is a decision about not being lonely and to marry is a decision to have a companion for life. Similarly, not to commit suicide is a decision to stay alive. By writing this book, I am making the decision of spreading financial education so that each and every one of us is financially free. Therefore we are constantly making decisions, whether we consciously realize it or not. When we are taking so many decision constantly in our life, there is no reason to fear money decisions. So don't fear money and take financial decisions bravely.
- Don't be too hard on yourself. Many a time I have seen people being very hard on themselves and cursing themselves for taking wrong decisions. Your aim is to use your best judgment, knowledge and experience while taking a decision. Once you have done your homework and taken a decision, the final outcome may or may not turn out in your favor. You need not be too harsh on yourself if the outcome of the decision goes against

you. Don't forget that we all make mistakes — and the biggest mistake in life is not to make any mistake.

- Avoid thinking too much. What I mean by this is that use your best judgment, knowledge and experience before taking a decision — but once you have decided, then act on it. If you keep thinking and re-thinking again and again, then your decision will become weak and you may never be able to take any decision. You must be intelligent enough to know where to draw the line or when to stop thinking and start acting.
- Every decision involves some risk. Learn to take intelligent calculated risks. The life of a person who does not take any risks becomes risky.

Common Financial Mistake 6: Selective Thinking

This is another common and dangerous money illusion. Selective thinking blocks your mind by not allowing all the relevant information to flow into it for taking a correct financial decision. Sometimes it might allow only those facts to enter your mind which are already unconsciously stored in your memory. This leads to multiple problems. For example, it may lead to "anchoring" which simply means holding on to facts which are unimportant for your decision making. Then there is other equally obstructive financial behavior called "confirmation bias". This is a cognitive bias whereby one tends to notice and look for information that confirms one's existing beliefs, while ignoring anything that contradicts those beliefs. Anchoring and confirmation bias paralyze your thinking and don't allow you to take a decision based on available facts and figures. They show you the wrong facts and figures which may completely distort your judgment. The common but dangerous financial mistake of selective thinking has a very deep implication for one of the most basic and important aspects of your life — the way you process and assess information. It's needless to say that selective thinking can have a big impact on the way you save money, spend, invest or take insurance.

If you think more closely, you will realize that the common financial mistakes of anchoring and confirmation bias are more likely to affect the more intelligent and knowledgeable persons. This is because they will have more facts, ideas and memories stored in their brain which will keep interfering with the new situations they encounter in life. Therefore such psychological behavior is a greater problem for the more knowledgeable people.

The problem of selective thinking can be detrimental when dealing with money, both at the time of buying as well as selling. For example, while buying a stock you may have some notions about a certain company and you may therefore think that the stock is not worth buying even when, in reality, the facts and circumstances have changed and warrant a fresh look. This may lead you to missing out an opportunity of profitable investment. As regards selling, suppose you want to sell your car and have decided on a price limit for it. Even when new and better models enter the market, you stick to your price with the result that you let great deals pass by.

Selective Thinking — A Devil Whose Potential You Don't Know

Selective thinking is a dangerous psychological behavior not only for your money but even in all aspects of your life. This is simply because it hijacks your thinking process. Suppose you have already decided what the correct facts are, then howsoever compelling the new facts may be, your mind will simply not accept them. Further, if you accept only a certain set of facts and don't let new facts enter your mind, then you are completely cutting off your mind from the real world. Bear in mind that knowledge is the foundation on which all your misconceptions will finally die. However, the process of selective thinking prevents fresh knowledge from entering your mind. So you can appreciate how dangerous this is because it fully hijacks your thinking and does not allow you to change at all. For example, even if the principles in this book are correct and make sense but you might reject them outright, or accept them only partially because of selective thinking, that would be to your disadvantage. Similarly, you might have a preconceived notion in your mind about a particular person. Now, whatever good things that individual might do, you will fail to see them because of your preconceived notion. This leads to forming a wrong judgment which may prove costly for your personal and professional life. You have to work very hard to change this sort of thinking pattern not only to improve your financial state but your life as a whole.

How to Recognize Whether You are a Victim of Selective Thinking

When you see the following tendencies in yourself while saving, spending, investing or taking insurance, it is very likely that you are a victim of selective thinking:

- You always surround yourself with people who only praise you and agree with your views, whether right or wrong.
- You almost always — and almost completely — disregard the advice of other people.
- You are always confident of your own knowledge, judgment and experience.
- You believe that you know everything whether it concerns saving, spending, investing, insurance or any other facet of life and do not require anybody's advice.
- You believe you don't need the services of brokers and analysts.
- You make spending and investing decisions without much research and thought.

Steps to Rectify this Mistake

- Be humble. The main causes of anchoring and confirmation bias are pride and ego. Remember that we are all just mortals and the creator is the Almighty God. When you have made a mistake, accept it. Don't fear failure because it is the greatest teacher in life. If you keep blaming others for your mistakes and failures, you will never grow as an individual. And if you can't grow as an individual, then there is hardly any chance that you would be able to grow financially.
- Always have an open mind and only then will you be able to learn. Always seek to learn something new. Keep challenging conventional wisdom and your own beliefs.
- Be reasonable in your expectations. When dealing with important money decisions, like investing, you should have realistic expectations. Selective thinking can block your mind and create unrealistic expectations from your investments. And when

unrealistic expectations, based on wrong notions, enter your mind, you are sure to suffer financially.

- Always seek advice — whether in doubt or otherwise. Remember, two minds are generally better than one. You may take the final decision based on your own judgment, knowledge and experience but you have to be receptive and open to new ideas. You have to respect the thoughts of other knowledgeable and experienced people in order to widen your own thinking and perspective.

Common Financial Mistake 7: Endowment Effect

Holding on to what you have is a financial mistake which very few people understand and acknowledge. People generally tend to overvalue what belongs to them relative to the value they would place on the same possession or situation if it belonged to someone else. This is called the endowment effect.

For example, a person will think that his son is the most intelligent or his daughter is the most beautiful girl of all. This is a very common and widely prevalent example of the endowment effect.

Endowment effect is also very common in the financial world. For example, you might think that your house is worth more than your neighbor's though the two houses are nearly identical. Because people place an inordinately high value on what they have, decisions to change become all the more difficult. However, contrary to other financial mistakes, people do manage to overcome this tendency. If they didn't, then human beings wouldn't sell their homes or divorce their spouses!

Businesses understand the endowment effect. That is the primary reason why they offer so many "trial period" or "money back" offers. Company executives know very well that once a consumer gets used to their product, it would then be difficult to live without it. Hence, the primary test for their product is that the consumer should like it in the first place and get habituated to it which, in essence, happens during the trial period. And once the trial period is over, due to the endowment effect the customer often continues buying the product. So the next time you go in for a free trial, pause and think twice because the free trial might in fact not turn out to be free for you!

One of the most costly and regrettable consequence of endowment effect is how people deal with their retirement planning. It's relatively easy to set aside small sums of money during one's earning years so as to accumulate a large retirement corpus due to the power of compounding. But many people fail to follow this basic principle. The main reason for that can be traced back to the psychological behavior of endowment effect — people overvalue what they have (today's income) and fail to properly value what they could have (financially independent retired life).

How to Recognize Whether You are a Victim of Endowment Effect

When you see the following tendencies in yourself while saving, spending, investing or taking insurance, it's very likely that you are a victim of endowment effect:

- You find it very difficult to save money.
- You think money today is worth more than money tomorrow; you don't think of the future but always want to live and consume what you have in the present.
- You believe that your investments, whether a house or a piece of art or anything else, is worth more than your neighbor's.
- You don't believe in retirement planning.
- You are always on the look out for "trial period" or "money back" offers.
- You believe investments are too risky.
- You can't determine the true value of your investments and always depend on others for it.

Steps to Rectify this Mistake

- Always view all situations and investments with the same eye — whether it is your own or that of somebody else.
- Be wary of trial period or money back offers because it's likely that the trial period might get converted into a permanent one.

- Learn to do a fair assessment and determine a proper value for your assets. The value should be the same — whether you own it or your neighbor does.
- Remember that retirement planning is one of the most important facets of financial planning and the gateway towards achieving financial independence. Go back to Commandment 1 — Thou Shall Make a Proper Asset Allocation Plan and put yourself on auto pilot.

Common Financial Mistake 8: Buyer's Remorse

If you have a tendency to spend money on buying things which you don't really require but end up buying them only because there is a discount available, or because there is some scheme, or because something is available with it for free, then you will suffer from buyer's remorse. That's so because after you have purchased the product, you are most likely to regret it. And, mind you, this is not restricted to buying only physical or material things but even financial products, investments, insurance, bank savings, etc.

For example, suppose there is an offer of a free music system on the purchase of a new Led TV. Now, if you otherwise don't require the TV but purchase it just because there is this offer, then you are in for buyer's remorse. Similarly, you will most likely suffer from buyer's remorse if you buy a useless insurance product which you don't require simply because of the gift of a free gold coin on its purchase.

Another example of buyer's remorse would be discount sales. If you don't require a particular product but buy it just because it is available at some kind of a discount, again you are in for buyer's remorse. Another symptom of it would be buying things which you don't require during special sales promotion seasons, like festivals, etc.

Advertisers and company managements know this human weakness very well and exploit it to the fullest.

Another trick that companies use to sell their products is that they set some kind of a threshold. Thus, if you purchase up to a value of, say, ₹ 10,000, then you get a gift voucher of ₹ 1,000.

There are many drawbacks to such schemes. Firstly, you have to purchase so many articles — some of which you may not really need — so that the value crosses the set limit. Once you have crossed that limit, most probably the company will not allow you to settle the discount in the current bill. In the given example, the gift voucher of ₹ 1,000 will not, in most cases, be allowed to be settled against the current bill of ₹ 10,000 but against some future bill. What it does is that it draws you back to the store to "cash in on the gift voucher". Once you are back in the store, it is more likely that you will purchase items whose total value crosses ₹ 1,000. And then there might be some other new scheme to lure you. So the cycle keeps continuing and you keep buying products which you don't require but which the company wants to sell to you by enticing you with "gift vouchers and discount coupons".

How to Recognize Whether You are a Victim of Buyer's Remorse

When you see the following tendencies in yourself while saving, spending, investing or taking insurance, it is very likely that you are suffering from buyer's remorse:

- You buy a certain item — whether physical or financial — just because there is something free available with it.
- You tend to shop more during discount sales, festival times, etc.
- You tend to shop more in stores which have certain kind of loyalty point system on the sales.
- You take an insurance policy or open a bank account because something like a gold coin comes free with it.

Steps to Rectify this Mistake

- Buy only what you want and not what the seller wants to sell to you.
- Concentrate on the product which you require and not on what is available for free.
- Don't stop buying a good product which you genuinely require only because some special scheme or offer on it has been closed.

Common Financial Mistake 9: Confusing Saving with Investing

If you assume that saving is equal to investing then you might be in for a nasty surprise. You are also living with a big delusion because you don't understand that the rules of money permanently changed in the year 1971 when the then US President Richard Nixon took the US off the gold standard and granted itself the license to print money. Since then, the US dollar and other world "currencies" have depreciated while prices of all commodities measured against it — be it precious metals like gold, silver or industrial metals like steel, copper, aluminum or agricultural commodities — have gone up and will continue to go up over the long term. That's why we call money as currency.

Although we all love money but invariably we are all fooled by it. The problem is that while most of us love money we don't realize how to value it. If you think closely, you will realize money is nothing but paper and has no value in itself except that it can be exchanged for goods and services. Thus, the value of money is not intrinsic but what it can be exchanged for in return. Which is why money today is nothing but a currency which can be exchanged for other goods and services. And the more the goods and services we derive for a given amount of money, the more the value of money, and *vice versa.* This is what is meant by knowing the value of money.

If you are still confused then let me give you a simple but a very common and practical example. As I mentioned earlier, most of us have illusions about money — the more the money we get, the better off we think we are, and *vice versa*. But this may not always be the case.

Let us consider the simple example of an employee Mr. X who got a 10% salary increment when the inflation was 12% while in another year he got 5% increment when the inflation was 3%. Which one would he prefer and which one should he prefer? In all likelihood, he will prefer the first case of 10% increment although the second one is superior. The reason is very simple and logical. In the first case, the employee is getting a negative real increment since inflation is higher than the salary increase while in the second case he is getting a real increment since inflation is lower than the salary raise. Thus, in the first case the value of money in his hand is lower while in the second case the value of money in hand is higher. I again repeat that money is just a currency with no real intrinsic value. Its value is derived from how many goods and services one can buy with it; the more the amount of goods and services which can be bought with a given amount of money, the more is its value, and *vice versa.* This is called the money illusion and one of the main reasons why people prefer investment in fixed deposit at negative real interest rates after tax rather than long term tax free gains through stocks.

One of the other facets of money illusion is taxes as these eat into your gross income. Although almost everybody hates to pay tax but people often don't realize how they can either actually avoid taxes perfectly legally or pay much lower tax. It's very simple. The government has made tax laws very discriminating. The rich know it and take advantage of it while the poor and middle class become its victims. As we saw earlier in the book, the government's regressive tax system puts maximum taxes on earned income which is the income that you work hard for like, say, salary. At the same time it totally exempts from income tax certain other forms of income, such as dividends, long term capital gains, etc., which all constitute passive and portfolio income — the income derived from your investment assets whether it be shares, real estate, etc. The tax is also regressive because it taxes the rich at a much lower rate, if at all. For example, the "net marginal tax rate" after deductions is much lower on a business than it is on salary. A salaried employee hardly gets any deductions and most of his earned income is almost fully taxed while a businessman gets all kinds of expenses — whether he actually spends or not — as deduction and the net taxed money is lower. I say whether he spends or not because there are certain expenses which the businessman actually spends money on, like staff salaries, telephone bills, electricity bills, etc., which are allowed as a deduction from income but there are certain other items, such as deprecation, which is not a cash expense but is still a deductible business expense. That is why the tax system is regressive and favors the rich. The middle class buy assets in their individual names while the rich buy assets in their businesses, typically the companies which they own buy the assets for them and enjoy all the legally allowed benefits on it. Thus, the rules of money are not fair and give the rich an unfair advantage. To own a company is very simple in today's information age; you don't need to actually own any plant or machinery for owning a company — it's just a document registered with the government. The only thing which you need to know is the relevant aspect of corporate laws, tax laws and securities laws to take advantage of this legitimate option.

Coming back to inflation, unlike income tax which goes out from our pocket and pinches us and hence we know it, inflation is a hidden monster with a double-edged sword. Although we may know it but we simply fail to recognize it and accept its presence. As the famous economist Milton Friedman said, "Inflation is always and everywhere a monetary phenomenon." That is why it is very important to understand the concept of "fiat money" as currency. Those who are "savers of money" and hold their savings as currency will be big losers over a period of time. The government can and will keep printing money which will result in larger and larger amounts of money chasing the same limited quantity of goods and services. And as we know from the basic premise of economics — demand and supply — when the supply of a particular item (money) increases without actual increase in output (goods and services), it invariably results in a fall in the value of money. The simple rule is that more the money chasing a fixed supply of goods and services, the more will the rise in price of those goods and services get expressed in terms of ever increasing money supply. Thus, by printing money the government is in effect "stealing money from your pocket" by diminishing its value.

After the 2008 global credit crisis, we saw lots of bailout packages announced globally. For example, the US bailed out of its troubled financial institutions such as the Citigroup, AIG, etc. in 2008. Many debt-ridden European countries kept crying out for bailout packages. What you must understand is that by bailing out these troubled institutions and countries, the governments were in effect "stealing" money from their people's pockets. Rather than paying for their mistakes, these institutions and countries used the non-existent savings of taxpayers. As a result, people will subsequently be taxed more — and the government will print even more money — leaving you with a lesser amount of money whose value is ever diminishing!

To drive home the point; if you believe that saving is investing then I think you are in for a rude shock. This is because you are saving in terms of money — currency whose value is continuously and incessantly losing its value. Therefore, in this modern information age of currency, savers are losers. You have to learn to convert your money into investment assets. Another benefit of converting money into investment assets is that you then actually profit from inflation. When you use money to purchase assets which increase in value with inflation, you are actually benefiting from inflation! For example, suppose you own rental real estate. Now, every time the value of money goes down because of inflation, you get the opportunity to increase your rent which, in essence, not only immediately increases your cash flow but also leads to an increase in the value of your property because inflation causes the replacement cost of your property to go up which, in turn, leads to an increase in the price of your property. This is how you can actually benefit from inflation by playing the rules of money correctly to your advantage.

How to Recognize Whether You Believe That Saving is Investing

When you see the following tendencies in yourself while saving, spending, investing or taking insurance, it is very likely that you believe that saving is investing:

- You believe money in the bank is safer than money in assets — whether it be stocks, gold or any other kind of real asset.
- You disregard inflation.
- You only look at gross income but not at after tax net income.
- You believe that the value of a rupee today will be the same tomorrow.

Steps to Rectify this Mistake

- Remember that saving is not investing, which is why English language also has two distinct words for them. Don't merely save your money but always try to convert money into investment assets.
- Never forget Commandment 1 — Thou Shall Make a Proper Asset Allocation Plan. It's worth repeating again and again that a proper asset allocation plan will automatically ensure that you won't hoard too much money in the form of savings but convert it into investment assets.
- Benefit from any fall in the value of currency with the help of investment assets which go up in value with inflation.

Common Financial Mistake 10: Bigness Bias

Most of us try to think big as far as money is concerned but often forget that small things when compounded over a period of time result into much bigger things. This is because of our ignorance of a basic principle of mathematics. For example, the tendency to dismiss or discount small numbers as insignificant can lead us to pay more than we need to for brokerage, commissions, mutual fund expenses and taxes. This has a surprisingly deleterious effect on our investment performance over time.

It's one thing to buy a pressure cooker when you are buying a new kitchen set which is a kind of one-off item but another thing to incur small expenses or losses repeatedly over a long period. They will become very big before you realize what's happening. In fact, many times the difference in performance of two competing products might just be those small items which have added up and become seemingly big over a period of time. Let us consider some practical examples.

People who trade very frequently in stocks or bonds might earn good gross profits but the commissions, transaction costs and income tax eat into their gross earnings and their actual net earnings might be much lower. Though apparently small, cumulatively these costs eat away into the extra profits, if any, you generate on trading. In my view, trading is a zero sum game; for every winner there has to be a loser — the only people who win are the brokers in the form of commissions, government in the form of taxes, and bankers in the form of interest on leveraged trading money.

A similar situation is seen in mutual funds where exorbitant salaries of fund managers and research analysts, legal and compliance expenses, and other operating expenses eat up into any kind of extra return (alpha) which they may generate. These expenses are charged to the fund and expressed in the form of expense ratio. The lower the expense ratio, the higher the probability of the fund outperforming its peers.

How to Recognize Whether You are a Victim of Bigness Bias

When you see the following tendencies in yourself while saving, spending, investing or taking insurance, it is very likely that you are suffering from bigness bias:

- You believe that by starting late with a larger monthly contribution you would be able to easily beat a person who has started investing early but with a slightly lower monthly contribution.
- You ignore the power of compounding.
- You look at the large picture but don't believe in capturing the details.
- You are ignorant of the principles of mathematics.

Steps to Rectify this Mistake

- Remember to always start early when building your financial wealth and never underestimate the power of compounding because small numbers add up to a large figure over a period of time.
- Read the fine print of fee structures, brokerages, commissions while investing in equities, bonds, mutual funds, private equity funds, etc.
- Remember the value of time and always try to keep it on your side.

Common Financial Mistake 11: Believing that Experts Can Consistently Beat Normal Market Returns

This is one of the most common financial mistakes which investors are prone to. Possibly, I am making a controversial statement because generally you will hear that equity investments are for experts and if you don't know how to pick the right stocks, you should entrust your money to an expert fund manager, etc. However, I dare say this is a useless advice. Hold on; I am not saying that you shouldn't entrust your money to experts and start picking your own stocks instead — no, there may not be bigger financial suicide than that. I just humbly submit that it's very difficult, if not impossible, to beat the stock market indices consistently over a longer period of time. If that were not the case, then approximately 75% of all "actively" managed stock funds would not under-perform the passively constructed stock indices over periods of a decade or more. The fact of the matter is that most people can't either pick winning stocks or time the markets on a consistent basis and their occasional success is simply chance.

Here, I would like to quote Dr. William Bernstein who said: "There are two kinds of investors, be they large or small: those who don't know where the market is headed, and those who don't know that they don't know where the market is headed. Then again, there is a third type of investor — the investment professional, who indeed knows that he or she doesn't know, but whose livelihood depends upon appearing to know where the market is headed."

Nothing more succinctly explains the real world of professional investing and stock picking. Merton Miller, Nobel Laureate and professor of economics in Chicago commented that "if there are ten thousand people looking at the stocks and trying to pick winners, one in the ten thousand is going to score, by chance alone, a great coup, and that's all that's going on. It's a game, it's a chance operation, and people think they are doing something purposeful, but they're really not." And as Rex Sinquefield, co-author of *Stocks, Bonds, Ills and Inflation* puts it: "We all know that active management fees are high. Poor performance does not come cheap. You have to pay dearly for it." Thus, active fund management is nothing but paying heavy fees for under-performing the passive indices!

For investors who are always on the look out for the next hot fund, the next great sector fund, etc., Bethany McLean, columnist for *Fortune* magazine, wrote that "skepticism about past returns is crucial, the truth is, much as you may wish you could know which funds will be hot, you can't and neither can the legions of advisors and publications that claim they can. That's why building a portfolio around index funds isn't really settling for the average. It's just refusing to believe in magic."

Further, let me quote John Bogle, founder and former CEO of the Vanguard group: "Index funds eliminate the risks of individual stocks, market sectors, and manager selection. Only stock market risks remain." In other words, when you invest in a passively managed index fund, all risks relating to the fund manager, his / her stock selection and market timing, selection of sectors, etc. are all eliminated and the only risk which remains is the risk of the stock market as a whole and that is precisely the risk which you would like to expose yourself to when you invest in equities.

Nicholas Taleb has written an excellent book titled *Fooled by Randomness* wherein he explains the role of chance in life and in the markets and I recommend this book to everyone who believes that he or she can consistently pick winning stocks or time the markets to perfection.

Last but not the least, I would like to remind you of the words of the legendary investor Warren Buffett who once said that "most investors, both institutional and individual, will find the best way to own common stocks is through an index fund that charges minimal fees. Those following this path are sure to beat the net results (after fees and expenses) delivered by the great majority of investment professionals."

The conclusion therefore is that you shouldn't believe that you can pick winning stocks or time the markets. The best solution for any equity investor is to stick to low cost, passively managed index funds because year after year they are likely to beat a majority of the actively managed funds — and over the longer term probably beat almost all equity funds.

How to Recognize Whether You Believe That You Can Beat the Markets

When you see the following tendencies in yourself while saving, spending, investing or taking insurance, it is very likely that you are suffering from the erroneous belief that you can beat the stock markets:

- You always believe in picking stocks and disregard the indices.
- You always aim at picking the next winning mutual fund.
- You always boast about your winning stocks and try to avoid or "explain away" your losing stocks.
- You ignore fund management expenses.

Steps to Rectify this Mistake

- Invest in equity through a low cost, passively managed index fund.
- Don't believe any expert at face value (including this author — although I don't claim to be an expert).
- Read analyst reports only for obtaining data and watch financial business channels only for getting news and as a source of entertainment — don't try to get stock ideas or market views from either of these sources.

Common Financial Mistake 12: Over Confidence

This is probably one of the most common mistakes but one which is difficult to identify. Even if identified, it is very difficult to accept and this not only affects the way you deal with money and finance but almost all facets of your life. It's difficult to identify because it is the very core of your beliefs — your very nature might be that of either over confidence or under confidence. And even if you are able to identify it, it may be very difficult to accept because that would hurt your pride and ego, things which are dear to most human beings.

We humans can learn from our mistakes and failures. Actually, few things can be a bigger teacher than our own mistakes and failures. We grow the most from our greatest challenges. But the problem is that our pride and ego make us over confident and help us explain away our mistakes and failures instead of learning valuable lessons from them. And since we don't learn our lessons, we continue to commit the same mistakes again and again, which leads to larger and larger failures in life, be it financial or otherwise. In the financial world, not learning from our mistakes and committing the same ones repeatedly is a sure formula for financial disaster. Therefore, there is no point holding on to your ego and being over confident. By identifying and understanding your behavioral shortcomings, you can correct them and enjoy greater financial freedom. I am not trying to suggest that you should not have confidence in yourself because confidence is the core foundation for doing anything. The only point I am trying to drive home is that you should never be over confident. The difference between confidence and over confidence is a very thin one and difficult for many to identify. When you take decisions based on your knowledge and experience and have the humility to accept responsibility when you go wrong, that is confidence. When you take decisions based on your ego and pride, that is nothing but over confidence.

As a result of over confidence, you might place too much reliance on what you know or what you think you know and this can cost your pocket dearly. Over confidence is very pervasive, even among the educated, knowledgeable and experienced people and often leads to their downfall. Numerous studies have shown that over confidence in the judgment of doctors, engineers, lawyers and fund managers has cost people dearly and this is more pronounced in the financial world, particularly the stock markets. Remember that market is famous for exposing human weaknesses. It will put you in the "ego trap" and fully exploit your over confidence, after which you will be ruined, losing both your money and your confidence.

Anyone, whether a professional or an amateur, who believes that he can consistently predict the markets or the value of any investment, be it a stock or bond, or any other financial or economic variable such as interest rates or inflation, is probably a victim of over confidence and is, in essence, fooling himself. He believes in magic which does not exist in the financial world. Such a person believes that it is easy to beat the general market indices which, as shown earlier, is an almost impossible feat and even if achieved, it's purely due to chance and randomness. Optimism and confidence are good and positive qualities but when ego and pride make you over confident, that is the first sign of your downfall, financially and otherwise, in life.

How to Recognize Whether You are a Victim of Over Confidence

When you see the following tendencies in yourself while saving, spending, investing or taking insurance, it is very likely that you are suffering from over confidence:

- You don't believe in using the services of a broker.
- You do more research when buying a sock than when buying a stock.
- You make spending or investment decisions without doing any home work.
- You think it's easy to out-perform the market consistently and over long periods of time.
- You believe research is a waste of time.
- You remember your winning investments while you shrug away the losing ones and don't learn any lessons from them.
- When you commit a mistake, you blame either someone else or the situation for it instead of taking responsibility and blaming yourself.

Steps to Rectify this Mistake

- Do proper due diligence and research before making any spending, saving, investing or insurance decision.
- Respect the opinion and views of others. You may take your own final decision but always consider and give due credence to the suggestions of others.
- Discount your own views. For example, while buying a stock buy it a few percentage above your buy price and while selling it, sell it a few percentage below your target price.

Common Financial Mistake 13: Under Confidence

This is the opposite of over confidence. Although it is not as prevalent as over confidence, it surely exists, particularly in the world of money. Under confidence might also mean you have more confidence in the financial abilities of others than in your own. Under confidence is likely to lead you to a big investment mistake called herd mentality. There are numerous examples of herd mentality in history, such as the Mississippi Scheme, South Sea Bubble, Tulip Bulb Mania, etc., instances of how the madness of crowds leads to big and widespread financial catastrophes throughout the world. How many times have you watched a movie only because others liked it, or went to dine in a restaurant because your friend went there, or wore a particular dress because your neighbor wore it? If you follow others most of the time then probably you are suffering from under confidence. While these small examples might not be so damaging for your pocket but when you start imitating others in taking your financial decisions, it can have disastrous consequences on your bank balance.

People commit the mistake of under confidence in today's world because they don't trust their knowledge, judgment and experience but surrender to the judgment of the crowd. It has been shown time and time again how completely rational and knowledgeable people take totally irrational and illogical decision when they are a part of a crowd. At such times, they surrender their own minds in favor of mass crowd psychology. Such behavior is suicidal in the world of money. There is a saying in the financial world that "either you act on your own judgment or entirely on the judgment of another." That another should be a family member or business associate with equal stake in the outcome of the decision and not just a friend or, worse, a financial advisor (yours truly included). Therefore, you have to know when to act on your judgment and when on that of others.

How to Recognize Whether You are a Victim of Under Confidence

When you see the following tendencies in yourself while saving, spending, investing or taking insurance, it is very likely that you are suffering from under confidence:

- You read financial and investment papers and reports or watch business channels for obtaining investment or stock recommendations. Actually, financial and investment papers and reports as well as business news channels should be used for getting news, information, data, etc., and not for specific investment or stock recommendations.
- You invest in popular stocks.
- You sell out shares of good companies only because they have grown out of favor.
- You don't buy financial products which you need but instead purchase those which your broker or advisor wants to sell to you.
- You spend on products and places that the most people are spending on.
- You find it difficult to buy stocks during bear markets after substantial price and time damage has already been done — or sell stocks during raging bull markets after substantial price and time gains are already behind it.

Steps to Rectify this Mistake

- Do not blindly believe in the abilities of your broker, investment advisor, fund manager, financial planner, research analyst, financial media, etc. Always do your own research and due diligence.
- Know your strengths and weaknesses and then try to consolidate on your strengths and minimize your weaknesses.
- Remember that financial magazines and research reports are only for data purposes and business channels for news and "entertainment" purposes.
- Always be on the look out for genuine contrarian opportunities but never try to be contrary just for its own sake. Kindly note that almost 90% of the time the market is right in its opinions on most things. So just being contrary will not help. It's only during

those 10% extreme circumstances when the market is not able to see or price some upcoming event or development which is the real time to be contrary — and 90% of the money is usually made during that 10% of the time.

Other Common Financial Mistakes

Now, let us briefly understand some other common financial mistakes which we are susceptible to committing.

Money Illusion — Not Knowing How to Value Money

Most of us have illusions about money — we measure money by gross increase rather than the real increase. Let me explain this with a simple example. In fact, I am repeating an earlier example to bring home the point. Suppose an employee got a 10% salary increment when the inflation was 12%, while in another case the same employee got 5% increment when the inflation was 3%. Which one should make him happier? There are chances that he will prefer the first case of 10% increment although it amounts to a negative real increment since inflation is more than the increment while in the second case it is a positive real increment since inflation is less than the increment. This is called money illusion and it's one of the main reasons why people prefer investment in fixed deposits at negative real interest rates after tax than long term tax free gains through stocks. One of the other facets of money illusion are taxes which eat into your gross income. Many people, particularly salaried employees with earned income, measure their progress on gross salary basis little realizing that it is only the net salary which they actually get to take home which in reality is theirs for saving, spending, investing or taking insurance.

Cash Fallacy

Cash fallacy is another common behavior which baffles many psychologists. We are living in the information age — the world of fast moving money and currency. There are lots of convenience and facilities which the modern day bank offers us. Most of the banks don't directly charge for those kind of services but they know very well how your mind works and most of these facilities are, in fact, for their own benefit. Many centuries back there used to be the barter system wherein goods were exchanged for goods. There was no paper money — real goods would be exchanged for real goods. For example, a grower of rice would exchange his rice with a poultry farmer who would give him chicken in return. This was the real and pure form of money in which many of the common financial mistakes which we discussed above were simply not possible. But today not only do we live in a world of paper money but also in the world of "plastic money", i.e. credit cards. Banks and companies selling goods and services try to take advantage of this plastic money. Suppose we go to buy an expensive gift item for, say, ₹ 1 lakh. If we have to actually withdraw the cash from our bank account and then pay for it we will feel the "pain" of losing cash and would probably think twice before buying it. On the other hand, if we pay through our credit card then we may be very comfortable and feel no pain of losing cash. This is called the cash fallacy and is the main cause of a lot of unwanted and avoidable expenses in the modern plastic world. Therefore, the next time before you recklessly indulge on spending on any kind of product or service with your ready-at-hand plastic money, always remember the advice the legendary investor Warren Buffett has to offer: "If you buy things you don't need, soon you will have to sell things which you need."

Price Fixation

This is another common financial mistake to which most of us are susceptible when investing, not only at the time of buying but even at the time of selling. For example, often when buying a house we have a price in mind, like, say, "I will pay ₹ 1 crore for this house." Now suppose in a period which is marked by a high interest rate environment or market buoyancy, the house does not quote below ₹ 1.10 crore, it would normally be wise for you to reconsider your "price fixation" of ₹ 1 crore. Otherwise, it is likely that when the general economic and market conditions improve further, the price of that same house may jump to, say, ₹ 1.25 crore and you might be left with nothing but the "price fixation" in your mind! You have to be smart enough to know when to stick to a price and when to let it go. The trick is that if your target price has still not come at the depth of an economic crisis / boom then probably you are underestimating / overestimating the asset's value. I don't say that you should not do your own research and determine the value of an investment. What I mean is that you should not get fixated to a price; you should be ready to adjust around it somewhat, otherwise you might miss a big opportunity. For example, after analysis you determine that the value of a stock is, say, ₹ 100 and it is currently quoting at ₹ 150. So, obviously you wait for it to fall. During a very bad market crash the price of the stock falls to ₹ 110 but you still don't buy it waiting for your target price of ₹ 100. The stock then bottoms out somewhere close to ₹ 100, but does not touch it, during the bear market. It then flies away to, say, ₹ 200 during the subsequent bull market. Because of your "price fixation" of ₹ 100 you would lose an opportunity of earning ₹ 90. Price fixation can also be another form of "over confidence" described earlier.

Does Living Cheaply Make You Wealthy?

Many of us believe that living cheaply will help us get wealthy. Sure, you have to save money and spend it in the right way but you can never hope to become wealthy merely by saving on living expenses. And even if you do become wealthy by saving on living cheaply, you will not be able to remain wealthy; for that you have to spend and invest like a wealthy investor and not just be stingy.

In this world there are only two kinds of money problems — the first problem is not having sufficient money and the second problem is having too much money. And it's a cardinal principle of finance that you can't have the second problem if you have the first one. You have, therefore, to solve the first problem first.

Being miserly is thinking that the world is full of scarcity while, in fact, the world is full of abundance. God wants all of us to be rich, happy and work in cooperation for the general benefit of humanity. Therefore, if you try to accumulate wealth by being a miser you believe in a world of scarce money. Instead, if you are talented, skillful, creative and cooperative, you see a world of abundant wealth. That is what will help you become really rich and wealthy, stay that way for your entire life and leave behind a legacy as well.

Deviating From Your Original Plan

For achieving financial independence, all you need is a simple, mechanical and boring plan. The reason why a majority of people simply fail to get rich — or if even they do get rich but then fail to stay rich — is because they cannot stand the boredom of following a simple, uncomplicated plan. Most people think there is some magic to getting rich through investing. Or they think that if it is not complicated, it cannot be a good plan. The truth is, that when it comes to investing, simple is better than complex. This is the reason why most people, particularly in the stock markets, make money one day and then give all of that back another day. So while they don't lose money, they are simply not able to keep the money which they made. The legendary Warren Buffett once commented, "The only reason I go to the market is to see if someone is about to do something silly." This again highlights the importance of Commandment 1 about making a proper asset allocation plan.

Lessons From This Commandment

1. Don't throw good money after bad money. The money that is lost is gone; forget about it and start afresh. Don't ever base your future financial decisions on the basis of the past.
2. Don't treat losses and gains separately. Both are money and their color is the same.
3. The pain which you get from losing a given amount of money must be equal to the pleasure which you get from gaining the same sum of money — you must be neutral about money.
4. Always treat money received from all sources as the same and equally precious. For example, a person may treat salary (earned money) as precious and be over cautious with it while treating gifts, unexpected bonus, unexpected tax refunds or huge inheritance as "free money" and be careless with it. The "importance" of earned money may lead a person to let the

money just remain idle in a savings account and thus get beaten down by inflation while carelessness about "free money" may lead one to spending or investing in risky ventures which lead to losses.

5. Whether it is saving, spending, investment, insurance or any other money matter, many a time we are unable to make a decision and just maintain status quo, not realizing that not making a decision is also a decision and that it is a vote to let things go on the way they are. Therefore, whether in the matter of money or anything else, never feel scared about taking a decision. Use your knowledge, judgment and experience to arrive at an appropriate decision.
6. Selective thinking is a common and dangerous money illusion which blocks your mind by not allowing all the relevant information to flow into it for taking a correct financial decision. Sometimes it might allow only such facts to enter your mind which are already unconsciously stored in your memory. This leads to multiple problems. For example, it may lead to anchoring which simply means holding on to those facts which are unimportant for your decision making. Then there is other equally obstructive financial behavior called confirmation bias which is a cognitive bias whereby one tends to notice and look for information that confirms one's existing beliefs, while ignoring anything that contradicts those beliefs. These two psychological behaviors of anchoring and confirmation bias actually paralyze your thinking mind and don't allow you to take decision considering the available facts and figures.
7. "Holding on to what you have" is a financial mistake which very few people realize and acknowledge. People generally tend to overvalue what belongs to them relative to the value they would place on the same possession or situation if it belonged to someone else. This is called the endowment effect.
8. If you have a tendency of spending money on buying things which you don't require but do so only because there is a discount or some scheme or free gift available then you are setting yourself up for buyer's remorse. Don't forget that if you keep

buying what you don't require, then very soon you will have to sell the things which you genuinely need!

9. If you believe that saving is equal to investing, then you are in for a big surprise. Bear in mind that income tax reduces your gross income; interest on loans, extravagant spending and luxury assets diminish your net income while inflation eats at your remaining income. Therefore when you save money in "currency" form which is constantly losing its value instead of in assets like gold, silver, stocks, etc., then you are holding on to something which is constantly diminishing in value.
10. Most of us try to think big as far as money is concerned but easily forget the small things which when compounded over a period of time result in much bigger gains and losses. Don't be a victim of the "bigness bias" by overlooking small items.
11. Don't ever believe in the misconception that experts can consistently beat the markets.
12. Don't be over confident that you know everything and don't require any advice. Optimism and confidence are positive qualities but when ego and pride make you over confident, that is the first sign of your downfall, financially and otherwise, in life.
13. Don't let lack of confidence stop you. Trust your knowledge, judgment and experience and don't surrender to the judgment of the crowd. Completely rational, knowledgeable people take totally irrational and illogical decision when they are a part of a crowd when they surrender their independent thinking to mass crowd psychology.
14. Cash fallacy is another common psychological behavior which has dangerous consequences in today's technologically advanced times. It simply means that you are comfortable spending through credit cards, cheques, etc. on things that you wouldn't if you had to actually pay on the spot, by cash.
15. Target price fixation is another common financial mistake to which a majority of us are susceptible when investing, not only at the time of buying but even at the time of selling. And because of this, many a time we miss out on good deals, both on the buying and selling side.

16. Many people believe that being stingy leads to getting wealthy. You can never become really wealthy by trying to live on the cheap. Even if by some luck you do become wealthy this way, you will not be able to remain so for long. In order to stay wealthy you have to spend and invest like a rich investor and not just be stingy.
17. Pay off high cost credit card debt or personal loans with the so-called "emergency funds" lying idle in your savings account.
18. Achieving financial freedom demands following a simple, mechanical and boring plan.

Self-Understanding Questionnaire

This commandment helped you look at the psychological behavior to which humans are susceptible. Now, honestly answer the following questions in yes or no to evaluate your understanding and acceptance of the principles explained in this commandment. The more the number of "no" answers, the better is your understanding of this commandment.

1. You don't realize the fact that although humans love money but they are also vulnerable to the most unimaginable mistakes while dealing with money? Yes/No?
2. Would you tip a hotel waiter whose service you did not like at all while bargaining to the last penny for the service of a shoe polish boy who really did a good job? Yes/No?
3. Would you keep your money in the bank even at negative real interest rates knowing that you are actually losing purchasing power? Yes/No?
4. Would you be happier with a 12% salary raise when the inflation rate is 15% and not with a 5% raise when the inflation rate is 3%? Yes/No?
5. Do you believe that insurance and savings go hand-in-hand and therefore a money back policy is far superior to a pure term policy? Yes/No?
6. Do you think that you have got a better bargain when you buy a dress with a price tag of ₹ 1,500 being sold at ₹ 1,000, i.e. at a

33% discount, as compared to the same dress directly priced at ₹ 1,000 without any discount? Yes/No?

7. Do you believe that you can successfully time the market and pick winning stocks and can therefore consistently beat the market on a long term basis? Yes/No?
8. Do you buy a stock because your friend and neighbor has purchased it and claims to have made lot of money in it? Yes/No?
9. Do you generally buy stocks after a big advance or sell stocks after it has already suffered a steep decline? Yes/No?
10. Do you believe that you don't require the services of a broker or financial advisor? Yes/No?
11. Do you believe that you can recklessly spend while using a credit card as compared to hard cash? Yes/No?

Appendix 5.1: The Incredible Human Brain

Triune Brain and Human Psychology

Psychology is a big subject and beyond the scope of this book. However, I would like to highlight its importance to human beings when dealing with money. I would like to explain how the structure of the human brain affects the various decisions which we take, including while dealing with money.

We may talk a lot about psychological behavior and how it is a very important factor in determining our success not only as investors, but also in other facets of life but do we really know how to make it work for our benefit and not otherwise? I am not a doctor, scientist or psychologist by qualification but I do think that understanding human psychology is of utmost importance in the world of money as well as in any field. Now, what is human psychology? For that we have to understand the human brain and how it functions because finally we are all controlled by our brains. Dr. Paul MacLean, a great neurologist and researcher, has propounded the concept of the "triune brain" or the three-layered brain.

The three major layers or "brains" were established successively in human evolution. Each of the three brain layers represents a distinct evolutionary stratum that has formed upon the older layer before it much like an archaeological site. The oldest layer is the reptilian (non-thinking) brain, the second oldest is the mammalian (emotional) brain, and the most recent is the cerebral (thinking) brain. Each of the three brains is connected by nerves to the other two. Each operates as its own brain system with distinct capacities for perceiving and responding to the environment and each can become dominant depending on the circumstances. The major problem with human psychology and irrational behavior is that the integration and coordination between the three brains is inadequate. This is a genetic problem in our species and has implications for human development.

Reptilian Brain or R-complex

The reptilian brain is the oldest layer — the most "primitive" of the three brain components and makes up the entire brain mass in reptiles. Functions of the reptilian brain are related to physical survival and body maintenance — digestion, reproduction, circulation, breathing, stress responses, territorial instincts, social dominance, ritualism, social dominance, status maintenance, deception, tendency to follow precedent, awe for authority, social pecking order behavior, compulsiveness, deception, prejudice and resistance to change, rigid, obsessive, compulsive, paranoid, etc. The functioning of the reptilian brain is activated when the organism perceives threat and the needs for survival and safety predominate. This part of the brain is active even in deep sleep. This is the only part of the brain which is *not* in human control — a lot of bad human behavior, wrong decisions and other psychological problems happen because of the reptilian brain and a lack of properly functioning mammalian brain.

Mammalian Brain or Limbic System

The second layer, or the middle part, of the brain occupies the lower fifth of the human brain and developed with the evolution of mammals. As a brain system, the mammalian brain consists of a series of brain structures around the brainstem which contains the reptilian brain. The mammalian brain functions as the primary seat of the emotions of fear, joy, rage, pleasure and pain, attention, and affective (emotion-charged) memories, what gets your attention, unpredictability, feeding, fighting, fleeing, memory and sexual behavior. The mammalian brain is the emotional brain — all the emotions which we humans experience is because of the mammalian brain.

Cerebral Cortex, Neo-Cortex or Rational Thinking Brain

The third layer which occupies five-sixths of the human brain is known the neocortex or the cerebral cortex. The cerebral brain is the latest evolutionary development of the brain. The cerebral brain is involved with most mental activity, including spatial and mathematical thinking, meditating, dreaming, remembering, processing and decoding of sensory information. The cerebral brain is divided into left and right hemispheres, called left brain and right brain. The left hemisphere is linear, rational, and verbal and controls the right side of the body. The right hemisphere is spatial, abstract, musical and artistic and controls the left side of the body. For example, generally speaking, highly educated people like doctors, lawyers, engineers, chartered accountants, etc. have a highly developed left cerebral brain while persons involving in creative professions like actors, singers, painters, musicians, etc. have a more developed right cerebral brain.

The interaction of the three brain layers forms the biological basis for the interaction of concepts, emotions and behaviors which make up the learning process. You might think that the cerebral brain dominates the mammalian and the reptilian brains. However, you will be surprised to know that the cerebral brain is generally the weakest of the three and that the mental functions of the cerebral (thinking) brain can be hijacked by the functions of the other two brain layers. This is the main reason why totally rational individuals take completely irrational decisions under specific situations of life, including while dealing with money. For example, the reptilian (non-thinking) brain runs automatically and not in our control (because it controls vital survival functions like breathing, digestion, circulation, reproduction, etc.) and it is that part of the brain which immediately starts functioning even without our knowledge. Suppose somebody gave you a complex mathematical problem. You will not have a direct answer, and will have to activate your cerebral (thinking) brain to solve the equation. On the other hand, the reptilian brain immediately gets activated even before we realize it — suppose you just see picture of a McDonald burger, your mouth might immediately start watering although your cerebral (thinking) brain knows that there is no burger. The reptilian brain, however, had stored the real burger picture in its memory which you might have eaten in the past and associates the picture with it. Hence, although we may be rational human beings and like to use our cerebral (thinking) brain but the automatic images of the reptilian brain "fool" the mammalian (emotional) brain to re-direct the power to it instead of to the cerebral "thinking" brain.

Let's now consider this in light of a stock market example. Let us take the example of the 4-year stock market period between 2008 and

2012. We all know that to make money in stocks (or for that matter anything) we have to buy low and sell high. We apply this rule to almost all items as we go shopping during times of "discount sales" and avoid buying when the items are unnecessary costly. Why, then, are we not able to apply this simple logic to stocks. Many of us might have invested when the BSE Sensex was around 21,000 in December 2007 when in fact we should have sold. Then, one-year down the line, many "frustrated" investors might have sold at 8,000 Sensex when in fact we should have bought. The same investors might again have purchased at close to 20,000 Sensex in October 2010, though they had sold at 8,000 Sensex in October 2008. And then in November 2011 those same "frustrated" investors might have contemplated and actually exited those loss making investments at 15,000 Sensex.

Why should rational investors behave in such an irrational manner? This is related to the three different brain systems explained above and the interaction and dominance of one over the other. Let us see what is actually going on through the investor's mind at each of the different stages. Kindly note, the cerebral (thinking) brain is the weakest and, unless consciously activated and used, succumbs to the power of the other two brains. At 21,000 Sensex in December 2007, the reptilian brain automatically tells the other two brains that the market has been going up and it shows the picture of the market going up (all pictures are stored and automatically retrieved in the reptilian brain). Next in line is the mammalian (emotional) brain which receives the "signal and picture" from the reptilian brain that the market has gone up. The mammalian brain is emotional and there are feelings of joy of earning money in the stock market or fear of losing money / not earning money. Now, at this time the cerebral (thinking) brain might be saying that logically the stocks are costly based on whatever evaluation like fundamentals, technicals, etc. But among the three brains its voice is very weak. In essence, the mammalian or emotional brain is the most powerful of the three because it now has the power to re-direct the situation back to either the reptilian (non-thinking) brain or the cerebral (thinking) brain. In most humans, the thought of earning more money which the reptilian brain has induced on the mammalian (emotional) brain is much stronger than the real correct picture which the cerebral (thinking) brain is portraying. Hence, the mammalian brain re-directs the power to the reptilian brain and that explains the illogical behavior. This kind of behavior is associated with most of our actions in our day-to-day lives under the influence of our reptilian (non-thinking) and mammalian (emotional) brains while ignoring our cerebral (thinking) brain in the process to our own peril.

Now let us consider another example related to the triune brain and a big social menace — sexual abuse and rape. When a male / female observes an attractive handsome / beautiful person of the opposite sex, the person may unconsciously get some kind of immediate sexual arousal. This is because the reptilian brain which stores the images and pictures and which is not in our active control immediately flash backs some kind of image picture of any person of the opposite sex which the person under question might have seen in the past and then he / she relates that picture to the person whom he/ she is currently viewing which in turn leads to some kind of excitement / arousal / interest in the person. Thus far the process is natural, unconscious and uncontrollable. From now onwards what happens within the three brains is most important. The picture from the reptilian brain then goes to the mammalian brain which is the emotional brain and which then attaches the joy of what it had or can experience with the person of the opposite sex in the past and at the same time it also experiences the fear of doing something wrong. The cerebral (thinking) brain is all the while saying that it should just keep quiet and not proceed any further because it is wrong. However, the cerebral brain is the weakest of the three unless the other two brains have relinquished their power in its favor. Now, in most cases the mammalian (emotional) brain will not heed to the reptilian brain and give the power to the cerebral (thinking) brain and hence the person will sit quietly. Unfortunately, in a few people, the mammalian brain will give the power to the reptilian brain which in turn will lead the person to do some wrong act like rape although his cerebral brain had been all the while signalling that it is wrong. Further, in a normal person the thinking is in a wide perspective but when he / she gets sexually aroused then due to the release of certain "natural drugs" like dopamine, norepinephrine, testosterone, oxytocin and serotonin the thinking becomes narrowly focused only on sexual arousal to the exclusion of other thoughts like social values, government laws, family, work, etc.

So, whether in money matters or any other phase of our lives, the problem happens with over-active reptilian brain and a weak mammalian brain. Hence, the key to succeed in money matters — for that matter in anything in life — is to slowdown our reptilian (non-thinking) brain, and have a very strong mammalian (emotional) brain so that it can re-direct the power to our cerebral (thinking) brain.

—

Chapter 6

Commandment 5

Thou Shall Remember These Principles While Investing in Equities and Fixed Income Securities

YOU WILL FIND INNUMERABLE BOOKS ON INVESTING IN STOCKS written by experts and investment gurus. This book is not a book only on stock market investing. It is a book to help you achieve financial freedom. The essential point, however, is that it is very difficult for anyone to achieve financial independence without investing in equity stocks.

This commandment deals with the principles which you need to understand in order to invest profitably in the stock market and fixed income securities.

Determinants of Equity Returns

When you own and operate a business like, say, a garment retail shop or a bread factory, you earn by selling garments and baking breads, respectively. Your profits are wholly and solely derived from your business activity. However, when you invest in stocks, your income comes from two sources:

1. From the earnings of the company in which you have invested, specifically from the distributed earnings called dividends.
2. From the fluctuation in the stock's price on the bourses — termed as capital gains.

Clearly, therefore, your earnings from stocks can be different than the earnings of the company in whose stock you have invested.

And many a time the difference and disconnect between the two can be vast. In the short term, most of the money from stocks is made because of the second source while over the longer term it is primarily made from the first. These two sources can be further divided into three main sources from which stock returns are derived:

1. Initial dividend yield;
2. Growth in earnings; and
3. Change in valuation, i.e. change in the stock's price / earnings ratio.

I will explain these three sources of return very briefly.

Dividend yield is nothing but the distributed earnings of the company, i.e. dividend when expressed as a ratio of its stock price.

Growth in earnings is the increase in profits made by the company over your holding period of the stock. Assume you hold the stock for, say, four years and suppose the company's earnings per share (EPS) is ₹ 100, ₹ 110, ₹ 125, and ₹ 140 in the first, second, third and fourth year, respectively. In this case, the growth in earnings for you would be 40%, i.e. ₹ 140 over ₹ 100, i.e. the fourth year' EPS over first year' EPS, the year in which you buy the stock.

The third concept is the change in the price / earnings (P/E) ratio or multiple of the company. P/E is nothing but the market price of a share divided by the company's earnings (profits) per share. It shows what multiple of the company's yearly earnings is the market ready to pay for its share. Suppose the P/E multiple of a stock is 10, it simply means the market is ready to pay ten times today's earnings for buying the entire company. If the expectations of future earnings and profitability of the company rise, the market would be ready to pay a higher multiple of, say, 12 times while if the expectation of future earnings falls, then the market would pay a lower multiple of, say, 8 times. This brings us to the third source of return from stocks which is change in the company's P/E multiple. An increase in the P/E multiple would result in an increase in its stock price while a decrease in the P/E multiple would result in a fall in its stock price. Kindly note that the first factor, i.e. dividend, can be positive or, at worst, zero while the second and third factors can be positive, zero or even negative if the company makes losses, in which case the P/E multiple may also then contract.

While You Buy Stocks, Businesses Sell Stocks

Remember that you buy stocks as investment. When you do so through the secondary market you buy them from another investor, trader, speculator, etc., and not from the company. However, when you subscribe to an offer from the company, then you are buying stock directly from the company which is itself selling its stock to you. Many people do not realize that major money in the stock markets is not made by those buying stocks but, in fact, by businesses selling their shares to the public. After all, it is the entrepreneur who has created substantial value in his / her own company and who is selling for a price the stock which he had "created for almost free". The entrepreneur created money out of "thin air" and that is why most of the richest people in the world are entrepreneurs and business owners and not equity investors. Such entrepreneurs work hard to create valuable business and then sell shares of ownership in the business to others, who then become shareholders. In other words, it could be said that as the selling shareholders, they printed their own money — legally!

Factors That Drive Stock Prices

There are five major factors which affect the market price of equities or, for that matter, any freely tradable instrument, like bonds, gold, etc. These are:

1. Macro economic factors;
2. Monetary factors;
3. Fundamental factors;
4. Technical factors; and
5. Psychological factors.

Further, the interaction and influence of each factor is different at various times. Let us briefly review each of these factors.

1. Macro Economic Factors

Macro economic factors would be very important in the initial stages of an investment cycle. We have to know whether we are within a structural bull or bear market and this can be determined with the help of macro economic factors. Please note, however, that investments in equity can't be made based purely on macro economic factors because the stock market is the barometer of the economy and moves about six to nine months in advance of the macro economic factors. So far as macro economic factors are concerned, therefore, we have to invest in stocks when the situation moves from the worst to bad and not wait till it turns good because by then the stock prices might have rallied substantially from their bear market lows.

2. Monetary Factors

Monetary factors or interest rates have a direct effect on equities as corporate profitability is affected by interest and finance costs. For example, a high rate of interest is one of the biggest enemies of equities because it leads to a fall in corporate earnings through increased interest costs, reduction in equity valuations (such as P/E multiple) through increase in discount rate, and lower investor surplus available for equities as high rates make debt attractive. An investor can't wait for all monetary factors to turn positive before buying shares. You have to invest when you believe interest rates are close to a peak, or will rise only slightly higher, because by then the worst would have played itself out.

3. Fundamental Factors

These are the fundamental reasons on which stock prices and valuations should ideally be based. These are also the factors on which an entrepreneur or the owner will value his / her own business enterprise. The major fundamental factors are earnings, sales, cash flow, book value, enterprise value, dividends, etc. Fundamental analysis is very important for stock picking but rarely helps in achieving above average market performance. This is because a business might be fundamentally good but the stock need not perform equally well because of other factors. Also, the fundamental value assigned to a business keeps on fluctuating. For example, we have seen throughout history that sometimes there can be buyers scrambling to get a piece of the action even at, say, an unreasonably high P/E multiple of over 25. At other times, frustrated sellers give up all hopes and sell at dismally low P/E multiple of, say, around 8 or even lower. Therefore, fundamental valuations are relative terms; costly can become costlier and cheap can become cheaper! It's a game of future expectations which nobody can predict with any stretch of confidence. Fundamental valuations are like pendulum; they swing from one extreme to another making equities alternately seem very cheap or extremely costly. When the markets are going up it seems that they will keep going up and up but in those times of euphoria we have to remember that "however tall a tree may grow it will never be able to touch the sky." Similarly, when stocks are crashing we feel depressed as if there is no bottom but in those depressing times we have to remember that at certain price a stock will become so cheap on earnings, dividends or replacement cost that somebody will just buy the whole company or business itself. In fact, over the past century most bear market bottoms in India, as also in developed markets like the US, have happened at single digit P/Es (7 to 10 times).

Talking about valuations, let us consider a very popular method amongst analysts known as discounted cash flow (DCF). I have seen many analysts take pride in doing DCF analysis and "sum-of-the-part" valuations. DCF is nothing but estimating the "free cash flows" into the future years and then arriving at their present value by applying a proper discount rate. Without going into the mathematical part of it, the discount rate is nothing but the risk free rate (yield on government securities) plus the beta (market risk or risk of investing in equities), multiplied by the risk premium, i.e. the extra risk which an investor demands for investing in equities as compared to bonds.

Theoretically, DCF is very elegant but is hardly ever attempted in practice! That is because there is no way that an analyst sitting in an air conditioned office in a big city can reasonably predict the future cash flows of a company producing something many miles away for so many years into the future. How can somebody calculate the discount rate when the country's central bank itself is not able to predict interest rates a few months down the line? If somebody can't predict interest rates a few months ahead with any accuracy, then how can it be done five years down the line with reasonable confidence? Again, how can somebody even dream of forecasting market risk premium and beta with so much confidence when these things are dynamic and changing constantly? How can somebody reckon the "terminal value" of a business many years or decades in future when the company management itself would not know it? When somebody can't predict the prices of commodities (which are raw materials for some companies and finished goods for others) and interest rates with reasonable confidence, how can one predict the future earnings and cash flows of a company? What a majority of the analysts actually do is that they pre-decide the target price of a stock and then accordingly change the different variables in the DCF model to arrive at that target price!

Thus, fundamental factors are important in stock market investments but with the caveat that they will not help in achieving above average market returns unless combined with other factors.

4. Technical Factors

In a sense, technical analysis begins where fundamental analysis ends. After we fundamentally decide what to buy and sell — then we have to technically see when to buy and also to sell it. Technical analysis is logical and can provide very good insights into price behavior. Unfortunately, here, too, most analysts work in a stereotype manner and first decide what they want and then try to justify how it will be achieved. The market never moves on the basis of what any person wants but on the basis of what the market itself wants to do and where it wants to go.

There are different kinds of charts, like line chart, bar chart, candlestick chart, three line break chart, renko chart, kagi chart, point and figure chart, etc., different kinds of patterns, such as head and shoulder, flags, wedges, saucers, rounding bottoms, double top, etc., various kinds of indicators like moving averages, trendlines, price and volume oscillators, bollinger bands, etc., and various theories and methodologies like Dow Theory, Elliot wave, Neo classical wave, etc. The detailed explanation of all these are beyond the scope of this book. Remember, however, that technical analysis is predicting future from the past and has only that much credence as you would put to predicting the future action of a person by looking at his / her past behavior.

5. Psychological Factors

Last, but certainly not the least, psychological behavior is perhaps the most important factor in the investment world which separates the successful investor from the novice.

For example, an investor does a thorough fundamental analysis on a company and concludes that its share is worth ₹ 150 while the stock's current market price is ₹ 100. Then he / she goes and buys it on that basis. Now suppose the stock falls to say ₹ 75 because of an overall market crash. In such a case, irrespective of whatever analysis the investor might have done, his / her faith might get shaken. How many of the so-called fundamental analysts will then still have the guts to hold the stock and believe that it is worth ₹ 150 in the long term? The same can be true of technical analysis. The important point is, whatever may be your investment method, the important and differentiating point is to follow it and be psychologically strong and sound to apply it in practice. Here I quote Sir John Templeton who said that "to buy when others are despondently selling and sell when others are greedily buying requires the greatest fortitude and pays the greatest reward." This quote explains psychological analysis in a nutshell. A psychologically sound person looks at market fluctuations as his friend and not his foe — he acknowledges the fact that when the gap between perception and reality is the maximum, the price is the best. An investor's worst enemy is not the market but his own emotions.

The confluence of all the above factors determines the price of stocks or, for that matter, of any easily tradable liquid investment. I further quote the great economist John Maynard Keynes who once commented that "there is nothing so disastrous as a rational investment policy in an irrational world". Warren Buffett has said that the "stock market is a place where people with money meet people with experience, the people with experience get the money while the people with money gain experience."

Stock prices are akin to a pendulum — just as a pendulum moves from right to left and *vice versa,* so do stock prices move from unjustifiably pessimistic under valuation to extremely irrational over valuation. Never forget the last of the determinants of asset and stock prices — psychological factors. Whether it is your success as an individual or as an investor, it would primarily be determined by how psychologically balanced you are. If you want further evidence then listen to what one of the greatest scientist and economist of all times had to state on the subject.

Sir Isaac Newton said: "I can calculate the motions of heavenly bodies, but not the madness of people." Appendix 6.1 gives you examples of extreme equity bubbles and periods when the "madness of people" broke all restraints.

Investor *versus* Speculator

Acquainted with how extreme human emotion leads to financial disaster, it should be your endeavor not to fall into that trap. You would be in safe waters provided you are an investor. However, the moment you become a speculator or a trader, you expose yourself to the market's pitfalls. So, let's now understand whether you are an investor or a speculator.

The words investor and speculator are often used interchangeably in the markets. In fact, many of you might not even know whether you are an investor or a speculator. And the worst situation is if you assume yourself to be an investor when in reality you are a speculator. Benjamin Graham, who is regarded as the father of value investing, wrote in his book *The Intelligent Investor* that "an investment operation is one which, upon thorough analysis, promises safety of principal and an adequate return. Operations not meeting these requirements are speculative."

Upon a closer analysis of this definition the following are the pre-requisites for being an investor:

- There should be a thorough analysis of the company, its business, market conditions, etc.
- This thorough analysis should promise reasonable safety of capital — based on premises like dividend yield, earnings yield, valuations, etc.
- The return expectation has to be "adequate" and not superlative.

And if these three criteria are not met, then you are not an investor but probably a speculator or trader. When you buy a stock, you have the choice of buying it on margin and not taking its actual delivery. Further, a person also has an option of buying or shorting (first selling and then buying) in the derivatives markets through futures (getting a position in a stock by just paying a small fraction of the actual cost) or options (getting a right to buy or sell the security at a particular price). It's very clear that investment has to be delivery based cash buying. If you are not taking delivery of stocks, or if you are buying on margin, or buying futures and options, etc., then you are not an investor but a speculator, trader or arbitrageur. The art of investment has one very specific characteristic which is not clearly understood.

Any lay investor can attain a respectable rate of return on his / her investments with minimal effort and application of mind. But if you aim for extraordinary returns using all sorts of esoteric techniques, then instead of getting a normal return you will probably end up in the red.

The virtues of a simple portfolio satisfying the above three conditions cannot be over emphasized. Any adventure beyond this would be outside the boundaries of investment and the role of luck and temperament then increases. Therefore, before investing in equities, you must know the difference between investment and speculation. An investor chases value while a speculator chases stock prices.

The Investment Cycle

In Commandment 1, we looked at the economic and business cycle in detail. Let's briefly revisit it here and try to address the important question of when, broadly, you should buy equities, and when, broadly you should be selling them. I use the word "broadly" because there is no clear cut formula for this. And both buying and selling are important because not all of us can be a Warren Buffett and keep holding our investments in perpetuity. Further, you may regularly require funds in your child's education, major medical expenses, buying a house for self occupation, etc. Or, you might get some income at specific periods of time, like the annual bonus, windfall gains, etc. which you need to invest. In other words, you might require funds at certain points of time and have surplus funds at other times.

There are different broad asset classes, like equities, bonds, commodities, real estate, currencies, art and, of course, cash. Different asset classes perform in different ways during different phases of the economic cycle. As a general rule, first interest rates come down and bond prices go up, then equities enter a bull market and, finally, commodities blossom. There are some interim periods when no asset class performs well and at such times we have to look at cash for preserving our capital. There are also periods when all or some of the asset classes move in the same direction and other periods when they move in different directions. The lesson, therefore, is that we don't have to be obsessed with any single asset class even when it is in a bear market because that will be against the principles of Commandment 1.

As we saw in Chapter 2, around the equilibrium line the economic cycle moves from extreme contraction to over expansion, in much the same way in which an equity market moves from extreme undervaluation to over-valuation. The economy and equity markets are like a pendulum — they swing from one extreme to another. This is also why different commodities like steel, cement, etc. move in cycles. It also explains why even agricultural commodities like, say, sugar move in cycles — although sugar demand might just vary marginally and not in big cycles. As shown in Commandment 1, the economic cycle results in the following movement of various asset classes; the preferred asset class to hold in each phase is also mentioned:

- Interest rates peak and bond prices bottom — government securities;
- Demand for credit declines — government securities;
- Central bank comes into action — government securities and corporate bonds;
- Equities bottom out — equities; and
- Commodities bottom out — cyclical and commodity stocks / commodities.

An understanding of the economic, business and investment cycles will give you an edge in planning your investment in compliance with Commandment 1 as well as for the different ups and downs of life without materially affecting or altering your long term goal of achieving financial independence.

Are Equities Risky? Understanding the Difference Between Risk and Volatility

Yes, of course, they are. Equities are risky because by buying into equities you are acquiring part ownership in a business and any business goes through up and down cycles. Further, the globalization of markets and the speed at which information, money and liquidity move in and out of individual countries, sectors and stocks has increased the volatility (though not necessarily the risk) in equity returns. Should you then own equities? Certainly you must because it has been statistically proven that adding some amount of equity to an all-bond portfolio actually increases the return from the portfolio while reducing risk. Figure 6.1 demonstrates this fact. Similarly, adding some amount of bonds to an all-equity portfolio considerably reduces the risk with only a minor dip in return. Hence, it's certainly not advisable to have only an all-equity (risky) portfolio or an all-bond (conservative) portfolio. It is much wiser to have a portfolio which is a combination of equity and bonds — the actual ratio of each would vary on a case-to-case basis.

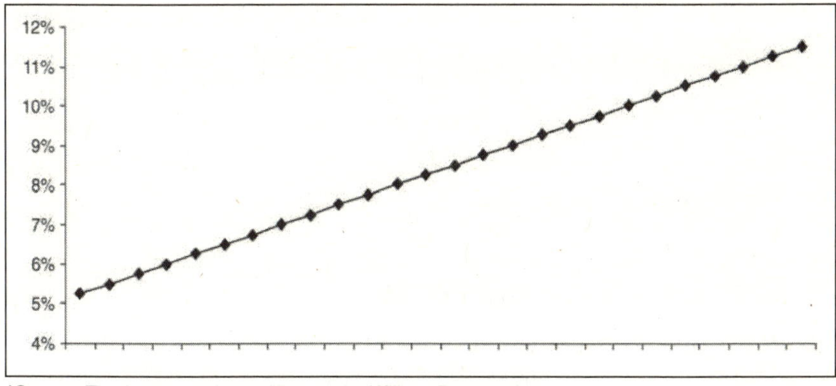

(*Source: The Intelligent Asset Allocator by William Bernstein*)

Figure 6.1: **Equity-bond risk return chart**

Equities Help You Beat the Biggest Risk of All — Inflation

The biggest risk of all is that one fine morning you wake up and find that while there is money in the bank but it can't buy you the goods and services which you had thought it would be able to. This is the risk of inflation. I have explained the monster of inflation earlier in the book, including how money has now become a currency which has lost, and will continue to lose, value against other basket of commodities. Fixation on risk alone, without considering rewards is a result of risk-averse behavior exhibited by the vast majority of people leading to over-exposure to bonds. The assets which can protect you against inflation are commodities, real estate and equities. Commodities would include precious metals, industrial commodities, agricultural goods and also alternative investments like art. Real estate would also shield you against inflation because inflation leads to an increase in the replacement cost of constructing property which, in turn, translates into higher real estate prices. Equities can also protect you against inflation because a reasonable level of inflation is healthy for corporate earnings. There are a lot of business sectors which benefit from inflation, such as consumer goods, metals, cement, oil and gas, etc. Then there are certain sectors like autos, engineering, construction, etc. which can pass on the inflation to their consumer through higher prices. So, a "normal rate of inflation" is beneficial for equities as it raises corporate earnings and leads to higher stock prices. Equities, thus, give you a hedge against the invisible monster of inflation which is constantly eating into the purchasing power of your money. By ignoring equities, you are inviting the biggest risk of all — inflation.

Equities and High Interest Rates

Abnormally high interest rates, on the other hand, are one of the biggest enemies of equities. This is because high interest rates impact equity returns in four main ways:

1. **Higher Interest Costs:** Interest rates increase the finance and interest costs of companies due to higher interest payment on borrowings. This would result in a reduction in corporates profitability.
2. **Availability of Finance:** Lots of projects become unviable due to increased interest rates. Companies find it difficult to service old borrowings where the return on their investments have fallen while the interest costs have increased. The banking sector's non-performing assets (NPA) might also increase leading to an overall squeeze in lending. This would, in turn, lead to a slowdown in business growth and consequently the revenues of companies.
3. **Stock Valuations:** Equities are valued by using a discount rate. As explained earlier, the discount rate is nothing but the risk free rate (yield on government securities) plus the beta (market risk or risk of investing in equities), multiplied by the risk premium, i.e. the extra risk which an investor demands for investing in equities as compared to bonds. When interest rates rise, the discount rate too goes up because of the increase in the risk free return. This results in reduced valuation of equities.
4. **Bonds Compete for the Same Funds:** If you are getting high, say double digit, return from bonds, then why would you take the risk (volatility) of investing in equities. At the same time, if the return on bonds is abysmally low then many new investors also invest in equities. Therefore, interest rates (bonds) compete for

the same available investor surplus. The more of their money investors put in bonds, the lesser the amount they have for equities thus affecting the funds available for equity investment.

Therefore, interest rates is one of the biggest, if not the biggest, enemies of equities affecting them through reduced earnings, lower sales, depressed valuations and lesser liquidity. For any meaningful recovery in equities, it is a *sine quo non* that the interest rates have to first stabilize and then soften.

Let's look at this in another perspective.

You might have heard of various metrics of equity valuations, such as price / earnings (P/E), price / book value (PBV), price / sales (PS), dividend yield, etc. but each of these values equities in isolation. Equities, however, are affected by a variety of factors, interest rates being a prominent one among them. Hence we have to look at a composite valuation metric. The best composite valuation for stock and bond markets comes from a comparison of the earnings yield (the inverse of P/E) of BSE Sensex with the bond yield, i.e. yield on the 10-year government securities.

Figure 6.2 shows the BSE Sensex along with the earnings yield to bond yield ratio. Note, how at higher earnings yield to bond

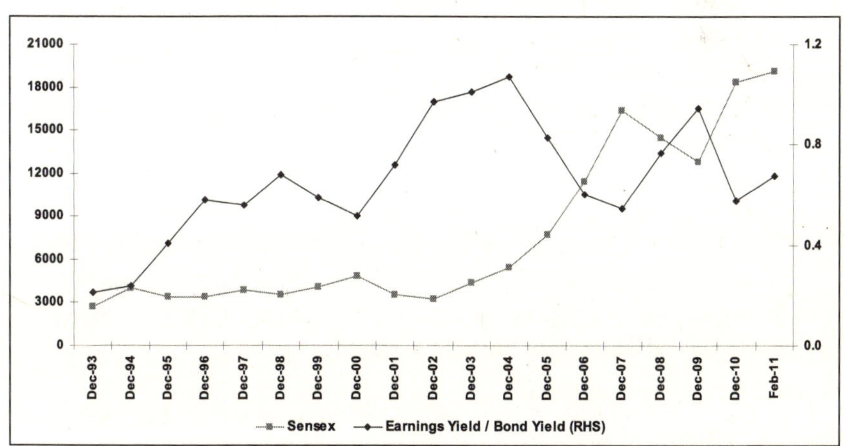

Figure 6.2: **BSE Sensex compared to earnings yield / bond yield**

yield ratio, the equity market bottoms out while at lower earnings yield to bond yield ratio, it becomes very vulnerable to a fall. A corollary is that bond prices top out at higher earnings yield / bond yield ratio, while at lower earnings yield / bond yield ratio, there is reasonable probability of a rally in the bond markets *via* a fall in interest rates.

There is another factor worth noting as far as interest rates are concerned. Financial history of the past more than hundred years of the US and other markets has revealed that first the government security rates bottom out, then the corporate bonds bottom out *via* a reduction in the spread between comparable same tenure best quality corporate bonds and government securities. Once that has played out, then it's the turn of equities to bottom out.

Therefore, look out for interest rates — and the expectations regarding interest rates — in order to get an idea of likely equity performance. Remember that equities seldom perform well in a high interest rate environment. At the same time, don't wait for the interest rates to completely bottom out before buying shares because by then their prices might have appreciated substantially. The ideal time for buying into equities would be when interest rates are close to their peak but have still not started to actually fall.

Different Techniques of Equity Investing

There are different equity investment techniques. Which ones to use depends on an investor's mental framework. All techniques are not necessarily wealth creators; some simply give investors a "feel-good" high. In fact, most of the techniques are just for the investor's short term entertainment at the cost of his long term wealth. The investor feels that he is doing a great job but in essence he is just destroying his wealth and future. Some of these well-known "long term wealth destroying" techniques include:

- **Buy, hold and pray:** When you by an investment — stock, bond, property, gold etc. — without really understanding its pros and cons for your portfolio and think that you will make money simply by holding it for a long period, it is probably going to lead to long term failure.

- **Frequent buying and selling:** If you buy and sell frequently, then you are probably a short term trader and not an investor.
- **Buying and selling futures:** If you buy and sell futures, then you are a speculator.
- **Selling and then buying (selling short):** If you first sell and then buy, you are a short trader or speculator.
- **Option buying and selling:** If you are buying and selling options, then you are a trader.
- **Writing options:** If you are an option writer, then you are a speculator.

Equity Investing Lessons from History

History repeats itself goes the saying. The importance of this saying is proved in the stock markets. Let us review what financial history teaches us about equity investing. Table 6.1 shows the primary and

Table 6.1
Sensex Levels and P/E along with Secondary Corrections

Date	*Sensex*	*P / E*	*% Increase / Decline*	*Comments*
Apr-2003	2,900	10.7		Bear market bottom
Apr-2004	6,035	17.3	108.1%	Intermediate top
May-2004	4,260	12.2	-29.4%	End of secondary correction
Sep-2005	8,750	19.4	105.4%	Intermediate top
Oct-2005	7,600	16.9	-13.1%	End of secondary correction
Apr-2006	12,670	24.2	66.7%	Intermediate Top
May-2006	8,790	16.8	-30.6%	End of secondary correction
Jul-2007	15,900	22.1	80.9%	Intermediate top
Aug-2007	13,800	19.2	-13.2%	End of secondary correction
Jan-2008	21,206	25.5	53.7%	Bull market top
Oct-2008	7,697	10.7	-63.7%	Bear market bottom
Jan-2011	21,108	18.4	174%	Intermediate top
Dec-2011	15,135	13.5	-28.3%	Intermediate bottom

(*Source:* BSE)

secondary movement of the bull market in Indian equities between April 2003 and December 2011.

Although the Sensex surged seven times during the period from 2003 to 2008, there were four secondary corrections which took away 15% to 30% from the market's intermediate tops in a matter of a few weeks, shaking the conviction of even the strongest of bulls. That is precisely what secondary corrections do; if money making in the market was so easy then nobody need do any other work!

Also note the subsequent movements. Once the secondary correction is over and the primary bull trend resumes, the gain was between 54% to 108%, i.e. much more than the secondary correction range of 15% to 30%. That's because it was a primary bull market. The scenario would be the opposite in a primary bear market.

Now, fundamentally, bear market bottoms generally came closer to a P/E ratio of 10 (April 2003 or even March 2009) while bull market tops can occur anywhere between 25 to 40 times P/E (*see* Figure 6.3). The important point here is that secondary corrections generally end at P/E of around 12 to 16 times. One more observation: the market underwent a secondary correction at 6,035 which

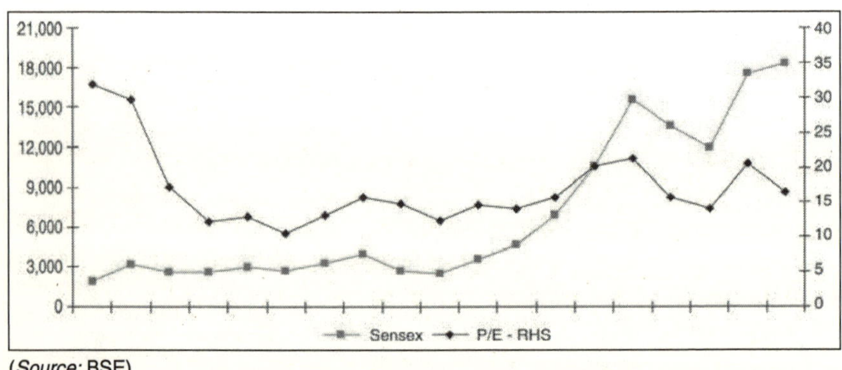

(*Source:* BSE)

Figure 6.3: **Sensex levels and P/E along with secondary corrections**

was around the same level of 6,175 it touched in February 2000 which was the previous bull market top before the technology bubble burst. The same thing happened again in January 2011 with the Sensex touching 21,108, which was within striking distance of the previous bull market top of 21,206 conquered in January 2008.

It is easier to predict bear market bottoms because at a certain price stocks become very cheap on replacement cost and dividend yield basis. It is much more difficult to predict bull market tops because of wide variance in PEs of previous tops.

Figure 6.4 brings out the 150-year history of US S&P 500 P/E ratio juxtaposed with long term interest rates. The great bear market bottoms of the past century in the US were 1907, 1921, 1932, 1949, 1974 and 1982. As you would see from Figure 6.4, the US markets formed major bull market tops at between 25 to 40 times P/E ratios while the bear market bottoms were closer to 8 to 10 times P/E. Also note that the earlier 20th century bear markets in the US were in conjunction with deflation, and thus low long term real interest rates. In the latter half of the century, on the other hand, the

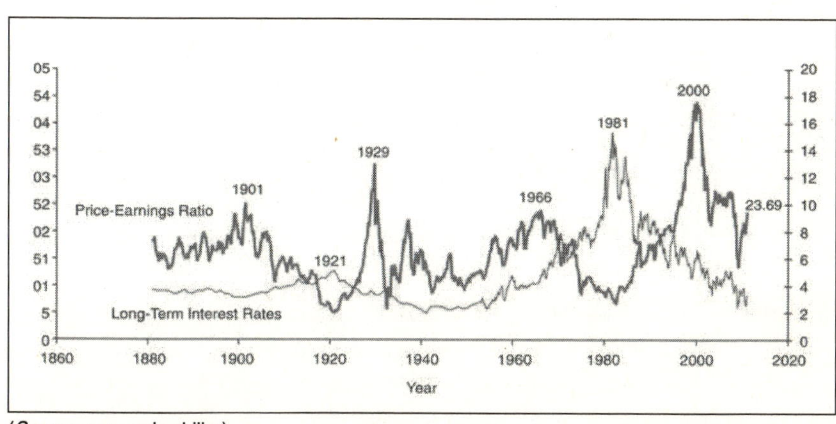

(*Source:* econ.yale.shiller)

Figure 6.4: **150 years of US S&P 500 P/E and long term interest rates**

Table 6.2

102-Year History of US DJIA Bull Market and Intermediate Tops and Bears Market Bottoms

Date	*US DJIA*	*P/E*	*Comments*	*CAGR Return from Bottom till it makes New High*	*Subsequent 5-year Return once index crosses above Previous high*
Jan-1906	103	19.9	Bull market top		
Dec-1907	58	10.6	Bear market bottom		
Aug-1919	107	12.8	Above previous high 162 months	4.4%	-3.4%
Jun-1921	64	4.9	Bear market bottom		
Nov-1924	110	3.8	Above previous high 63 months	10.8%	19.8%
Sep-1929	381	32.9	Bull market top		
Nov-1932	41	5.8	Bear market bottom		
Nov-1954	385	12.8	Above previous high 264 months	10.6%	7.4%
Dec-1968	1,050	22.3	Intermediate top		
Jul-1974	600	8.9	Bear market bottom		
Feb-1983	1,080	9.6	Above previous high 182 months	3.9%	13.1%
Jul-2000	11,500	44.2	Bull market top		
Oct-2006	11,600	26.1	Above previous high 75 months	0.1%	
Jan-2008	14,200	24.1	Intermediate top — all time high		
			Average return	6.0%	9.2%

(*Source:* Dow Jones)

bear markets were accompanied by high inflation and high interest rates. Note especially the 1981 high when long term interest rates were around 16% when the 50-year multi-decade bear market in bonds ended and one of the longest bull markets in US equities commenced. This practical example of US — the largest and most developed economy and market in the world will help you appreciate with the economic, business and investment life cycle which I explained earlier in the book.

Table 6.2 shows a 102-year history of US DJIA bull market tops, intermediate tops and bear market bottoms. The purpose of this table is to help you understand how many years it takes for the market to re-conquer its previous bull market high and what kind of returns it generates for investors. The table reveals that it took anywhere between 5 to 22 years for the market to go from one peak to the next peak. Hence, the cycle of a primary bull market top to a bear market bottom and back to again conquering the previous primary bull market top can be anywhere between 5 to 22 years.

Now, if somebody invested just when the previous bull market top was tested, for example at 21,000 on Sensex in India in January 2011, then it generates CAGR returns of anywhere between -3.4% to 17.8% over the subsequent 5-year period (average of 9.2%).

That investing at bear market bottoms would give excellent returns is also far from true because investing at a bear market bottom and waiting till the next bull market top arrives yielded around 4.4% to 12.6% (average of just 6.0%) returns.

In fact, the major portion of the returns did not come by investing at bear market bottoms or when the market made new highs above the previous bull market tops but by investing during the secondary correction which happened after the market made a new high — or touched or approached it — during the later or last leg of the bull market.

Now, let us study this in light of India's BSE Sensex (Table 6.3).

The Sensex made a bull market top at 4,580 (P/E 61 times) in April 1992 during the Harshad Mehta scam. The subsequent bear market led to a 57.3% erosion in its value to 1,956 (P/E 24.1) by April 1993 at the bear market bottom. However, that did not mean that a new bull market started immediately — it only meant the end of the bear market. However, markets do rally from bear market bottoms, as have we seen in the last 120 years of US equity market history or the Indian markets. The Sensex rallied by 135% from a bear market

Table 6.3

India: 20 Years of Sensex History of Bull Market Tops and Bottoms

Date	*BSE Sensex*	*P/E*	*% Increase / Decline*	*Comments*	*CAGR Return Bottom till it makes new high*	*Subsequent 5-year Return once crosses above previous high*
Apr-92	4,580	61.0		Bull market top		
Apr-93	1,956	24.1	-57.3%	Bear market bottom		
Feb-94	4,600	35.6	135.2%	Intermediate top		
Jun-96	4,200	26.8	-8.7%	Intermediate top		
Aug-97	4,580	17.2	9.0%	Intermediate top		
Apr-98	4,400	15.1	-3.9%	Intermediate top		
Dec-99	5,050	18.1	14.8%	Above previous high 92 months	1.3%	5.7%
Feb-00	6,120	21.9	21.2%	Bull Market Top	3.7%	2.0%
Jan-04	6,250	18.0	2.1%	Above previous high 49 months	0.2%	10.0%
May-04	4,240	12.2	-32.2%	Intermediate bottom		
Jan-08	21,206	24.5	400.1%	Bull market top	54.4%	0.0%
Mar-09	8,050	9.8	-62.0%	Bear market bottom		
Jan-11	21,100	19.6	162.1%	Intermediate top		

(*Source:* www.bseindia.com)

low of 1,956 in April 1993 to an intermediate top of 4,600 (P/E 35.6) in February 1994. However, the Sensex then went into hibernation for many years and made a new high only in December 1999 (P/E 18.1) giving meagre CAGR returns of 1.3% over a seven-and-a-half year period. It then hit a bull market top of 6,120 (P/E 21.9) in February 2000 before the technology bubble burst. This high of 6,120 in February 2000 gave a paltry CAGR return of just 3.7% since the previous bull market top of April 1992. Also note, the subsequent 5-year CAGR return since the bull market top of 6,120 in April 2000 was a measly 2% although the great bull market of 2003-2008 was very much underway.

However, if we see the returns from the bottom of secondary correction of May 2004 to the bull market top of January 2008, it comes to 400% absolute return or, importantly, CAGR return of 54.4%.

To conclude, the big money in market is not made by investing at bull market tops or even at bear market bottoms — unless somebody sells after the initial rally from the bear market bottom to the intermediate top, say from Sensex 8,040 in March 2009 to Sensex 21,100 in January 2011. The major sustainable long term return comes from investing in the subsequent secondary correction — after the intermediate top has been made — to the next bull market top. When the rally from the bear market bottom (April 2009 — Sensex 8,050) to the intermediate top (January 2011 — Sensex 21,100) got over, the initial more than 100% return had come and gone — as was the case in US during the years 1907, 1921, 1932, 1949, 1974, 1982 and in India in the years 1993 or, more recently, in 2009).

Bear Market Bottoms

There is so much to learn from bear market bottoms in equities and what better way of learning than to study the past 116-year price history of the US Dow Jones Industrial Average (DJIA) — one of the oldest indices of the best developed and the most mature market in the world.

First, let's see the full course of the DJIA from its inception. It was started in 1896 by the late Charles Dow editor of the *Wall Street Journal* and founder of the Dow Theory. It began with ten stocks (currently 30) and on a price weighted basis. In November 2012, the DJIA was close to 13,000. However the ride from 41 to 13,000 over 116 years was very choppy and volatile, with unbelievable swings between times of tremendous over- and under-valuations. Table 6.4 captures the history of the DJIA over the 116 years since its inception showing major market tops and bottoms.

As highlighted in Table 6.4, the DJIA witnessed wild swings from time to time and moved from highly over-valued to extremely

Table 6.4

Major Market Levels of DJIA Since Inception — 116-Year History

Year	*DJIA*	*Q Ratio**	*Returns*	*Comments*
1896	41			Inception
1905	98		139%	Multi year high
1907	48		-51%	Bear market bottom
1919	110		129%	Bull market top
1921	64	0.28	-42%	Great bear market bottom
1929	381		495%	Bull market top
1932	41	0.30	-89%	Great bear market bottom
1937	190		363%	Bull market top
1938	92		-52%	Multi year low
1942	87		-5%	Multi year low
1946	211		143%	Multi year high
1949	150	0.35	-29%	Great bear market bottom
1968	1,050		600%	Bull market top
1974	600	0.35	-43%	Bear market bottom
1981	1,000		67%	Multi year high
1982	769	0.27	-23%	Great bear market bottom
2000	11,500		1395%	Bull market top
2007	14,198		10%	Multi year high
2009	6,470		-55%	Multi year low
2012	13,000		100%	

(*Ratio of the stock price to the replacement value of assets)

(*Source:* Dow Jones & Co.)

under-valued zones in a matter of few years giving investors great buying and selling opportunities. The table shows that the bear market bottoms of the last century were in 1907, 1929, 1932, 1949, 1974 and 1982. The table also shows that from the bear market bottoms of 1921, 1932, 1949 and 1982, investors made returns of 495%, 363%, 600% and 1,395% in the subsequent period ranging from 8 to 19 years. Generally, the markets fell anywhere between 30% to 55% from their previous peak to the next bear market bottom, though the Great Depression triggered a heart-stopping market fall of 89% from 381 to 41 in just 3 years from 1929 to 1932. The valuations (by valuations I mean the Q ratio — the market cap to replacement value of assets), have however, been in the range of 0.28x to 0.35x in all these bear market bottoms. Thus, equity valuations did not fall much beyond the normal bear market bottoms; it was at 0.30x which is well within the range of the other bear market bottoms after the Great Depression. However, the significant difference between that bear market and the others is the pace at which equities moved from extreme over-valuation to under-valuation — namely in just 3 years — while in other cases it was a grind over many more years. Therefore, it's not a rule of thumb that equities become cheap after a significant and fast decline. In fact, the bear market of 1929-1932 was an exception in the history of financial markets. Generally, equities move from over-valuation to under-valuation over many years of relative under-performance of stock prices while the underlying economy and profits keep growing.

Lessons from Bear Market Bottoms

So what can we learn from bear market bottoms? How do we identify a great bear market bottom? An excellent study by Russell Napier in his book, *Anatomy of the Bear*[*] shows that while it's very difficult to predict a bottom, there are lots of factors which are

---

[*] Napier, Russell, *Anatomy of the Bear*, published by Vision books (www.visionbooksindia.com).

common to great bear market bottoms. Some of the common factors which we find at bear market bottoms are as follows:

- **Price (inflation) stabilization:** Improving demand for certain goods at lower levels, particularly autos.
- **Commodity price stabilization:** There should be stabilization in prices of commodities before an equity market rally can take place. Historically, the most important commodity in determining the stabilization of commodity prices turns out to be copper.
- **Improving economic news is ignored by the market.**
- **Reduction in Fed (central bank) controlled interest rates:** This has worked in all the above bear market bottoms, except in the 1929-1932 period where markets fell a further massive 69% after the first Fed interest rate cut in October 1931. We may consider the 1929-1932 Great Depression as an exceptional period in modern financial history.

  Fed (central bank) policy is one of the most powerful tools in determining equity market bottoms. There are few other factors as important for equity valuations as is interest rates.
- **Rally in government bond prices:** A rally in government bond prices has always preceded a rally in high grade corporate bonds which, typically, precedes a rally in equities with the exception of the 1949 bear market bottom. However, that was an abnormal period when the Fed was controlling its policy interest rates due to the extraordinary deflationary fear prevailing at that time after World War II.
- **Rally in corporate bond prices:** Rally in prices of high grade corporate bonds follows a rally in government bonds (except in 1949 as described above), while it precedes the rally in equities.
- **There is increase in trading activity and market volumes** on days when the market ends in the positive as compared to the days when the market ends in the negative.
- **Reluctance of the market to fall on incremental bad news.**
- **Rising short interest and the reluctance of shorts to cover on rising equity prices.**
- **Positive signals from Dow Theory:** Of all the technical methods, Dow Theory was the only one which correctly predicted the bottom

for all the four major US bear market bottoms of the 20th century.

These are the major factors which we have to look at in determining a bear market bottom. The purpose of studying bear market bottoms is not to try and suggest in any way that you try to time the markets. No — that is not the purpose of this book and if you try to do it then it could be very dangerous for your wealth and may substantially delay your financial freedom. Remember that in the markets money moves from active traders to passive investors. The purpose of writing all this was to give you a perspective on investing in equities, their financial history and performance, the risk and volatility involved, and how you can benefit from equities over the longer term and its role in your achieving financial independence.

Different Market Phases

Now that we have become familiar with the lessons from history and bear market bottoms, let us understand the market's different phases.

Phase 1: Market Begins to Ignore Good News and Starts Falling

This is the start of the bear market. If the market shrugs off even all good news and starts going down it is the market's way of saying that the bull market has ended; the general underlying economic scenario is not as good as it seems from the news and so it must go down.

Phase 2: Market Listens to the Bad News and Continues its Downward Journey

This is when the market is in the midst of a full fledged bear phase. Everything is gloomy. There is all kind of bad news around, such as an economic downturn, falling corporate sales and profitability, job losses, persistent high inflation, rising interest rates, economic scandals, increasing political and social unrest, etc.

Phase 3: Bad News Continues but the Market Refuses to Fall Further

This phase marks the death of the bear and the birth of a new bull. When the market refuses to fall further even on incremental bad news, it's the markets way of saying that it has fallen enough, that it has already discounted all the negative news, and that going forward the economy and the general business conditions are not as gloomy and, in fact, things will improve.

Phase 4: Market Continuous To Go Up With Good News

This phase is the normal full fledged bull market. Everything around looks good and rosy; businesses are making big money, companies are announcing huge expansions and acquisitions, the government's tax collections are good, people have lots of money to spend, etc. The economic environment, business conditions and ground level realities are all good — the full fledged bull market is up and running.

11 Common Mistakes in Equity Investing

Now it's time for us to consider some of the common mistakes investors make when investing in equity shares. Irrespective of whether they are experienced and seasoned professionals or first-time amateurs — all investors are susceptible to these mistakes. Remember what Fran Williams observed: "If you are intelligent the market will teach you caution and fortitude, sharpen your wits, and reduce your pride. If you are foolish and refuse to learn a lesson, it will ridicule you, laugh you to scorn, break you, and toss you on the rubbish-heap." The market has its own method of finding and exploiting human weaknesses.

We will try to explore and explain the eleven most common mistakes which investors commit while investing in common stocks.

Mistake 1: Trying to Catch the Market's Top and Bottom

This is a very common mistake which most equity investors commit, i.e. trying to catch the market's very top and bottom. Only fools believe that they can catch the market top or bottom. No government, no central bank, no company management, no fund manager, no analyst or anybody else knows what will be the next exact top or bottom of any stock. How then can an investor believe that he or she will be able to catch the market's very top or bottom?

Instead, determine the value and target price of any stock in which you intend to invest by whatever method you follow — fundamental, technical or any other — and then buy it within 5% to 10% range of that target price. You may also pace out the purchase over a period of time keeping in mind the current performance of that company and / or the overall market conditions. But once you have decided your correct price for buying a stock and once that price is approached, then don't wait to "buy at the bottom" because you will probably never be able to do that. Remember that if you wait too long to buy, until every uncertainty is removed and every doubt is lifted at the bottom of a market cycle, you may keep waiting . . . and waiting. The same rule also applies while selling. Therefore, never aim to buy at the bottom and always sell slightly earlier than others.

Mistake 2: Believing "The Price Will Come Back!"

This is another common mistake which most investors commit while investing in equities both when buying and selling shares. If they miss buying / selling a stock at a certain price, they then keep waiting in anticipation that the same price will come back, irrespective of market or stock considerations.

For example, based on his analysis somebody might have decided to sell Unitech. He had seen the price of ₹ 530 in January 2008 but "missed" selling at that price. After that the stock started falling because of general market weakness and fundamental deterioration in the company. But investors who waited for the "price to come back" — might still be waiting. The stock's price hit a low of around ₹ 17 — and who knows whether or when the price of ₹ 530 will ever come back! The lesson to be learned is that if the price of the stock has gone up — or gone down — because of a change in the company or sector's prospects then there is no point holding on to the illusion that the "price will come back".

Mistake 3: "It has already Fallen So Much — It Can't Fall Any Further"

This is another serious mistake which many investors commit while investing in equities. A stock falls "considerably" and they believe that it cannot then fall any further. Nothing can be farther from truth. In fact, this is one of the gravest mistakes which results in multiplication of investor losses.

Continuing with the Unitech example, the stock fell from ₹ 530 in January 2008 to ₹ 240 by March 2008, a massive fall of 45% in just two months. An investor who believed that it couldn't fall further because it had fallen 45% in two months and hence held on to it — or purchased it — was in for a rude shock as it fell to ₹ 20 by December 2008, a massive 96% fall from the top and also a substantial fall of 92% from the March 2008 level of ₹ 240. Unless the stock again becomes attractive on a stand alone basis, there is simply no logic in thinking that "because it has already fallen so much, it can't fall further."

Mistake 4: "It's Already Gone Up So Much — it Can't Rise Any Higher"

This is the corollary of mistake number three — many times investors believe that since a stock has risen so much, it cannot rise any further.

For example, Titan rose from around ₹ 5 in July 2004 to ₹ 42 by March 2006, a stupendous, jump of more than 8-fold in less than two years. Anybody who sold it believing that the stock had already risen a lot and therefore wouldn't rise any more was in for a rude surprise as the price rose to ₹ 290 by November 2012, not only swelling 58-fold from its July 2004 price of ₹ 5 but even multiplying by around 6.9 times from its March 2006 level of ₹ 42. Hence, unless the stock becomes expensive on the basis of valuation, expectations of future growth, or any other "price determination" parameter which you might be applying, there is no reason to sell a stock simply because it has risen so much.

Mistake 5: Protecting Your Profits Or Cutting Your Losses

Many readers might not agree with me on this point. Unless you are a short term trader or investing using costly leveraged funds, there is no point in simply trying to "protect the profits" or "cut losses". You should sell if the stock becomes costly on valuation basis, or its fundamentals deteriorate on a long term basis. Just because a stock on which you are making money corrects, it does not mean that you panic and sell it to "protect your profits". Let's continue with the example of Titan.

After rising about 8-fold from ₹ 5 in July 2004 to ₹ 42 in March 2006, i.e. in just two months, Titan's stock price corrected to ₹ 21 by May 2006, i.e. it fell to almost half of its peak price of March 2006. An investor who panicked and sold the stock then would have been in for a nasty surprise as the stock then went up to ₹ 85 by December 2007, i.e. a 4-fold jump from its May 2006 low — and then beyond that to touch ₹ 290 in November 2012.

The same principle would apply for cutting losses as you might be cutting your losses just before the stock is on the verge of embarking on its dream run. Let's continue with the Titan example. Suppose you purchased the stock at ₹ 42 in March 2006. It halved to ₹ 21 in the subsequent two months and you were nursing a massive 50% loss. Now, had you sold the stock at ₹ 21, then you would have sold it just before it was getting ready for its next dream run which led to manifold price multiplication over the next few years. So, the lesson is: sell the stock only if after your analysis you feel that the price is right for selling and not on the misleading notion of protecting your profits. By doing the latter you might in fact be eliminating any probability of serious wealth creation in the future. The same applies to the "cut your losses" fallacy as well.

Mistake 6: Price Averaging

This is another loss-making mistake which equity investors make.

There is a wrong notion that bringing down the purchase cost by averaging would enable you to sell at some marginal profit or, at least, closer to your cost price.

Let us return to the example of Unitech.

Suppose you invested in the share at ₹ 530 in January 2008, then "averaged" by buying another share at ₹ 300 in February 2008 and further averaged by purchasing another share at ₹ 240 in March 2008. Now your reduced "average cost" per share is ₹ 357. But what purpose has that served? At the time of this writing, the stock was quoting around ₹ 33, down by a phenomenal 91% from the reduced "averaged cost".

One caveat: sometimes an investor might get an opportunity to exit the averaged stock at close to the "average cost" but such opportunities are rare, exist only for a short time, and are therefore very difficult to capitalize on.

Finally, if you would not otherwise buy a stock at a particular price then what is the logic for averaging just because you already own it? Remember, never throw good money after bad. If you have made a mistake in selecting a wrong stock, humbly accept your mistake, sell it, book your loss move ahead, and utilize the proceeds to buy better investments with potential of future price appreciation.

Mistake 7: The Market Trap — "Stock's Gone Up So I Am Right" or "Stock's Gone Down So I Am Wrong"

Ego and lack of self confidence are both negative qualities for an investor. If you buy a stock and it goes up for no real reason but because of irrational market behavior, then be smart and sell it and get out instead of pampering your ego by thinking that you are an astute investor or a great stock picker. In other words, never confuse bull markets with intelligence. Remember, that the market is a great deflator of all egos. The same holds true when you might have invested in a stock at a decent price after a thorough analysis and the stock falls not due to any deterioration in the company's performance but for some uncontrollable market reasons. At such times, there is no need to panic, lose self confidence and start believing that you were wrong. Remember that the market can also be wrong and is, in fact, wrong most of the times. Try to take advantage of its abnormalities by using your knowledge, experience and judgment instead of getting swayed by it and losing your self confidence.

Mistake 8: Efficient Market Theory

Don't blindly believe in the efficient market theory. In fact, remember that the market is inefficient almost 95% of the time — it's like a pendulum moving from over-valuation to under-valuation, and *vice versa*. Like a pendulum moving from one side (over-valuation) to the other side (under-valuation), the market only sometimes that it passes through the middle (fair valuation). Having said that, over the long term the pendulum does move in the right direction — if the country, economy, sector and the individual stock perform well, then over the longer term, the pendulum, too, puts its weight behind them.

Mistake 9: Blindly Following a Guru

There is a saying that either you completely trust your judgment or the judgment of another person. And that other person in the market is the investment guru or fund manager, etc. You may trust any investment guru of your choice — and, indeed, some investor gurus will periodically beat the market — but it's worth noting that even all investment gurus together cannot beat the market on a continuous basis because they themselves make up the market! Simply put, everybody can't beat everybody — for there to be a winner, there has also to be a loser. And, kindly note, the buyer and seller are always on the opposite side of the trade and they both mysteriously believe that they are right — but one of them is, in fact, wrong! So don't trust any of the so-called investment gurus at face value (including myself, although I don't claim to be an investment guru but just a student of investing). Most of the time, the guru will not advise what he believes is right but in fact say what you want to hear. Research and analysis do not always work in the stock market but the jobs of analysts are always secured. So, bear these points in your mind before selecting your guru.

Mistake 10: Buying Penny Stocks

This is another common mistake which most investors commit — they buy penny stocks, i.e. stocks with low prices, thinking that the price is already "so low", most probably in single digits, that it can't go any lower, little realizing their folly. In the pursuit of buying "cheap stocks", they end up investing in "cheap companies". The amount of loss in stock investing is reported in percentage terms and measured in rupee terms, whether it be a penny stock of ₹ 1 or a high priced stock of ₹ 1,000. Therefore, if a ₹ 1 stock falls to 10 paisa or a ₹ 1,000 stock falls to ₹ 100, the loss in both cases is 90%. And, most importantly, if you invest, say ₹ 1,000 in either of the two stocks and both of them become zero, then you lose your entire investment of ₹ 1,000, irrespective of the stock's initial price. So, remember the old saying: "penny wise, pound foolish". The stock price is just a quote in the market and on its own does not have any significance whatsoever. It has to be measured in conjunction with the company's performance, earnings, book value, dividends, etc. A high priced stock may actually be cheap on valuation basis while a low priced penny stock may in reality be very costly if the underlying business does not support even that.

Mistake 11: Failure to Pass the Test of Patience and Character

The market is a place which will test your patience and character. Many times you might have bought a stock for all the right reasons and at the right price but the stock may still not go up for a long period. You may have just hung on thinking that the day you get frustrated and sell it off, there are chances the stock will then start rising. Hence, patience and character are key virtues which will be repeatedly tested by the market. Remember, whether in life or in the markets, you must never quit when things seem to be the worst. Inevitably, good times follow bad times.

To recapitulate, there are many elementary — and avoidable — mistakes which investors commit while investing in stocks. We have tried to highlight some of the most common ones. Always remember that simple, logical things work far better in the marketplace rather than complex algorithms, theorems, valuations principles, DCF, etc. And there is no better place to test your virtues than the market — be it common sense, logical thinking, patience, perseverance, mental balance, emotional intelligence, performing under stress, etc. All the qualities which make a successful human being will be tested by the market which has its own method of finding and exploiting human weaknesses. Investing is not about beating the market or anybody else, it's more about simply overcoming your own self — your own negative traits. Once you are able to master your own self and become a mature human being, you will also become a successful investor.

Characteristics of Successful Equity Investors

Investing tests the character of human beings, and none as much as equity investment. Chinese philosopher Lao Tse observed that "He who knows much about others may be learned, but he who understands himself is more intelligent. He who controls others may be more powerful, but he who has mastered himself is mightier still."

Successful equity investing is nothing but battling with yourself to master yourself. This section provides an illustrative list of some characteristics which are common among successful investors.

Be a Smart Investor and Not Just a Hard-Working One

There are two categories of investors in the market — the hard worker and the smart worker. More than 90% fall into the category of hard workers (or at least those who believe working hard is important in the market) and less than 10% fall in the category of smart workers. Whether in the stock market or anything else in life, there has to be plan and clear cut goals to be achieved. You can't just be a workaholic and hope to succeed. Hard work alone does not lead to success. There has to be proper focus and direction. Therefore, learn to work smart and not just hard. One of the most important qualities in the market is not fundamental or technical analysis, DCF, complex algorithm, etc., but emotional maturity.

Philosophy and Methodology

You must develop your own investing philosophy and methodology — never try to copy or imitate another successful investor or trader because it's almost certain that it would lead you to financial disaster. In stock markets, what has worked for another person will not work for you — and *vice versa*. Therefore, always develop your own philosophy and methodology. You may follow whatever technique you like — fundamental, technical, macroeconomic, monetary, etc. — whatever style — growth, value, momentum, etc. The styles and techniques don't determine whether you will succeed or not in the stocks markets; it's how you develop those styles and techniques into a proper philosophy and methodology that will work for you through bull and bear markets.

Discipline and Patience

One of the biggest enemies of long term success, whether in stock market or life, is the lack of mental character and ability to postpone gratification. Everyone wants instant success. This leads people go in for short-term gain which results in long-term pain. For example, a young person who takes a short term job for earning money and in the process sacrifices his or her long term career, or labor unions fighting for higher wages which in the long run cripple the company and the industry itself. Patience is a virtue which will help you in a big way in achieving success in the stock markets.

Independent Thinking

This is one of the most important attributes of successful investors which most of us lack. Today there is so much information, research, news, etc. that we often get lost in just reading and accumulating information. We have an information cascade with no real knowledge or creative thinking. We can collect and assimilate information but can hardly make sense of that information. Often, investors believe independent thinking means being a contrarian, but being contrarian by itself will not help — what will help is trying to understand why the crowd might be wrong. If you don't have independent thinking, then you will rush to sell your good stocks at the slightest market panic. You may listen to all the experts, fund managers, analysts, gurus, etc. but always make a final judgment based on your independent and creative thinking.

Pragmatism

You may have high hopes and dreams but it's important to always have your feet well grounded. Be optimistic but at the same time also be realistic in the market. You may hope for the best but should also be ready for the worst. If you are not ready for the worst, then you will be taken unawares by sudden market moves and be stampeded into taking immature market decisions at inappropriate times.

There are a host of other qualities which help in making a successful equity investor, but detailing all of them is unnecessary. What's important to remember is that most qualities which go into making a successful human being will be needed to become a successful equity investor because nothing probably tests a human being more than the stock markets.

Classic Equity Investment Principles

I give below an illustrative list of classic equity investment principles. Kindly note that this is just an illustrative list and not a comprehensive one. Probably, there simply can't be a comprehensive set of principles for equity investments — there can be as many principles as the number of investment vehicles, multiplied by the number of investors!

- Bull and bear markets run for several years. Hence determine the primary trend of the market and generally don't go against the primary trend.
- Market is supreme and above everybody — and no government, central bank, industrialist or operator can alter the primary trend of the market. They can only complicate its wave structure somewhat.
- Once a low is made, it typically gets tested once or twice. If it gets tested again and again, it probably means that it is not the real low and the market is eventually going to break it.
- Correct asset allocation and getting the macro view right are far more important and profitable than individual investment ideas.
- In the stock market, a small percentage of people end up being successful in the long run whereas a majority of the people, in spite of being successful in the short run, end up losing money in the long run.

- Never invest or trade more than you can reasonably afford to lose.
- Put stop loss at a logical, not convenient, place — and always adhere to it.
- Cut losses and let profits run. Don't let a profit get converted into loss.
- Giving excess weight to the most recent past history as opposed to a longer view, is a common judgment error — and not just in the stock market.
- If you wait too long to buy, until every uncertainty is removed and every doubt is lifted at the bottom of a market cycle, you may keep waiting — and waiting. So the opportune time to buy might not necessarily be when the conditions have become good but, in fact, when they have moved from worse to bad.
- Either act on your own judgment or entirely on the judgment of another.
- Tips are for waiters, not for investors.
- When in doubt, stay out — and don't get in when in doubt.
- Don't overtrade.
- Don't invest or trade based on hope.
- Learn to accept your mistakes in the market otherwise the market will cruelly force you to accept them. Then analyze and learn from your mistakes.
- Wherever possible, trade liquid markets.
- Don't believe everything that a corporate official says about his or her company's stock.
- Beware when opinions in the market are nearly unanimous because markets are famous for doing the unexpected.
- Never be sentimental about an asset class or an individual stock.
- Investing in the stock market is more of an art than science.
- Simple, logical things work far better in the marketplace rather than complex algorithms, theorems, valuations principles, DCF, etc.
- Buy stocks of companies that have shown consistent growth in earnings and which produce goods and services that people cannot do without.

- When the gap between perception and reality is the maximum, price is the best. The time to buy is when the gloom is the deepest.
- Last but not the least — never try to catch the market's very top and very bottom. Only fools think they can do so.

The Determining Factor — Psychology of Equity Investments

In the beginning of this chapter we had looked at the factors driving stock market prices — economic factors, monetary factors, fundamental factors, technical factors and psychological factors. There has been a lot of research, and many books and material are available, about these four factors but the most important — and, I would say, the deciding — factor is the fifth category, i.e. psychological factors about which very little is written. Whatever may be our method of investing, whether fundamental, technical or any other, the crucial point is whether we actually do what we had initially decided to. What if the price goes against our decision — do we still stick to our conviction? For example, an investor after doing full fundamental research on a stock whose current price is ₹ 100 concludes that its value is ₹ 150 and buys that stock. Now, with all the original fundamental factors intact, the stock falls to, say, ₹ 75 because of a general market fall or some rumor surrounding the stock, etc. What does the investor do then? Do you panic and exit the stock at a loss? Or, do you hold on as the original premise for which you bought the stock has not changed? This issue deals with investor psychology. Whether in stock market or any other walk of life, while beating the external factors is difficult enough but beating oneself is the really difficult part. Beating oneself simply means mastering one's own emotions and the ability to think rationally and independently in the face of all the "noise" surrounding us.

There is a difference between just thinking about investing or trading and actually committing money in the market. During the latter, objectivity often falls by the wayside and emotion takes over. Markets have their own method of probing human weaknesses. I have seen young people with hardly any experience or knowledge of the market jump in thinking that it is a quick, easy and effortless way of making money. Nothing is farther from the truth. Can anybody imagine becoming the CEO of a big company with just six months experience, or becoming a star cricket player after six weeks of training and practice, or a university professor with just an under graduate degree? Clearly, no. How, then, can a young person without any investing experience dream of becoming rich overnight when even seasoned and experienced players often fail to do so?

Psychology is a big subject and beyond the scope of this book but, very broadly, it deals with understanding one's own self. Similarly, whether you are speculator, a trader or an investor, you need to be aware of your strengths and weakness and then consolidate on your strengths and minimize the weaknesses. We don't have to believe any expert or guru at face value. Instead, we should inculcate independent thinking, and be patient and persistent. We should know when to follow the trend and when to go contrary, how to profit from news breaks and media (rather than just getting carried away by the noise around us), how to deal with brokers and fund managers for whom it's a "compulsion" to be always bullish, etc. Never underestimate the fact that pride is an investor's biggest enemy. The market is the biggest deflator of the human ego. The great Charles Dow (founder of the *Wall Street Journal* and the all-season Dow Theory) had once said that "pride of opinion has been responsible for the downfall of more men on Wall Street than any other factor."

The fact that while equity as an asset class has given handsome returns but investors have fared poorly only highlights the fickle-minded behavior of investors. We are all human beings with minds and hearts. Many of the gurus will tell you to invest through the mind. In fact, I end the equity section with the simple advice that make equity investment decisions based on the mind — and then stay the course by having a strong heart.

Investing in Fixed Income Securities

Fixed income securities are an essential component of an investor's portfolio.

Interest Rate Risk

There are different types of risks associated with investing in fixed income securities. The major ones are credit risk, interest rate risk, yield curve risk, liquidity risk and basis risk.

The most common risk which an investor faces with fixed income investments is credit risk. Having said that, there is one more risk which is as important as credit risk, and that is interest rate risk. Few people understand this latter risk. For example, a long term government security may have zero credit risk because the government can literally "print notes" and pay back the loan or tax you to pay back your own loans, but it has one of the highest interest rate risks. Interest rate risk is directly related with the maturity of a security. I will now cover two very important contributors of interest rate risks — duration and convexity.

Duration

Many investors confuse duration with maturity. However, they are both distinct and different. Maturity is simply the time period after which the fixed income security will mature and pay back the principal. For example, the maturity of a 10-year paper will be ten years at the time of issue. On the other hand, duration is the time within which the investor receives back all the cash flows related to the security, i.e. interest and principal. For example, a 10-year maturity paper paying yearly coupon at the interest rate of 8.0% p.a. issued at par (₹ 100) will have the following cash flows, 8 + 8 + 8 + 8 + 8 + 8 + 8 + 8 + 8 + 108 which will be paid at the end of every year for the next 10 years till it matures. The ₹ 8 is the interest at 8% p.a. on ₹ 100 face value. Kindly note that at the end of the 10th year the investor will receive ₹ 108, i.e. ₹ 100 of principal + ₹ 8 of the 10th year's interest. This example clearly shows that although the maturity of the security is ten years, the investor receives cash flows frequently and at regular intervals much before the final maturity of the security. That brings us to the concept of duration.

The duration of a bond is defined as the "weighted average term to maturity of a security's cash flows". Since the cash flows on a security are received piecemeal before the actual maturity of the security, the duration of any coupon paying bonds will be less than its maturity. And as a zero coupon bond does not pay any interest during its life, its duration is equal to its maturity.

There are different forms of duration. The basic one is the Macaulay Duration or Unadjusted Duration. The one which we use for our calculation is the adjusted or Modified Duration. I would not go into the mathematical formulae of computing these but will explain the concepts which are necessary for understanding interest rate risks associated with fixed income securities.

Duration is useful primarily as a measure of the sensitivity of a bond's market price to interest rate (i.e. yield) movements. It is approximately equal to the percentage change in price for a given change in yield. For example, for small interest rate changes, the duration is the approximate percentage by which the value of the bond will fall for a 1% per annum increase in market interest rate. So a 10-year bond with a duration of 7 years would fall approximately 7% in value if the interest rate goes up by 1% per annum. In other words, duration is the elasticity of the bond's price with respect to interest rates.

The summary of duration characteristics is as follows:

- The duration of a zero coupon bond is equal to its term to maturity.
- The duration of a coupon paying bond will always be less than its term to maturity.
- There is an inverse relationship between coupon and duration. The higher the coupon of a bond, the lesser its duration — and *vice versa*. The logic is simple because the higher the coupon, the sooner will the cash flows accrue to the investor and hence the lower the interest rate risk associated with future cash flows.
- There is generally a positive relationship between duration and term to maturity. Note that the duration of a coupon bond

increases at a decreasing rate with maturity and the shape of the duration / maturity curve will depend on the coupon and the yield-to-maturity (YTM) of the bond.

- There is an inverse relationship between YTM and duration.
- Sinking fund and call provisions can cause dramatic change in the duration of a bond.

Convexity

Duration is a linear measure of how the price of a bond changes in response to interest rate changes. As interest rates change, the price does not change linearly. Rather, it is a convex function of interest rates. Convexity is a measure of the curvature of how the price of a bond changes with changes in interest rates. Convexity deals with the curvature of the price / yield relationship or chart. Specifically, duration can be formulated as the first derivative of the price function of the bond with respect to the interest rate in question, and convexity as the second derivative.

Convexity also gives an idea of the spread of future cash flows. Just as duration gives the discounted mean term, so convexity can be used to calculate the discounted standard deviation, say, of return.

Note that duration can be either negative or positive depending on the way the interest rates move but convexity is always a positive feature of the bond. The exception to this rule is in the case of "callable bonds" where the convexity is a negative feature. Positive feature of convexity means that for a given change in interest rates and the modified duration of a bond, the change in price of the bond will be in favor of the investor. For example, because of the positive feature of convexity, when interest rates rise, the price of the bond will fall less than that indicated by the duration — and when interest rates fall, the price of the bond will rise more than that indicated by the duration. This is because when we study the price / yield relationship of a coupon paying option free bond, the larger the increase in the YTM, the greater is the magnitude of the error by which the modified duration will overestimate the bond's price decline. Correspondingly, the larger the decrease in the YTM, the greater the magnitude of the error by which the modified duration will underestimate the bond's price rise.

As the YTM changes, the bond's duration changes as well. Thus, modified duration is a near accurate predictor of price change. Yield to maturity, or YTM, is simply the discount rate at which the sum of all future cash flows from the bond (coupons and principal) equal the bond's price.

Summary

Without making this section on fixed income securities too long and complicated, the change in price of a fixed income security is duration times the change in yield, i.e. for a security having a modified duration of 7 years, for every 1 % (100 bps) decrease in yield (interest rates), the price will go up by 1 * 7 = 7% — and *vice versa.* Due to convexity of the bond, the gain will be a little more than 7% in case of interest rate decline and the loss will be a little less than 7% in case of interest rate increase.

Debt Funds Which Combat Interest Rate Risk

Now let us understand which category of debt instruments you should invest in at different points in the interest rate cycle. Since mutual funds offer a variety of debt instruments, the concepts are explained primarily in the context of debt investments through the mutual fund route.

- **Bank Fixed Deposit or Fixed Maturity Plan:** A bank fixed deposit (FD) or a fixed maturity plan (FMP) offered by a mutual fund is for a fixed period of time and hence locks in your money at the prevailing interest rate for that period of time. It, therefore, does not have any interest rate risk. However, the FD or FMP has a very high "opportunity loss risk" in the sense that if you lock in long term FD or FMP just before the beginning of an interest rate hike cycle then you will lose the opportunity of earning higher yields. Therefore, investment in an FD or FMP should ideally be done at the peak of the short term interest rate hike cycle.

- **Liquid or Money Market Funds:** These are suitable for parking your surplus funds earmarked for meeting liquidity needs and hence interest rate considerations are not important.
- **Ultra Short Term Funds:** If the liquidity need can be stretched to a couple of weeks, then the interest rate risk in ultra short term funds will smoothen out and most probably give better returns then would a liquid fund.
- **Short Term Funds:** These should be considered when there has already been substantial hike in short term policy rates and, importantly, it should have resulted in the yield curve being inverted or flat.
- **Income Funds:** These funds become attractive when there has been substantial hike in short term policy rates and, importantly, the yield curve is steep, or at least upward sloping, and the spread between government securities and corporate yields is high.
- **Gilt Funds:** These funds are ideal when there has been a substantial hike in short term policy rates and, importantly, the yield curve is steep, or at least upward sloping, and the spread between government securities and corporate yields is low.

It is important to know when to invest in short term funds, income and gilt funds. The common feature is that you should invest in all three after a substantial hike in short term policy rates but in short term funds when the yield curve is inverted or flat, in income funds when the yield curve is steep / upward sloping with high yield spreads as compared to government securities, and in gilt funds when the yield curve is steep / upward sloping with low yield spread as compared to corporate bonds.

To conclude this commandment, the essential thing to understand is that investing in equities is not actually risky over the long term; it is the volatility over the short term which makes it appear risky. It's therefore important to learn to distinguish between risk and volatility. The behavioral traits of the investor in particular and the crowd behavior of the markets in general make equity investing appear a risky proposition. Also, remember this: whatever you don't know is risky. For an accountant to draw up a balance sheet is very easy because he does it daily as it is for a doctor to prescribe medicine because that is the job he is accustomed to doing daily. Now if you tell the accountant to prescribe medicines or the doctor to draw a balance sheet, they will fail miserably and would find it risky. That's why there is nothing inherently easy or difficult, risky or safe. If you know something, it's easy; otherwise, it's difficult. Similarly, if you understand the pros and cons of investment then it is safe and not risky. And always bear in mind that the life of a person who does not take risks becomes risky. Therefore, instead of writing off an investment as risky learn more about it, take up some course or seminar on it, or read some books on it and increase your financial literacy. The reason that you are reading this book means that you want to increase your financial literacy. Congratulations — and keep up the good work!

Lessons From This Commandment

1. There are three sources of return from equity — initial dividend yield, growth in earnings, and change in valuation (price / earnings ratio).
2. While investors buy shares in companies, entrepreneurs sell shares of their companies. The biggest money in this world is made by successful entrepreneurs selling shares of their companies and not by investors who invest in equity shares.
3. Learn the difference between good and bad quality stocks and businesses. Benjamin Graham commented that "the risk of paying too high a price for a good-quality stock — while a real one — is not the chief hazard confronting the average buyer of securities. Observation over many years has taught us that the chief losses to investors come from purchase of low-quality securities at times of favorable business conditions."
4. The five major factors which affect the price of equities — or, for that matter, any freely tradable instrument like bonds, gold, etc. — are macroeconomic, monetary, fundamental, technical and psychological factors.
5. History is full of examples of the "madness of crowds" — of rational and intelligent people succumbing to irrational crowd behavior and psychology.

6. Know the difference between investing and speculating. An investor chases value while a speculator chases stock prices.
7. Understanding the economic and business cycle is of paramount importance. As a general rule, first interest rates come down and bond prices go up, then equities enter a bull market, and, finally, commodities blossom.
8. Understand the difference between risk and volatility. Equities might be volatile in the short term but provide higher returns with much lower risk over the longer term. The biggest risk might be posed by inflation which eats into the purchasing power of your money.
9. Interest rates are one of the biggest enemies of equities affecting them through reduced earnings, reduced sales, depressed valuations and lower liquidity. For any meaningful recovery in equities, it is a *sine quo non* that the interest rates have to first stabilize, and then soften.
10. There are very important lessons to be learnt from history and bear market bottoms. As a general rule, look for price (inflation) stabilization, commodity price stabilization, reduction in central bank controlled rates, rally in government bond prices followed by corporate bonds and positive signals from Dow Theory to identify bear market bottoms.
11. There are different market phases wherein news has different impact on stock prices. It makes sense to know which phase of the market we are in at any given point of time.
12. The market has its own method of finding and exploiting human weaknesses. There are certain common mistakes which investors commit while investing in common stocks. Beware of them so as to not to become their victim.
13. Successful investors have certain characteristics or traits. Try to imbibe those characteristics. Also, remember the classic equity investment principles and always try to abide by them.
14. If you think equities are too risky and not for you, then remember that whether in investments or in life — the biggest risk of all is not taking any risk whatsoever. The life of a person who does not take risk becomes risky. Try to reduce your risk by increasing your financial knowledge.

Self-Understanding Questionnaire

This commandment took you through the fascinating journey of equity and fixed income investments. It sought to remove various myths which you might have had about equities while at the same time making you mentally and psychologically equipped to be a successful equity investor. Now, honestly answer the following questions in yes or no to test your understanding of the principles explained in this commandment. The more the number of "no" answers, the better is your understanding of this commandment.

1. Do you think equities are too risky for any common person to invest in? Yes/No?
2. Do you imagine that to become a successful equity investor you need to be equipped with the latest news, research reports, views of fund managers, expert opinion, etc.? Yes/No?
3. Do you believe that common investors have no chance of competing against the might of highly educated professional investors? Yes/No?
4. Are you of the opinion that the most important form of return from equities comes from capital gains, i.e. an increase in the price of the stock? Yes/No?
5. Do you believe that markets are always rational and adhere to the efficient market theory? Yes/No?
6. Do you think that a short term trader will be able to multiply his money many times and will therefore be more successful than a long term investor? Yes/No?
7. In your view, do all asset classes generally move in the same direction? Yes/No?
8. Do you think equities are a bigger risk than inflation? Yes/No?
9. Do you believe that only knowledge is important in the equity markets while human psychology, crowd behavior and behavior finance have no relevance? Yes/No?

—

Appendix 6.1:The Madness of Crowds*

"Markets can remain irrational longer than you can remain solvent".
— John Maynard Keynes

I have studied human behavior, mass psychology, behavior finance and the "madness of crowds" going back around five hundred years, including the minor financial revolution of the 1550s, troubles of Henry VIII, Francois I, the Fuggers, the Genoese and the "madness of crowds" in the eighteenth century like the South Sea Bubble, Tulip Bulb craze, the Mississippi bubbles and the 1857 and 1866 crises in England. The law of a crowd is mental unity. Individuals comprising the crowd lose their conscious personality under the influence of emotion and act as one, directed by the lower, crowd intelligence.

History shows that financial markets are neither rational nor efficient and any investment strategy that ignores this fact is doomed to fail. The market is not there to oblige any individual. Instead, it has its unique ways of exploiting individual weakness to the maximum. I will take you back by three hundred years in human financial history to show you how rational, knowledgeable investors made totally irrational and illogical decisions when part of a crowd — how they submitted their independent thinking to irrational crowd thinking. The study of crowd behavior and market psychology is of paramount importance if you want to be a successful investor. Rational and successful investing is all about channelizing your emotions correctly and understanding behavior finance. If you haven't studied big books on investments, are not aware of valuations, modern portfolio theories, efficient market theories, etc., don't feel that you lack knowledge on investing — all these are actually quite irrelevant in the real world of investments. Such knowledge and qualifications might help you get a job but will certainly not make you a successful investor. You might have witnessed

---

* For a *tour de force* on the subject *see Extraordinary Popular Delusions and the Madness of Crowds*, published by Vision Books (www.visionbooksindia.com).

many market crashes over your years of stock investing. You might have wondered why stocks of so many good companies consistently trade at below par valuations for long periods and why investors are ready to pay billions of dollars in market capitalization for companies with no sales or earnings. This has always happened throughout history because, finally, we are all emotional human beings. If you want to win the investment battle, you don't have to defeat anyone else but you have to win against your own self. Let me give you three examples of the incredible mistakes and madness to which crowds can succumb by taking some examples from financial history.

South Sea Bubble

During the late 1990s you might have wondered why investors were ready to give billions to Internet companies which had no assets, sales or earnings. Most of those companies eventually lost money and vanished as if they never existed. Don't be surprised for our forefathers had also made similar mistakes. At the time of the South Sea Bubble, the British were ripe for throwing away money. A long period of British prosperity had resulted in fat savings and few investment outlets. In those days, as even today, owning a stock was considered a privilege and stock was one of the properties in which British women were allowed to invest in their own right. The South Sea Company was formed to oblige this appetite for owning stocks. It was incorporated to restore faith in the government's ability to meet its obligations. Formed in 1711 by Robert Harley, the South Sea Company was created to convert £10 million of government war debt (incurred during the War of Spanish Succession) into its own shares. It took over Government IOUs of around £10 million and in return it was given monopoly to trade over the South Seas. The public believed that enormous wealth was to be made in such trade and everybody wanted to buy stock of the company. It seemed to make no difference that the company did not have any real sales or profits. From the very beginning it enjoyed profits at the expense of others. There was news in December 1719 that there would be peace with Spain which would benefit the South Sea trade as Mexicans were waiting to empty their gold mines in return for England's cotton and woollen goods. The directors, a greedy lot, decided to fund the entire national debt of £31 million. The South Sea stock jumped from

£130 to £300. Slowly the stock increased to £340, then £400 (another issue announced), then £550, further to £800 and, finally, to £1000 when the speculation and madness was at its extreme.

The demand among people for speculative investments had soared to such insurmountable levels that all kind of fraudulent issuers came to the market with their issues. The greater their bad intention, the more the demand for their stock! One prospectus stated that "A Company for carrying on an undertaking of great advantage, but nobody to know what it is". And the issue got over subscribed multiple times within a few hours — that was the ultimate height of the madness of crowds. But all bubbles eventually burst. Realizing that the price of the stock bore no relevance to its actual prospects, the avaricious directors of the company sold their shares. As this news leaked, the stock fell off the cliff — from £1000 to £100 in a matter of a few weeks! That was the end of the speculative craze for the South Sea stock. To protect the general public from such fraudulent issues the parliament passed the Bubble Act, which forbade the issuing of stock certificates by companies. This prevented such activities for more than a century until the act was repealed in the year 1825. In short, the British people had a lot of money and wanted some investment for their newly earned wealth. They got it in the form of the South Sea Company, which then robbed them of their hard earned wealth and prosperity. The South Sea project remains the greatest example in British history of the infatuation of people with commercial gambling. From the bitter experience of that time, we may learn how dangerous it is to allow unrestrained speculation to take enormous profits from inadequate causes.

The Mississippi Scheme

While the South Sea Bubble was going strong in England, across the Channel another stock company was formed by an exiled Englishman named John Law. This man was a great gambler who had settled in France.

He was thoroughly acquainted with the philosophy and true principles of credit. He understood monetary question better than any man of his day; and if his system fell with a crash so tremendous, it was not so much his fault as that of the people amongst whom he had erected it. He did not reckon on the avaricious frenzy of a whole nation; he did not see that confidence, like mistrust, could be increased, almost ad infinitum, and that hope was as extravagant as fear. Law's dream in life was to replace metal as money and create liquidity through a national paper currency backed by the State and controlled through a network of local agencies. To fulfill his dream, he acquired an abandoned concern called the Mississippi Company and went ahead to build a conglomerate that became one of the largest enterprises of its time. The word "millionaire" was invented at that time. The house and road where he stayed and trade used to be crowded and flocked by people of all kind. Lots of robberies and murders used to take place as everyone, including the rogue thieves, wanted their share of the newly founded wealth. Women would be crazy to have a glimpse of John Law. No wonder the stock price of Mississippi Company rose from 100 to 2,000 in just two years. At one time, the market capitalization of the Mississippi Company in France was more than eighty times that of all the gold and silver in the country! When the bubble burst, Law fled to England and then finally moved on to Venice where he eventually met with a very embarrassing death.

The Tulip Mania

This was the mother of all bubbles. Imagine someone telling you that he is ready to pay you a bag full money or a box full of gold or barter his personal belongings like land, jewels, furniture for a flower! That was the craze at the height of this bubble. The Tulip Bulb mania is a great story of a get rich quick story gone wrong. It happened in Holland between the years 1634 to 1637. The events leading to this spectacular frenzy were set in motion in the year 1593 when a botany professor from Vienna brought to Leyden a collection of unusual plants that had originated in Turkey. Over the next decade, the tulip bulb became a costly but popular item in Dutch gardens. Subsequently, a virus caused the tulip petals to develop contrasting colored stripes or frames. The Dutch highly valued these infected bulbs. Slowly but surely the price of the tulip bulbs went up and the more bizarre the bulb, the higher the price. The more costly the bulbs became, more it made the people believe them to be smart investment. Doesn't it sound familiar: the more the stock prices increase, the more the investor feels that he is smart and safe investing in it? People who believed that prices of tulip bulbs could not go up any further were left flabbergasted — the same way as rational investors who may believe that the price of certain speculative stocks can't go up further are left astonished when they do.

Today we regularly trade futures and options but the term "call option" was invented at that time. A call option gave the holder the right to buy tulip bulbs at a fixed price during a specified period with a call premium of around 15% to 20%. If the price of the bulb doubled, which was quite common at during the height of the bubble, the call value would jump by three to four times, allowing the call holder to multiply his so-called investment. As with any kind of bubble, this period was also filled with tragic episodes. As in the case with any bubble, finally a time comes when some investors say that enough is enough and the price can't go up further. And if at that time, there is no "greater fool" to buy the asset at the inflated price, the price starts coming down. As the price starts coming down, more and more of investors flock to sell it which results in further selling pressure. And with insufficient buying interest, the prices start falling rather rapidly. Then comes a stage where there is "seller's panic" as lack of buyers results in the price crashing down the cliff. The same thing happened with tulip bulbs during the early part of 1637. Government ministers stated officially that there was no reason for tulip bulbs to fall in price — similar to how governments and central banks today try to "talk up the markets". But when a bubble bursts, no government, central bank, industrialist or operator, can stop the inflated balloon from bursting. A government plan to settle all contracts at 10% of their face value was frustrated when bulbs fell even below that mark. Prices had a free fall until the price of the tulip bulb reached its correct price — the price of a potato because, finally, all flowers are worth only about that much. The plight of a person who might have sold his house or gold to buy a tulip bulb would be the same as the plight of an investor who sells his house to buy the next hot speculative stock.

Our financial systems might have become advanced and we can get all the modern financially engineered tools like derivatives, pass through certificates, asset and mortgage backed securities, etc. (ironically, these were the primary reasons for the credit crisis of the year 2008 which hit the advanced Western markets), but we cannot change human psychology and folly. We cannot change the madness of crowds, we cannot change a rational person's totally irrational behavior as a part of the crowd and we cannot change the perception of fear and greed when related to financial decision making. Nothing is farther from truth than the argument put forward by some experts that government and central bank bailouts and interest rate cuts, etc. can avoid any such crisis. They were not able to do that a century ago and they will not be able to do that even a hundred years from now. What they can do is just complicate things and make the market more volatile. They can increase the complexity of the wave structure but cannot certainly change the primary movement of the wave. No government, central bank, industrialist, operator or anybody else can alter or manipulate the "primary movement of the entire market over a reasonable period of time."

To sum up, innumerous bubbles have occurred across the globe in the past. Volumes of books can be written about them but that is not the purpose of this book. My only objective is to highlight that while markets may change, time may change, instruments may change, traders may change but human psychology and crowd behavior does not change. What happened three hundred years ago is happening today and will happen three hundred years later as well. You cannot change the crowd behavior and mass psychology but you can surely learn behavior finance and be a master of your mind and emotions. Ultimately, investing is not about beating anybody else; it's about mastering your own self — you have to become emotionally strong and mature before investing in stocks. As Rudyard Kipling astutely remarked: "If you can keep your head when all about you are losing theirs, yours is the earth and everything that's in it."

Chapter 7

Commandment 6

Thou Shall Use the Power of Positive Leverage

THIS IS ONE COMMANDMENT WHICH YOU MIGHT FIND DIFFICULT to understand, accept and practically apply in your day-to-day financial transactions. Yet it's a very important and powerful commandment. It is a commandment which will give you the power of positive leverage.

Leverage

In simple accounting or legal terms, leverage means debt. But for financial freedom fighters, leverage need not be debt. Instead, it's a simple concept that money in your hand is worth more than money in the hand of your neighbor. Leverage simply puts your neighbor's money into your hand. And once the money comes into your hand, you can then invest and make more money with that money, i.e. make more for yourself with "other people's money." In other words, leverage is a multiplication. Whatever may be the thing — money, time, effort, etc. — leverage is just its multiplication. With leverage, you can extract more out of a given portion of something.

You will find different definitions of leverage depending on who you are dealing with. For example, leverage might mean different things in accounting, corporate finance, banking, investing, legal, etc. We are not concerned with all those definitions and meanings and will not go into them here. We are interested only with leverage which is positive — leverage which will give you power and freedom over your finances and help you achieve your goal of financial independence faster, better and, most importantly, with lower risk.

The Magic of Positive Leverage

As leverage is multiplication of what you have, it is of prime importance to use it in a positive way. Once you learn to use leverage in a positive way, which is what this commandment is all about, you will recognize its power and magic. And the more the positive leverage, the higher will be your returns and the more the money you will have for nothing.

Is Leverage Risky?

Yes, it is, if you don't understand it and don't believe in the power of positive leverage. But if you familiarize yourself with it and understand how to use the power of leverage then it becomes a boon, just like magic. Never fear taking risks in life as being within your comfort zone in the biggest risk of all since it is the most dangerous and uncertain place on this planet. Thus leverage in itself is not risky — it becomes risky when you are not familiar with it and you don't know the difference between positive and negative leverage. As you increase negative leverage, your risk multiplies. On the other hand, as you build positive leverage, your risk reduces. Whether you are an individual, company or government, unless you know the power of positive leverage and understand how to use it to multiply your money, you cannot become truly rich and wealthy and may not be able to achieve financial freedom.

Positive and Negative Leverage

Let us now distinguish between positive and negative leverage.

As explained earlier, leverage is multiplication of money through the use of debt.

Thus, positive leverage is debt which multiplies your money by putting money into your pocket while negative leverage is debt which reduces your money by taking money away from your pocket.

But what exactly is positive leverage and how to distinguish it from negative leverage?

Characteristics of Positive Leverage

There are certain attributes and characteristics of positive leverage. You have to learn to recognize the difference between positive and negative leverage. The following points will help you do that.

1. Recognize the Difference Between an Investment Asset and a Liability Disguised as an Accounting Asset

As explained in Commandment 1, an investment asset is an asset which puts money into your pocket. However, in the accountant's language an asset is quite different.

In textbook accounting terms, an asset is something whose use and value generally last for more than one year. In accounting terms, any expense can either be written off to the income statement in the same year in which it occurs or it can be taken to the assets column in the balance sheet if its use extends for more than one year. In the latter case, it is then "written off" partly every year as "depreciation" in the income statement over the "useful life of the asset". For example, car, furniture, computer, TV set and such other items would be classified as assets in accounting terms. However, once out of the showroom the value of all these items immediately falls by almost 25% to 40%. Further, additional money is needed for their maintenance. Table 7.1 shows a simplified version of the

Table 7.1

Income Statement — Expenses of Accounting Assets

Expenses	*Income*
Petrol for car	No Income from these accounting assets
Utility Bills for using computer / TV	Deficit carried forward to balance sheet
Maintenance of car / furniture / computer / TV	
Car driver's salary	
Depreciation on accounting assets	

Table 7.2
Balance Sheet — Accounting Assets

Liabilities	*Assets*
Net Worth	Car
Less: Deficit brought forward from income statement	Furniture
	Computer
	Television set
	Less: Deprecation on the above assets

income statement and Table 7.2 the balance sheet of a person classifying such items as an assets.

Just notice what happens when you classify such items as assets in your balance sheet. It simply takes away money from your pocket in the form of maintenance, petrol, utility bills, etc. And all that money is then reduced from your net worth in the balance sheet. If something takes money away from your pocket then how on earth can you classify it as an asset? Which is why from a financial freedom view these, and many other items which are usually shown as assets, are in fact nothing but liabilities which rob you of your money year after year.

2. Using Leverage to Buy a Liability Disguised as an Accounting Asset

This is the worst possible combination — using leverage to buy a liability disguised as an accounting asset. This not only takes money out of your pocket in the form of maintenance and running expenses on the accounting asset but also in the form of interest payments on the debt. Table 7.3 shows a simplified version of the income statement of a person who uses leverage to buy a liability disguised as an accounting asset and Table 7.4 is the corresponding balance sheet of the same person.

You can easily note the damaging effect of this worst combination of using negative leverage to finance a liability disguised as an accounting asset on the income statement and balance sheet. Along with the expenses of maintenance and other running costs, it adds another cost in the form of interest payment. All these eat into your profits and create further deficits which, in turn, eat into your net worth. The negative leverage creates a "bad debt" in the form of

Table 7.3
Income Statement — Effect of Negative Leverage on Accounting Assets

Expenses	*Income*
Petrol for car	No Income from these accounting assets
Utility bills for using computer / TV	Deficit carried forward to balance sheet
Maintenance of car / furniture / computer / TV	
Car driver's salary	
Depreciation on assets	
Interest on loan (negative leverage)	

Table 7.4
Balance Sheet — Accounting Assets Financed by Negative Leverage

Liabilities	*Assets*
Net Worth	Car
Less: Deficit brought forward from income statement	Furniture
	Computer
Loan (negative leverage)	Television set
	Less: Deprecation on the above assets

loan which is a real liability in your balance sheet. This is the worst kind of debt which a person can go in for — a debt to finance a liability mistaken to be an asset. This form of debt will be termed as negative leverage.

3. Leverage Used for Creating an Investment Asset

To reiterate, an investment asset is an asset which puts money into your pocket. Ideally, your money should go only into buying investment assets and not liabilities disguised as investment assets. This rule becomes even more important when you are using leverage because leverage is, finally, nothing but multiplication. So, if you use leverage to buy investment assets then your investment assets will multiply providing you with life long income. On the other hand, if you use leverage to buy liabilities disguised as accounting assets then only your liabilities will multiply giving you life long costs in the form of maintenance and other running expenses.

Leverage or debt should, therefore, be used sparingly and only for buying investment assets.

Now have a look at Table 7.5 and Table 7.6 and then notice the difference between these two tables and Tables 7.1 to 7.4. Money is created by borrowing, i.e. leveraging, to invest in investment assets like bank fixed deposits, equity shares, rental real estate, etc. These investment assets yield income in the form of interest, dividend and rent, respectively. The interest on the loan — which I call as positive leverage — is an expense in the income statement. If the income from investment assets is more than the interest payable on the loan, there will be a surplus which will add to your net worth. If it is less, then there would be a deficit which will reduce your net worth. Whatever be the case, the point I am making here is that if the income from investment assets is used to pay interest on the loan, and if you can manage the cash flows by taking from one hand and giving to the other hand, then once the loan is repaid, the investment asset is yours for life — and so is the income from it.

Table 7.5

Income Statement — Effect of Positive Leverage

Expenses	*Income*
Interest on loan (positive leverage)	Income from investment assets
	Interest on bank fixed deposit
	Dividend on equity shares
	Rent from rental real estate
Surplus carried forward to balance sheet	Deficit carried forward to balance sheet

Table 7.6

Balance Sheet — Effect of Positive Leverage

Liabilities	*Assets*
Net Worth	Investment assets
Add: Surplus / *Less:* Deficit brought forward from income statement	Bank fixed deposit
	Equity shares
Loan (positive leverage)	Rental real estate

4. Net Positive Cash Flow after Tax

I will call this state — net positive cash flow after tax — as the ultimate state which you should aim for in order to harness the full power and potential of positive leverage. Once you reach this stage, you would be making money out of thin air. Basically you get money for nothing; in essence, you are printing your own money. No, I haven't gone crazy. Just have a look at Table 7.7 and Table 7.8.

If your income from an investment asset is more than the interest cost on the loan taken to finance the investment asset, after considering the effect of tax, then you have attained the ultimate nirvana state as far as leveraging your money is concerned. Once you reach this stage, you would have reached the stage of positive cash flow. The more you borrow, the more you invest, the more positive cash flow you generate — and therefore you are doing nothing but simply printing your own money.

Table 7.7

Income Statement — Effect of Net Positive Cash Flow after Tax

Expenses	*Income*
Interest on loan (positive leverage)	Income from investment assets
	Interest on bank fixed deposit
	Dividend on equity shares
Surplus carried forward to balance sheet	Rent from rental real estate

Table 7.8

Balance Sheet — Investment Assets with Cash Flow Positive Leverage

Liabilities	*Assets*
Net worth	Investment assets
Add: Surplus brought forward from income statement	Bank fixed deposit
	Equity shares
Loan (positive leverage)	Rental real estate

More Cash Flow, Positive Leverage, Higher Returns — Money From Nothing

Yes, the heading for this section says it all — more cash flow, positive leverage, higher returns — money from nothing or, literally, printing your own money. You might wonder how one can reach that stage. Tables 7.9 and 7.10 will take you through that journey to your destination.

Assume you invest in a rental real estate worth ₹ 25 lakh, which gives you rental yield of 12%, by putting ₹ 5 lakh (20%) as down payment and borrowing the rest ₹ 20 lakh from a bank at 9% p.a. rate of interest. Now, as depicted by Table 7.9, after paying for property tax, maintenance and income tax, you are left with a cash

Table 7.9
Income Statement — Money for Nothing

Expenses		*Income*	
Interest on loan (₹ 20,00,000 @ 9%)	1,80,000	Rent from rental real estate	3,00,000
Property tax	30,000		
Maintenance	36,000		
Income tax	16,200		
Surplus carried forward to balance sheet	37,800		
Total	3,00,000	Total	3,00,000

Table 7.10
Balance Sheet — Owning Your Own Printing Machine

Liabilities	*Year 0*	*Year 1*	*Assets*	*Year 0*	*Year 1*
Net worth	5,00,000	5,00,000	Rental real estate	25,00,000	25,00,000
Add: Surplus brought from income statement		37,800	Free cash		37,800
Loan (positive leverage @ 10% p.a.)	20,00,000	20,00,000			
Total	25,00,000	25,37,800	Total	25,00,000	25,37,800

flow of ₹ 37,800. Kindly note the principal repayment of the loan is not assumed because if the transaction can provide free cash flow after paying the interest, there is no need to repay the loan — the arrangement can run for perpetuity, throwing up free cash flow every year. To substantiate, take the balance sheet of any company. Most of them carry loans in perpetuity. Does it mean they don't repay their loans? Certainly not. They keep repaying old loans which had financed earlier assets and then take new loans to finance newer assets. Both their loan and assets keep expanding. The trick is to manage the cash flow to keep this cycle of creating new assets out of new loans running. In the process, you will generate life long free cash flows for yourself.

This is your positive cash flow from the transaction — the money which you printed out of nothing. And, remember, so far we have not assumed any increase in the value of the real estate, i.e. we have assumed no portfolio income but only passive income from rent. Of course, over a period of time the increase in the asset's price could be significant simply because the value of money will come down due to inflation. Since we are concentrating only on cash flow, we are not concerned with the short term vagaries and price movements in the real estate market — we earn rent (passive income) and over a period of time will also earn capital gains (portfolio income).

What If You Have No Money to Start With?

You might argue that you don't have ₹ 5 lakh to put up as down payment. When you think this way, it's worth reminding yourself that God has given each one of us some unique talent or gift. Identify your unique ability or skills and work towards earning some money using those. And once you have accumulated some wealth, learn the tricks of the game; start small initially and then graduate to bigger and bigger play over a period of time.

What If You Initially Generate Negative Cash Flows?

It's true that there are chances of generating negative cash flows initially. Remember, however, that if you have selected your investment asset correctly, whether it be real estate, stock or bond, and at a reasonable price, then over a period of time it is sure to rise in value, if for no other reason than simply because the value of money will go down. You may wonder how, for example, the price of a bond would go up when the value of money goes down. As we saw in Commandment 5, the price of a bond rises when interest rates fall, and *vice versa*. Therefore if you buy a bond at a high yield, its price would eventually rise when the yields start coming down. The price of an equity stock will rise when the company's earnings rise while that of real estate would rise with inflation and the improvements which you make to the property so that it commands better rent, e.g. new paint, new fans, air conditioners, geysers, etc. And once the value of your investment asset increases, you would get higher income from it while the interest cost will remain the same. Thus, over a period of time a stage would come when your increased income will become more than your fixed interest cost, thus producing positive cash flow for you. Sure, the initial pain would have to be endured but once that phase has passed you will reach the stage of cash flow positive leverage.

Never Leverage for Portfolio Income

Caution: never leverage for portfolio income. You should always decide upon leverage on the basis of your passive income — the asset generating income — and not income from an increase in value of the asset.

You will recollect that incomes from investment assets, such as interest, dividends, rent, etc. are passive incomes while capital gains through an increase in the value of an investment asset is portfolio income. If you incur debt in the expectations of an increase in the market price of your investment asset, like, say a stock or real estate — you are committing financial suicide and this is totally against the principles of this commandment. Always remember that when you take on leverage, you need to service the debt by way of interest payments and you need to generate income or cash flow to service the debt — otherwise the bank would foreclose your loan by selling off your asset. This will make you a loser from all sides; you will lose your asset, you will lose on interest and penalties and, the biggest loss of all, you will lose your credit worthiness and market standing. Remember that the multiplication power of leverage does not distinguish between the good and the bad — either will simply be multiplied. Always use leverage to multiply positive cash flows so that it makes the leverage positive and allows you to multiply your money and wealth.

Never Leverage with Margin Money

This brings me to another very important point about using leverage when investing in equities.

Nowadays, derivatives such as futures are very common. In simple terms, a futures contract allows you to buy a certain amount of a stock, or the entire market, at a fraction of the actual price. For example, you may be able to buy popular stock market indices, like the US Dow Jones Industrial Average or India's NSE Nifty, at around 15% of its prevailing price. Now, what is the danger with that kind of leverage — the multiplication factor which I mentioned earlier?

Suppose that you are long a popular index future by paying 15% of its actual price. Now if the index were to fall by just 5% it would actually wipe out 33% of your capital because ₹ 5 is just 5%, on the total cost of ₹ 100 but 33% on the future's position of ₹ 15. Worse, a 15% fall in the popular index will wipe out your entire capital.

Buying a future also violates the important rule stated earlier; namely, never leverage for portfolio income. Leverage has to be used for investing in investment assets which give you passive income and not for portfolio income or capital gains. When you buy a stock future, in effect you are betting on the price movement of the stock, i.e. on capital gains or portfolio income — which can be financial suicide as explained above. Therefore, use the multiplicative power of positive leverage only to create income earning investment assets with net positive cash flow.

Inflation is Your Partner With Positive Leverage

People generally believe that inflation is always bad and that they are its victims. Not any more. Remember that one man's loss is another man's profit. Inflation is your friend when you are a borrower. That's because you borrow in costlier money today and repay the loan in tomorrow's cheaper money since inflation reduces the value, i.e. the purchasing power, of future money.

For example, say you borrowed ₹ 100 today and purchased a shirt with it. Now if the inflation rate is 10%, the price of the shirt would be ₹ 110 after one year. So after one year when you repay the loan, the borrower would not be able to buy the same shirt then with ₹ 100. Thus, using leverage, you were able to buy something today which you would otherwise not have been able to purchase after a year — or would have had to shell out more money for it. Of course, you have to pay interest on the borrowed funds and that's why I again stress the importance of positive leverage and net positive cash flow from leveraged money.

Unleashing the Ultimate Power of Positive Leverage

We've seen earlier in the book that banks have the legal authority to print their own money through a process called money multiplier. When you deposit, say, ₹ 100, in your bank, the bank then gets the power to lend about ₹ 1,000 against your deposit of ₹ 100. Thus, it multiplies your money by ten times and this process continues. Remember, the bank gets this power from you and multiplies its money with your money. So, why shouldn't you also apply the same technique and multiply your money with the help of the bank's money? If this sounds too good to be true, just take a look at Table 7.11.

As demonstrated by Table 7.11, you can use the money multiplier to your own advantage and print your own money just as a bank does. In the given illustration, suppose you owned a self-occupied house worth, say, ₹ 5 million. Now, a self occupied house property is otherwise a dead investment because it does not produce any cash flow. At the same time it's a necessary investment because it saves you unnecessary recurring expense in the form of rent which you would otherwise have to incur. However, you can unleash the power of your self-occupied house by using the power of the money multiplier.

Table 7.11
Balance Sheet — Your Money Multiplier

Liabilities	*Before Money Multiplier ₹*	*After Money Multiplier ₹*	*Assets*	*Before Money Multiplier ₹*	*After Money Multiplier ₹*
Net worth	50,00,000	50,00,000	Own self occupied house	50,00,000	50,00,000
Loan against own house (90% value)		45,00,000	Rental real estate	0	2,25,00,000
Mortgage against rental real estate (80% value)		1,80,00,000		0	
Total	50,00,000	2,75,00,000	Total	50,00,000	2,75,00,000

Here is how.

Your house has value with which you can create and multiply your own money. Let's see how it works. Suppose on the ₹ 5 million value of your house, the bank grants you a loan up to 90% of that value, i.e. ₹ 4.5 million. You then buy a rental real estate worth ₹ 22.5 million by paying 20% down, i.e. the ₹ 4.5 million bank loan which you got on your self occupied house plus ₹ 18 million which you borrow against your rental real estate (up to 80% of its value). The effect of all this is shown in the next column of your balance sheet under the title "After Money Multiplier". You have now expanded your balance sheet size from just ₹ 5 million to ₹ 27.5 million by using bank (other people's) money and the money multiplier in your favor. The only thing which you have to take care of is that the loan against your own house property and the mortgage against the rental real estate should be positive leverage, i.e. they should provide net positive cash flow to you. If you are able to achieve that, which is not difficult with some knowledge, you would literally be printing your own money. What's more, once the loan and mortgage are paid off after a few years, the rental real estate of ₹ 22.5 million plus your own house of ₹ 5 million are yours to keep. And, mind you the rent will keep flowing to you for life! Does this not imply printing your own money for life? This is what I would call unleashing the ultimate power of positive leverage.

Create Your Own Investment Assets

I will give you one more example of how you can create your own investment assets out of thin air. You will get something for nothing and that something will be an investment asset, such as equities, which will give you dividends (passive income) for life along with the potential of capital gains (portfolio income). Have a look at Tables 7.12 and 7.13. Don't let the amount of columns, rows or figures worry you — in reality it is quite simple and logical.

You start initially with ₹ 5 million worth of your self-occupied house property. You then borrow from the bank against this property. The bank gives you a loan of up to 90% of the property's value, i.e. ₹ 4.5 million at 10% p.a. rate of interest. With that ₹ 4.5 million, you purchase equity shares. Further, you pledge the same equity shares of ₹ 4.5 million with the bank which, in turn, sanctions you a loan to the value of 70% of the shares, i.e. ₹ 3.15 million. With the new loan you buy further equity shares of ₹ 3.15 million, taking the total tally of your shares to ₹ 7.65 million. Therefore, with that initial ₹ 5 million worth of house property, you have extracted additional ₹ 7.65 million of equity shares, with the original house property remaining fully intact on your balance sheet. As shown by Table 7.12, your balance sheet size multiplied from ₹ 5 million to ₹ 12.65 million, simply by using positive leverage.

Now let us move ahead to your income statement which is depicted in Table 7.13. Kindly note that the interest rate on bank deposit is 10%. However, the dividend yield on equities is generally close to 2%. So how do you fund the gap of 8% (10% less 2%) or ₹ 6,12,000 in the first year? Remember that over the long term equities appreciate in value because of increased corporate earnings and the reducing value of money (inflation). Over the 32 years, 1980 to 2012, Indian equities as represented by the BSE Sensex, returned around 17.5% compounded annual growth. This provides you with portfolio income. The trick is to encash or sell that much value of

Table 7.12

Balance Sheet — Creating Investment Assets — Equity Share

Liabilities	*Year 0*	*Year 1*	*Year 2*	*Year 3*	*Assets*	*Year 0*	*Year 1*	*Year 2*	*Year 3*
Net Worth	50,00,000	50,00,000	50,00,000	50,00,000	Own self occupied house	50,00,000	50,00,000	50,00,000	50,00,000
Add: Surplus from Increase in value of equities			5,35,500	12,23,235					
Loan against own house (90% value)		45,00,000	45,00,000	45,00,000	Equity shares	0	45,00,000	45,63,000	47,07,360
Loan against equity shares (70% value)		31,50,000	31,50,000	31,50,000	Additional equity shares	0	31,50,000	36,22,500	41,65,875
Total	50,00,000	1,26,50,000	1,31,85,500	1,38,73,235	Total	50,00,000	1,26,50,000	1,31,85,500	1,38,73,235

Table 7.13
Income Statement — Investment Assets out of Thin Air

	Year 0	*Year 1*	*Year 2*	*Year 3*
Income				
Dividend (passive income) 2% yield	0	1,53,000	1,63,710	1,77,465
Capital gains (portfolio income) 8% realized		6,12,000	5,40,090	4,72,326
	0	7,65,000	7,03,800	6,49,791
Expenses				
Interest on loan (10% on outstanding loan)		7,65,000	7,03,800	6,49,791
Net cash flow	0	0	0	0
Investment asset created (equities)	0	76,50,000	81,85,500	88,73,235

shares every year so as to fill up the gap between the dividend you receive and the interest you have to pay, thus making the net cash flow nil. The computations for the next three years are shown in Table 7.13.

One point to bear in mind is that the return from equities is anything but linear. There will be bull and bear markets and ups and downs in your return. Your financial acumen will be tested in how you manage your cash flows from equities to enhance the power of positive leverage in your favor. The most important point is to notice how your balance sheet expands every year. As your equity value kept compounding at 15% p.a. over the next three years, the balance sheet expands to ₹ 13.87 million as against the small beginning of ₹ 5 million. Over a period of time, your equity shares will reach such a value that you will be able to pay down your entire debt and still have the same value of shares with which you started. Again, "money out of thin air"! You have created investment assets out of nothing. Therefore, the argument that you have to be rich to have money does not hold true any more — the only thing which you require is the knowledge of the ten commandments of money and how to apply them as efficiently as possible in your financial life.

Rental Real Estate Has the Highest Leverage Factor

Although positive leverage helps in the multiplication of your money with any investment asset, its effectiveness is the maximum when rental real estate is used as the investment asset. This is simply because the leverage factor of rental real estate is the highest. Leverage factor is the amount of rupees which you can get as loan for every rupee of your own money. In equities, the leverage factor is generally slightly lower than one while in real estate it is typically closer to four. For example, if you want to buy a property worth, say, ₹ 10 million, generally you may have to fund ₹ 2 million on your own and the balance ₹ 8 million will be funded by the bank as mortgage loan. Therefore, for every single rupee of your own money, the bank loans you four rupees. Which is why the leverage factor of real estate is the highest and why property makes it easier to unleash the power of positive leverage. However, you have to be cautious because the leverage factor can work both ways. If there is positive leverage then it would multiply your wealth four-fold. On the other hand, if you end up with negative leverage, then it would have the potential of destroying your wealth by almost four times.

Know the Difference Between Cheap and Costly Leverage

Till now we have concentrated on the end use of leverage and classified positive and negative leverage on that basis. Now let us understand another important factor, namely the source of leverage. This concept is very important because just as all money is not the same, so, too, all leverage, or debt, is not the same. Leverage, or debt, is nothing but a claim by somebody on you to pay them a certain sum in future, along with a certain rate of interest. You may be offered debt on the basis of different factors, including your name, reputation, credit rating, etc. However, whatever may be the factor the pertinent thing to note is that you may or may not be required to put some asset as security to get a loan. The rate of interest varies considerably depending on whether you are required to put up a security. And when you are required to put up some asset as security, there is also a lot of variation in the rate of interest. Let us now understand this in some detail.

Leverage Where No Security is Required

The worst kind of leverage is where no security is required because not only is the rate of interest very high in such cases but since no security is required, you would tend to borrow recklessly and use the money on extravagant and wasteful expenses or for buying bad assets, both of which are harmful for your money. The popular forms of unsecured loans are unsecured personal loans and credit card loans. The rates of interest are the maximum for such loans, ranging from anywhere between 18% to 36% p.a., or higher. Further, since you get such loans without any security, there is all the more likelihood that this money will be squandered away. Generally speaking, therefore, loans where no security is required, such as personal loans or credit card loans, would never qualify as positive leverage.

Leverage Where Security Is Required

This is a better form of leverage because such loans are generally cheaper. Also, since you have to give some security in order to get such loans, there is lower likelihood that you will throw away the borrowed money on extravagant expenses or bad assets.

Even within this category, there are certain loans which are cheaper and others which are comparatively costlier. The cheapest is a mortgage on your property while a car loan or a loan for buying furniture would be comparatively costlier. This is probably because the bank also recognizes the value of real estate and its potential as an investment asset as against a car or furniture which are just liabilities disguised as accounting assets.

Reverse Mortgage

Till now we have talked about mortgages wherein you take loan from the bank and repay it in EMIs every month. There is also the opposite of a mortgage in which you pledge your house to the bank and it pays you EMI every month for a fixed tenure. This is called reverse mortgage. It is a type of mortgage in which a homeowner can borrow money against the value of his or her home. The rules may vary from country to country but typically it is available to senior citizens, i.e. people who are 60 years and more. It is generally available for a period of 15 to 20 years. The owner can continue to stay in the house even after the EMI period expires. Of course, after that he or she will not receive any further payment from the bank. After accounting for the initial mortgage amount, the rate at which interest accrues, the length of the loan, and rate of home price appreciation, the transaction is structured so that the loan amount will not exceed the value of the house over the life of the loan. Moreover, the lender will require that there can be no other liens against the property and that any existing liens must be paid off with the proceeds of the reverse mortgage.

A reverse mortgage provides income that people can tap into for their retirement. The advantage of a reverse mortgage is that the borrower's credit is not relevant, and is often not checked, because the borrower does not need to make any payments. Because the home serves as collateral, it must be sold in order to repay the mortgage when the borrower dies though in some cases the heirs have the option of repaying the mortgage without selling the home. These types of mortgages have large origination costs relative to other types of mortgages. These costs become a part of the initial loan balance and accrued interest. Senior citizen borrowers with good credit should carefully analyze the options of a more traditional mortgage, such as a home equity loan *vis-a-vis* a reverse mortgage. In fact, I feel very bad for senior citizens who have to take recourse to the reverse mortgage route in their retirement years. They probably did not plan for their future and retirement as they should have when they were young. If you are already old and have no choice, then you might be forced to take recourse to the reverse mortgage route. I don’t want anyone to ever be forced to take this route; I want everyone to achieve financial independence.

The Most Important Leverage of All — Your Financial Knowledge

This commandment would be incomplete without emphasizing this point.

Throughout this commandment I have talked about money and how you can leverage it, i.e. take debt and multiply your investment assets through the power of positive leverage. Leverage cannot be only in respect of money. Finally, today money is nothing but currency whose value is daily compromised and lost to inflation. Over the longer term, the money that you hold is going to be worth less and less because of ever greater ravages of inflation on the purchasing power of your money.

The one thing which will hold you in good stead in this modern day of money, finance and currency is your financial knowledge, something which is not taught in school. It is knowledge about how to deal with money when earning, protecting, budgeting, saving, spending, leveraging, investing, insuring. This is what you need to know if you aim to achieve financial independence.

So, remember, the biggest leverage is financial knowledge because that is the only real leverage in the modern world of information and currency which will help you achieve financial independence. Therefore, increase this leverage and you will unleash the power within you which will open the boundaries of wealth and happiness. Don't be afraid of committing mistakes while acquiring financial knowledge because all lessons in this world, whether it be riding a bicycle or learning to deal with money, have to be learnt through mistakes — but learn the rules of the game and never repeat the same mistake again. You can reduce uncertainty while dealing with life, money or debt by improving the most important leverage of all — your own financial knowledge and wisdom.

Once you are able to unleash and leverage your financial knowledge, you would have fully mastered this commandment simply because the biggest reservoir of positive leverage is within your own self.

Are You Caught in a Debt Trap?

A debt trap is simply a situation in which your debt has grown to such large proportions as compared to your current income and repayment capacity that you are not able to repay the debt either through your income and / or through additional borrowings. Debt trap is one of the most difficult traps from which to emerge unscathed because neither your current income supports such kind of debt repayment nor are there any additional lenders willing to lend you further money to fund your debt repayment. Therefore, it is very important for you to know whether you are facing a debt trap or not. I have developed a very simple questionnaire for you. Each question has four alternatives. Select the one which fits your situation the best. Take this important questionnaire and then I will tell you how to compute your score and your debt position.

Debt Trap Questionnaire

1. Your loan EMI accounts for:
   a. Less than 10% of your after tax income;
   b. Between 10-20% of your after tax income;
   c. Between 21-50% of your after tax income;
   d. Over 50% of your after tax income?
2. How much of your loan EMI goes into non-mortgage loans:
   a. Less than 10% of your after tax income;
   b. Between 11-20% of your after tax income;
   c. Between 20-25% of your after tax income;
   d. Over 25% of your after tax income?
3. Have you missed an EMI or credit card payment in the past year:
   a. Never
   b. Only Once
   c. Between 2-3 times
   d. More than 4 times?
4. When unable to pay a credit card bill, what do you do:
   a. Cut your expenses and stop using the card till your financial position improves
   b. Take a loan to settle the bill
   c. Pay the minimum amount required
   d. Transfer the balance to another card?

5. How often do you roll over your credit card bill:
    a. Never, always pay the entire amount on time
    b. Once in a year
    c. Occasionally — 3 to 4 times in a year
    d. Almost every month?
6. You use a credit card because:
    a. Of its convenience; you don't need to carry cash with you
    b. Of its utility and wide acceptance
    c. You are always short of money
    d. You can spend recklessly without needing hard cash?
7. When your loan EMI is due:
    a. You don't bother as you always have surplus cash in your account
    b. Just confirm your account balance in case it falls short
    c. Always fall short and hence arrange the money through other loans
    d. You are not able to arrange for money as no lender is ready to lend you money?
8. Do you make a loan repayment strategy?
    a. Yes, I always do so.
    b. I do have a rough idea.
    c. I am not sure and assume everything will fall properly in place.
    d. I am totally oblivious and don't know how I will be able to repay my loan.
9. On what basis do you take loans:
    a. Based on present after tax income?
    b. Based on present after tax income plus assumed pay hikes in future?
    c. Based on present after tax income plus current realizable value of investments?
    d. Based on assumed big rise in after tax income plus increase in the value of investments?

Once, you have answered these questions honestly, compute your score as follows:

A - 4 points
B - 3 points
C - 2 points
D - 1 point.

Once you get your score, check out your debt trap status below.

Safe and Excellent (score of 30 and above)

Great. You are doing perfectly fine as you have not overleveraged yourself.

Comfortable (score between 25 and 30)

You are comfortable as of now. But take care that you don't fall in the debt trap.

Tipping Point (score between 20 to 25)

You are on the tipping point. If you don't take immediate remedial steps like cutting expenses, repaying debt, etc., then you could very soon fall into a debt trap.

Debt Trapped (score of 20 or below)

You are in a hellish debt trap. Immediately cut your expenses, try to increase your income, repay as much debt as possible (all the bad loan first) and consult an advisor (such as this book).

Never, never fall into a debt trap. It's really difficult to come out of one.

Lessons From This Commandment

1. Leverage can be compared to the mathematical sign of multiplication. It is simply the multiplication of your money and wealth.
2. Contrary to popular opinion, leverage is not risky if you know how to harness the power of positive leverage. In fact, lack of

proper leverage could hinder your goal of achieving financial freedom.

3. Positive leverage is debt which multiplies your money by putting money into your pocket while negative leverage is debt which reduces your money by taking away money from your pocket.
4. Learn to recognize the difference between an investment asset and a liability disguised as an accounting asset.
5. Never use leverage to buy a liability disguised as an accounting asset because not only will it take money out of your pocket in the form of maintenance and running expenses but also in the form of interest payments on your debt.
6. Leverage or debt should be used to buy only investment assets. This is called positive leverage.
7. To unleash the ultimate power of positive leverage, you must aim to reach the stage of net positive cash flow after tax because once you reach that stage, you start making "money out of nothing".
8. You should never leverage for portfolio income, i.e. capital gains, but only for passive income, i.e. regular income in the form of rent, dividends, coupon interest, etc.
9. Never leverage with margin money, e.g. for buying equity derivatives because that will pit the power of negative leverage against you. It also has the potential of multiplying your losses.
10. Inflation is your partner with positive leverage simply because you borrow in costlier money today and repay back your loan in cheaper money tomorrow.
11. When you properly harness the power of positive leverage, you can use other people's money to multiply your own wealth by using the money multiplier factor, thereby creating your investment assets out of thin air.
12. It is important to understand the leverage factor of your investment because that will determine the quantum of positive leverage which you may be able to apply.
13. Understand the difference between cheap and costly leverage — remember that leverage without security may not be cheaper

and might, in fact, turn out to be very costly leading you to financial disaster.

14. Don't forget the most important leverage — and the most important investment asset of all — your own financial knowledge.
15. Never fall into a debt trap because it's really difficult to come out of one unscathed.

Self-Understanding Questionnaire

This commandment took you on a journey of debt and how to unleash the power of positive leverage. It dealt with the myth that leverage is risky by explaining the difference between positive and negative leverage and how you can use the power of positive leverage to create investment assets out of thin air which provide positive net cash flow after tax. Now, honestly answer the following questions in yes or no to test your understanding of the principles explained in this commandment. The more the number of "yes" answers, the better is your understanding of this commandment.

1. Do you believe that borrowing is not risky? Yes/No?
2. Do you consider that debt can actually enhance your return and multiply your wealth? Yes/No?
3. Do you think that debt can also be of two kinds — positive and negative leverage — and while the positive leverage multiplies your wealth by enhancing it several times, negative leverage diminishes your wealth considerably? Yes/No?
4. Do you understand that when positive leverage is properly used for buying investment assets which produce net positive cash flow after tax, it can actually take you to a stage where you get money for nothing and are able to practically print your own money? Yes/No?
5. Do you appreciate the fact that there can be liabilities disguised as accounting assets? Yes/No?
6. Do you understand the difference between portfolio and passive incomes and in lieu of which kind of income should you go in for leverage? Yes/No?

7. Do you acknowledge the fact that leverage without security may not be superior as compared to leverage with security and can prove fatal to your financial health? Yes/No?
8. Do recognize that your comfort zone is the most dangerous place to be in and the biggest risk in life is to not take any risk? Yes/No?

—

Chapter 8

Commandment 7

Thou Shall Buy Your Own House for Self Occupation

THIS COMMANDMENT RELATES TO THE MOST PRECIOUS and perhaps the most valuable asset among all your possessions — your own house.

The title of the commandment suggests that you should buy a house of your own to live in, a house which you can call your home, a place where you can relax and spend time with your family — your parents, spouse and children, — a place where you can unwind after the strenuous work day.

But does the title of the commandment in any manner suggest that your house should be your biggest asset? Are you of the view that you should buy your own house to live in because it is an investment asset?

Let us answer these questions first before proceeding further.

Is Your Own House An Investment Asset?

I have already emphasized the difference between a liability disguised as an accounting asset, an asset, and an investment asset. Let us quickly revisit some of these and related terms in the context of your own home.

Liability

A liability is something which takes away money from your pocket. In the traditional accounting sense, a loan would be a liability as it takes away money from your pocket in the form of interest payments. Having said that, we learnt in Commandment 6 that all loans are certainly not bad; that there are positive and negative leverages and how we can use the power of positive leverage to make money out of thin air.

Liability Disguised as An Accounting Asset

There are many items which are classified on the assets side of the balance sheet in conventional accounting practice. But that does not mean that they automatically become assets. Just because you classify something as an asset on your balance sheet would not make it one. It has to pass the litmus test of being an asset, i.e. it must not take away money from your pocket. If it takes away money from your pocket then it certainly cannot be your asset. Further, in order to become an investment asset, it has to actually put money in your pocket. Let us understand all these concepts more clearly.

Bad Capital Asset

Any thing which is classified on the asset side of your balance sheet but which does not put money into your pocket should be classified as a bad capital asset. Your self occupied house will be classified under this category — I shall explain why a little later.

Very Bad Capital Asset

Anything which is classified on the asset side of your balance sheet but which actually takes away money from your pocket will be classified as a very bad capital asset. Examples of very bad capital assets would include a luxury car, a vacation home, etc. For example, no sooner is a new car out of the showroom, it's immediately worth 30% less than what you paid for it. Further, you have to continuously incur costs to maintain it, costs such as fuel charges, service and maintenance, insurance, parking charges, etc. Hence, although a car might be classified as an asset in accounting practice but it is certainly not an asset but a very bad capital asset. As had been already explained in Commandment 6, any debt taken to finance such an asset would be termed as negative leverage which is detrimental to your financial interest.

Investment Asset

I don't think that I need to re-define the term investment asset because I have been doing so again and again — and stressing on its importance. An investment asset is an asset which puts money into your pocket. Examples of investment assets would include rental real estate, equity shares, bonds, etc.

You Own House Is a Bad Capital Asset

The above caption might annoy you but before your blood boils, listen to what I have to say. What is your house? No doubt, it is the place where you and your family live, the place where you can entertain your friends, a place where you can love your loved ones, a place where you can have your own space — all these facts are true. But, finally, what is your house? Does it put any money into your pocket? I regret to say that the answer is no. Your house does not put any money into your pocket. Contrary to that, your house actually takes away money from your pocket in the form of property tax, maintenance, society charges, utility bills and other expenses. Therefore, in the strict sense your house could well be a bad capital asset which takes away money from your pocket. However, one factor saves it from becoming a very bad capital asset and we can classify it as a bad capital asset. That factor is necessity — the undeniable fact that everyone requires a house, a roof above one‘s head. If you don't buy or can't buy your own house, then you would be forced to stay in rented premises. That would be totally against the principle of this commandment because the rent which you pay is nothing but an unnecessary expense which does not result in the creation of any productive investment asset. Further, it is an avoidable hindrance in your life because you have to constantly keep searching for new rental houses, disrupting your family life, children's school, etc. Finally, time is the biggest and most important asset of all, and if your time is wasted in moving houses periodically then you are losing the most valuable asset which is used in the creation of all other assets. Therefore, to avoid the unnecessary expense in the form of rent, it is advisable to try to buy your own house as soon as possible.

Your House — Whose Investment Asset?

If your house is a bad capital asset for you, taking away money from your pocket, then for whom is it an investment asset? Keep in mind that each of your expense is someone else's income, and each one of your liabilities is someone else's asset. Therefore, if your house is not your investment asset then whose is it? Have a look at Tables 8.1 and 8.2 to get a clearer picture and the answer to this most important question.

When you take mortgage loan to buy your own house, it becomes an investment asset for your bank. Table 8.1 shows your income statement and balance sheet. You receive earned income in the form of salary, etc., with which you pay the interest and EMI (equated monthly installment) to the bank on your house mortgage loan. The house appears on your asset side as a bad capital asset while the home mortgage loan is shown on the liability side of your balance sheet.

Table 8.1

Your Income Statement — Earned Income to Pay House Mortgage

Expenses	*Income*
House mortgage, EMI	Earned income

Your Balance Sheet — Your House — Accounting Asset and Actual Mortgage Liability

Liabilities	*Assets*
House mortgage loan	Self occupied house property

Table 8.2

Bank's Income Statement — Bank's Income on Your House Mortgage

Expenses	*Income*
	Interest income on your house mortgage

Bank's Balance Sheet — Your House Mortgage Bank's Investment Asset

Liabilities	*Assets*
	Your house mortgage

Now have a close look at Table 8.2 which shows the bank's income statement and balance sheet. The interest which you pay to the bank on your house mortgage becomes income for the bank. Further, your house mortgage loan is an investment asset for the bank which earns interest for it. Therefore, your expense (mortgage interest) is the bank's income and your liability (mortgage loan) is the bank's asset.

How Should You Finance Your House?

Should you buy your house with your own money, or with money borrowed from a bank? In Commandment 6, we'd discussed the leverage factor of an asset and also the difference between cheap and costly leverages. Always remember that real estate is the asset with the highest leverage factor, generally around 1:4, i.e. you put in one rupee and your bank puts in four. Therefore, the maximum power of positive leverage can be utilized in real estate. In Commandment 6 we had also examined the difference between cheap and costly leverages and loans without and with security. We had concluded that a loan with security is much cheaper and easier to procure and that mortgage is probably the cheapest form of loan which banks give. Further, in most countries tax deductions / tax benefits are available on interest and even repayment of housing loan. Therefore, a housing loan offers unique and multiple benefits which probably no other kind of loan offers:

- The highest leverage factor.
- The cheapest kind of loan with the lowest rate of interest.
- Tax deductions and benefits on interest payment.
- Tax deductions and benefits even on repayment of principal. This is actually ridiculous as it does not make any sense that the government should allow tax deduction on repayment of the principal of a housing loan but then there are lots of provisions in the tax laws which do not make sense and this is one provision which benefits you; so take advantage of it!

Notwithstanding the fact that a mortgage loan is a liability. as far as possible you should take mortgage and get your house financed by the bank who will shell out the lion's share of the cost of the house at the lowest possible rate of interest — and the taxman will then also shower you with all the deductions and exemptions in respect of payment of interest and repayment of the principal capital. Remember the golden rule that emerges here: government generally gives tax benefits to buy liabilities and not true assets.

Fixed or Floating Interest Rates?

Once you are clear that it makes sense to borrow from a bank to buy your own house, the next point is the kind of mortgage you should go in for — fixed or floating. Before moving forward, let's briefly review the concept of fixed and floating rate mortgages.

A fixed rate mortgage is one in which the rate of interest remains fixed throughout the tenure of the mortgage loan.

On the other hand, in a floating rate mortgage the rate of interest fluctuates with changes in the level of interest rates in the economy during the tenure of the mortgage loan.

In Commandment 6, we had looked at the factors which affect bond prices. We had also looked at the concept of investment cycle and how different asset classes and sub-classes, such as equities, bonds, real estate and commodities move in cycles. While buying a house on mortgage you are, in effect, dealing with two variables at the same time — real estate prices and interest rates. Both of these are very difficult to predict and there is little point trying to do so. In fact, it is the endeavor of this book to discourage you in timing any investment or other decision relating to money because nobody can do so with precision on a sustainable basis. Instead, be simple, logical, methodological and follow the principles as far as possible.

Figure 8.1 shows the typical interest rate cycle. Interest rates move up and down in a cyclical fashion. The chart shows the points where you should go in for floating rate mortgage and when you should opt for a fixed rate mortgage.

- You should go in for a floating rate mortgage loan when there has already been a substantial hike in central bank controlled interest rates over a period of time.

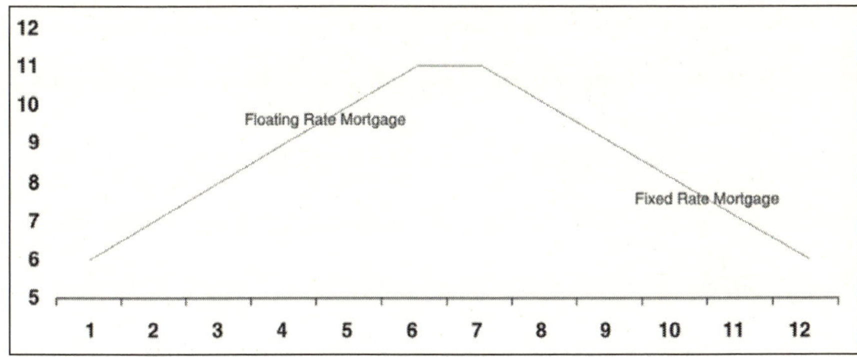

Figure 8.1: **Interest rate cycle — the fixed and floating rate mortgage puzzle**

- On the other hand, you should settle for a fixed rate mortgage loan when there has already been a substantial fall in central bank controlled interest rates over a period of time.

Table 8.3 lists some typical factors which you should watch out for in the bond markets, interest rates, banking system, money market liquidity, etc., while taking a decision on fixed or floating rate mortgage. You could use these factors as a guide to enable you to take an informed and educated decision on the type of mortgage you should take on.

Table 8.3

Assessment — Fixed or Floating Rate Mortgage

Fixed Rate Mortgage	*Floating Rate Mortgage*
Interest rates have been on the rise for a reasonable period of time	Interest rates on have been falling for a reasonable period of time
After substantial hike in interest rates	After substantial fall in interest rates
Tight banking system money market liquidity	Easy banking system money market liquidity
Increase in bond / deposit ratio of banks	Increase in credit / deposit ratio of banks

The Best Time to Buy Your House

This is not a book on timing the markets. At the same time, you have to take decisions.

Figure 8.2 shows the same interest rate cycles chart as was shown in Figure 8.1. However, here, instead of the floating and fixed rate argument, the point is about deciding when to buy your own house.

Figure 8.2 shows that interest rate cycles typically move up and down in cyclical waves. The best time to buy your house would be just before the peak in interest rates when property prices would either have come down, or cooled off from the highs, or stabilized. This is probably the best time to buy a house. The reason is that when interest rates have stayed high for a significant period of time, liquidity in the banking system becomes tight, and money and credit are neither easily nor cheaply available. That is probably the time when your dream house would be available at close to the best price. Look out for following factors to gauge the situation:

- Interest rates should have been on the rise for a reasonable period of time.
- Interest rates should have been raised several times by the central bank during this period.

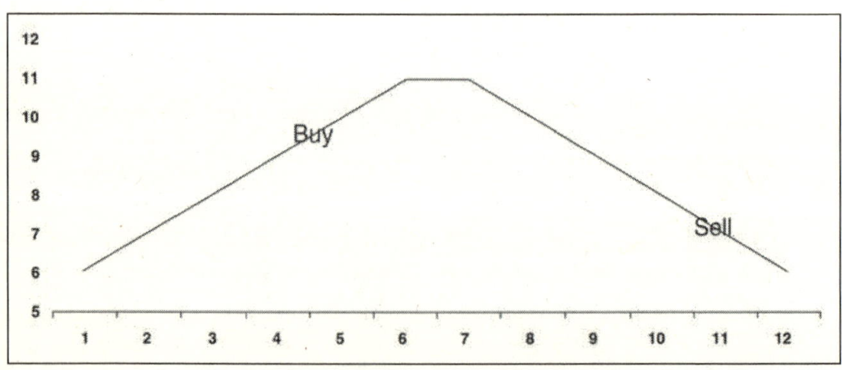

Figure 8.2: **The best time to buy your house**

- The central bank should still be worried about inflation but also, for the first time, introduces growth concerns in its reports.
- The banking system and money market liquidity should be very tight.
- Bank deposit growth is high while credit growth has slowed down.
- Ideally there should be an inverted — or at least — a flat yield curve, i.e. short term (1-year) interest rates should be higher than, or equal to, long term (10-year) interest rates.

Look out for all or some of these factors and then make your judgment. There are chances that you would be buying your dream house at the bottom, or close to the bottom, or at a price point after which a reasonable rise in real estate prices commences.

Although I don't recommend you to sell the house you live in because that goes against the tenet of this commandment, but in case you do have to sell it out of some compulsion or problem beyond your control, or if you are shifting to a bigger house, then you should sell it when interest rates have stayed low for a substantial period of time, liquidity conditions are easy, and money and credit are cheaply available — that is probably the time when your house will fetch you the maximum price and value.

Who Should Own Your House?

Surprised by this question? Your obvious answer would be "Of course, I." People take pride in being the owners of the house they live in. However, what I mean here is whether you believe that holding the house in your own name is the safest and the most efficient way of owning it. Perhaps you don't know the power of corporatization and are unaware of corporate, tax, securities, property and succession laws and how they favor a company over an individual. I will offer the following factors why holding your assets, including your own house, through a corporate structure would be safer and more efficient than holding it in your own personal name.

- **Protection from Legal Financial Predator 1:** It was highlighted in Commandment 2 how the government is the number one and the biggest financial predator of all among those who legally take away money from your pocket. And the government's taxing power falls more heavily on individuals and less so on a corporate. Thus, if you are owner of a corporate and your company owns your assets then the tax is reduced to a large extent. Therefore, it makes sense to hold your assets, including your own house, through a company and not in your individual name.

- **Protection from Legal Financial Predator 5:** Commandment 2 also highlighted a residual category of financial predators called the blackmail predators. These are people who use the legal system to cheat and blackmail you with the nefarious aim of taking away your money. If they are able to win, they may get an order from the court to attach your assets and property. Hence, if you own your assets, including your own house, in your individual name they would be able to pounce on your house with a court order. However, if you hold your assets, including your house, through your company, the blackmailer may win against you but not against your company since it is a separate legal entity in the eyes of law. So, while he can attach your individual assets he cannot attach the assets which your company owns.
- **Succession Planning:** Have you ever realized what will happen to your wealth, including your house, after you are no more? Have you thought of succession planning? I would strongly advise you to contact your legal advisor and immediately prepare your Will so that there are no death predators after you die. As we learnt in Commandment 2, death predators are worse even than vultures. The best way of succession planning is to hold all your assets, including your own house, through your company. In the eyes of the law, you are separate from your company. The company is a separate legal entity and has perpetual succession, i.e. the company never dies, even if you do, unless it is wound up as per law. In my view, one of the superior and safer methods of succession planning is to hold your assets, including your house, through a corporate structure rather than in your individual name.

Should You Consider Shifting to a Bigger House?

This is a question which most of us will mull over from time to time. As noted earlier, a house is a place where we wind up after the whole day's hard work with our loved ones and family members. It is a place where our parents, spouses and children reside, play and pray. Therefore, everyone wants as big a house as possible. Further, due to the common and prevalent misconception that "a house is the biggest asset", everyone strives to buy as big a house as possible. It appears to be such a heady combination — your biggest asset combined with the best comfort and luxury for you and your family.

As discussed earlier, however, your house is nothing but a liability disguised as an accounting asset. It allows you to save on unnecessary rent expenditure, and therefore you have to buy your own house. The answer to this delicate question of owning a bigger house is that you should own a house wherein you and your family members can stay with reasonable comfort. It is certainly not advisable to own a large house with super luxuries because a large house will entail two types of costs:

- Property tax, maintenance, utility bills and other charges relating to house property.
- Opportunity cost in the form of the same funds not being available to invest in true investment assets.

You must decide about the size of your house after taking into account the above two factors. Of course, you can and should enjoy the luxuries of life. After all, God wanted all of us to be happy. For that, you have to reach a stage where your investment assets grow to a level that the return from them pays for your luxury expenses and bad assets. Once you reach that stage, you would have achieved financial freedom — and then you can buy as big a house as you want.

The Break-Even Price of Your House

Let me now consider another concept, namely the break-even price of your house. I will explain it with an illustration. Take a look at

Table 8.4

Break-Even Price of Owning Your Own House

I. Renting a House	₹
Term deposit interest (1,00,00,000 * 10%)	10,00,000
Tax	3,00,000
Net after tax interest income (A)	7,00,000
Rent paid on rented home (B)	3,30,000
Net income (A - B)	3,70,000

II. Owning Your Own House	₹
Property tax	60,000
Maintenance	48,000
Total cost (A)	1,08,000
Interest lost (opportunity cost) (B)	7,00,000
Aggregate cost (C = A + B)	8,08,000
Rent saved (D)	3,30,000
Net loss (C - D)	4,78,000

Table 8.4. Those of you who don't have an accounting or mathematical background might find this table challenging. However, nothing is more challenging than to become a servant of money and keep working for it your whole life. This table will inspire you to learn something new which will be very interesting and thought provoking. Also, while the illustration might look difficult but in reality it's very simple and logical.

Let us assume that you have ₹ 10 million. Now, you have two options:

- To put the money in the bank, earn interest on it, and live in a rented house.
- Buy and live in a house worth ₹ 10 million.

Let us examine both the options.

In Option I, you will put that ₹ 10 million in a bank fixed deposit at, say, 10% p.a. rate of interest and earn ₹ 1 million, on which you will have to pay around 30% tax (might vary depending on your tax bracket). Hence, your interest income after tax would amount to

₹ 7,00,000. Now you will have to rent a house to live in. Let us say the rent is ₹ 3,30,000 p.a. — residential rental yields are generally one-third of the prevailing long term interest rates. Hence, your net income would be ₹ 3,70,000, i.e. net interest income after tax *minus* rent paid on rented premises to reside in.

Let us now examine the second option of owning your own house. You utilize the ₹ 10 million and buy a house for self occupation. Once you buy your house, the government charges you property tax and you will also have to incur the cost of maintenance of your house. Let's say these amount to ₹ 1,08,000 p.a.

The other cost which you incur is the opportunity cost. Since you've utilized the money for buying a house, you will now have to forego the interest which you could have otherwise earned from the bank. So, your aggregate cost for owning your own house amounts to ₹ 8,08,000 (₹ 1,08,000 + ₹ 7,00,000). However, since you have bought the house for self occupation, you would not require the rented premises and hence save on the rent of ₹ 3,30,000 p.a. and therefore the net loss to you for owning your own house worth ₹ 10 million amounts to ₹ 4,78,000 (₹ 8,08,000 *minus* ₹ 3,30,000). I have kept the calculations simple by not including mortgage, corporate ownership and tax benefits, etc. as my purpose was to explain the concept. Once that is clear, the numbers can change and vary.

Ideally, the break-even point should be zero — you should be monetarily unaffected between renting a house or owning one. However, this may never happen because the rental yield on residential real estate is always lower and closer to one-third of the prevailing interest rates. On the other hand, your house is an asset and over the very long term, notwithstanding intermediate fluctuations, its value will rise against the artificial thing to which it is measured, i.e. paper currency or money. Accordingly, the differential should be such that the opportunity loss in current income gets compensated by the increase in the value of your house over the long term.

Will Your House Appreciate in Value?

While it's difficult to predict whether the price of a particular house will appreciate in value but the general level of real estate will surely appreciate over the long term, notwithstanding any short and medium term fluctuations. This is due to the simple fact that your house is not paper currency like money — it is a real asset. And, over the long term, real assets appreciate against paper currency because of fall in the purchasing power of money.

Over the very long term, the price of real estate as a whole will always tend to go up because:

1. The supply of real estate in aggregate is limited while the supply of paper money, against which it is measured, it practically unlimited — the government can, and actually does, print money at will. If the supply of one of the things (money) keeps increasing while the supply of the thing it is measured against (real estate) does not increase, then it's common sense that more and more of paper currency would be required to buy the same quantity of the real asset. Hence, the price of real estate is bound to increase over the long term, not because it might be something invaluable but simply because of the fall in the value of paper money.
2. Due to inflation, the replacement cost of the house — or in other words the construction cost — increases. For example, over time due to inflation the price of cement, steel, labor, etc., keep on rising and therefore the price of the house has to rise commensurately for the developer to make money on it.

Because of the above two reasons, the price of real estate in general will always tend to rise over the very long term. However, whether the price of your own house will rise or not depends on several factors, which is the point discussed in the next section.

Factors Influencing Real Estate Prices

Having understood that the price of real estate always tends to go up over the long term, let us consider the factors which generally affect real estate prices.

Economic Growth Leading to a Rise in Real Income Levels

Rising incomes enable people to spend more on buying a house. If economic growth of country is high, it will lead to a general rise in the income levels of people. However, you have to note here that there has to be rise in the real income levels (nominal income rise *minus* inflation) rather than just an increase in the nominal income. In essence, people's purchasing power has to increase.

Interest Rates

This is perhaps one of the most important variables affecting property prices in general. A fall in interest rates leads to a rise in real estate prices — and *vice versa*. While the correlation is high but the impact would generally be after a time lag, i.e. the interest rate movement would precede movement in real estate prices.

Demographics

Demographics are the data that describe a population's composition, such as age, race, gender, income, migration patterns and population growth. These statistics are an often overlooked but significant factor that affects how real estate is priced and what types of properties are in demand. Major shifts in the demographics of a nation can have a large impact on real estate trends for several decades. For example, the baby boomers who were born in the US between 1945 and 1964 are an example of a demographic trend which significantly influenced the US real estate market. The transition of these baby boomers to retirement was one of the more interesting generational trends in the last century, and the retirement of these baby boomers, which began in 2010, is bound to be noticed in the market for decades to come.

Government Policies, Legislation and Subsidies

Whether you like it or not, government influences the price of a lot of assets, and none so more than real estate. Legislation is a factor that can have a sizable impact on property demand and prices. Tax credits, deductions and subsidiaries are some of the ways government can boost real estate prices in certain areas. Being aware of government policies and initiatives might help you in taking the right decision as regards the locality to buy property in.

Availability of Credit

As mentioned earlier, interest rates affect the price of real estate. So, too, the development of the banking system and the availability of credit. A marked improvement in the banking system and the availability of easier and quicker credit go a long way in the development of the real estate market.

Factors Influencing the Price of Your House

An increase in general real estate prices might not necessarily translate into an increase in the price of your house. Sometimes the price of your particular house might rise or fall to a lesser extent than that of your neighbor's. This section attempts to answer the important question of what influences the price of your house.

Development In Your Locality

Anyone buying real estate will say that the most important factor to watch for is locality. However, I will change this statement slightly and suggest that the most important factor affecting the price of your house is the "change happening in your locality". When you buy a certain house in, say, the best of localities, the price of the house would have invariably included all the advantages offered by the locality at that point of time. Hence, the price will not increase in future just because the locality is good since that is already factored into it. Instead, the price will rise in future when there is some additional development in the locality; for example, a new school, hospital, railway station or shopping mall, etc. coming up in the vicinity.

Improvements / Additions to Your House

The amount of improvements / additions, such as re-painting the house in a new color, installing air conditioners / heaters, electric lights and fittings, geyser, etc. certainly increases the value of your house since it now provides additional benefits to potential buyers.

Economic Activity and Job Availability in the Neighborhood

The value of your house property will also depend on jobs being created in and around your locality. These factors have a direct positive correlation with prices of property. The more the number of jobs and the higher the salaries and wages earned, the higher would be the demand for house property as well as rental property, consequently leading to overall higher house property prices.

Rental Real Estate

The discussion on house property and real estate would be incomplete if we were not to discuss rental real estate, which is one of the best investments assets.

Remember the definition of an investment asset? It is an asset which puts money into your pocket. And rental real estate does just that by putting real hard cash into your pocket month after month. As we learnt in Commandment 6, when the return on an investment asset attains the state of net positive cash flow after tax then the debt on it becomes a positive leverage. For example, consider the figures given in Table 8.5.

Table 8.5
Break-Even Price of Owning Your Own House

Particular	*Value (₹)*
Rental Real Estate Value	2.5 Million
Down Payment	0.5 Million
Mortgage Loan (10% rate of interest)	2.0 Million
Rent Received	2,50,000
Mortgage Interest	2,00,000
Property Tax and Maintenance	25,000
Net Cash Flow	25,000
Net Cash Return on Investment	5%

Let's assume you purchased a rental real estate worth ₹ 2.5 million by paying a down payment of ₹ 0.5 million and borrowing the rest from the bank at 10% p.a. rate of interest. Now, let's suppose you are able to rent it at ₹ 2,50,000. After paying the mortgage and the maintenance, you are still left with ₹ 25,000 in net cash flow. As your investment in this project was ₹ 0.5 million, so your actual net cash return on investment is 5% (₹ 25,000 ÷ ₹ 5,00,000). You are, therefore, earning this return of 5% literally free. This is your actual net cash return on investment after making all the payments, such as mortgage, property tax, maintenance, etc.

How did the rental yield go up so much in this example. Your rental yield can be raised due to the following reasons.

Commercial Property

Rental yield on commercial property is generally higher than that on residential property. This is simply because your tenants are doing business and are therefore ready to pay you a higher rental income for the premises. However, commercial property prices and rentals are very volatile and you must therefore grow your knowledge and understanding before investing in it.

Distressed Sale

You should be on the look out for a good property being sold at distressed prices because the seller has some cash crunch, or the seller is in hurry to sell it, or the seller's mortgage has been foreclosed, etc.

Distressed Property

You should also be on the look out for any distressed property available at cheap bargain prices. Distressed property is one wherein the owner has been disinterested and has not maintained it. By making simple improvements like re-painting, and installing air-conditioning, heaters, geysers, etc., the value of the property can be improved and, importantly, by providing these simple facilities the rent from it can be increased.

Shopping in Foreclosure Auctions

You should be shopping in auctions where the foreclosed properties are forcibly sold off. Some of the best bargains are sometimes available in such auctions.

These are some of the ways by which you can try and increase the yield from your rental real estate. Just as a child learns to walk by practice and gathering experience, you can also learn to find good rental real estate at bargain prices offering high rental yields through constant trying and experience.

Price Risk in Rental Real Estate

What about price risk of rental real estate? To start with, I am not suggesting that you buy real estate with an expectation of an increase in its value so that you can sell it at a higher price and get capital gains (portfolio income). No, I am not recommending that you buy an investment asset, such as rental real estate, primarily for capital gains. In fact, I never suggested that you buy any investment asset, be it rental real estate, equity shares, bonds or anything else, just for capital gains or portfolio income. You should invest in investment assets for earning income and with the aim of generating net positive cash flow after tax (passive income). That is the major premise for investing in any investment asset, rental real estate being no different. And once you follow this discipline, you are not worried about the price of your investment asset. As explained in Commandment 1, prices will go up and down, and bull and bear markets will come and go. All those need not worry you so long as you are investing for passive income and not for portfolio income. And, remember, it is a cardinal principle of investment that if you are investing for passive income, then portfolio income would also invariably follow. The reason is very simple. When you invest for passive income, it is but natural that you would be buying assets at fair value because only "value gives higher yield". Don't forget that you make money in investments not at the time of selling but at the time of buying; if your purchase price for any investment asset is reasonably correct, you will eventually make money. Which is why money is made at the point of buying; you only realize it at the time of selling.

To sum up, you should invest in rental real estate for rental yield and net positive cash flow. The value of your property will be determined by the amount of rent your tenants pay you and not the vagaries of the market. In fact, in a housing market crash, many people's houses would be getting foreclosed and therefore the demand for rental house goes up — and so does the rent!

Brokers and Property Managers

Never underestimate the utility and value of good brokers and property managers so far as rental real estate investing is concerned. For a small brokerage, a good broker will help you find excellent assets at reasonable prices. Never try to undercut the brokerage. Remember that a broker is not just a person who introduces two people. S/he is an intermediary who makes two people meet both of whom have equal — but contrary — interest in the property, i.e. buying and selling. When shopping for a broker, don't go for any high flying big name because such a broker would seldom have the time for you. Even if he does, he would rarely be in a position to provide you value because many customers would be chasing the limited valuable investment options which he might have. Instead, try to find a broker who is himself a student of investment — a student of his own asset class, a constant learner. Avoid all those self proclaimed gurus and experts and go in for an eager student of investment.

The other set of important people who provide indispensable service are property managers. I don't think you would like your tenant calling you at midnight and complaining that there is no water in their toilet. But that kind of worry should not deter you from owning rental real estate. The solution is to appoint a professional property manager whose job it is to look after your property and get the toilet tap fixed even at midnight. They are the people who take care and maintain your property in proper condition thus enhancing the probability of finding good tenants with higher rents. And higher rents enhance the value of your property over the long run.

Avoid the Wealth Effect Trap of Your Owned House

This is a very important principle which you must always remember so that you don't fall into a trap.

Only because of inflation, which is not really a genuine increase in the value of an asset but a decline in the value of paper money, many people feel wealthier as the price of their home appears to go up. When they feel wealthier, they borrow more money (negative leverage) and spend more on liabilities (a double-trouble combination!).

In simple terms, wealth effect is spending money which you don't have but imagine you do simply on the basis of an increase, or a perceived increase, in the price of an asset which you own. When the asset price falls, or the value which you thought it commanded does not hold true, you helplessly watch yourself fall into the wealth effect trap — a situation in which you are left with diminished asset prices along with high cost debt which your current income is not able to service.

For example, a few years back home prices in the US were constantly rising due to the credit market bubble. Many people borrowed money against their inflated home values. When the credit bubble burst, their homes were worth much less that what they had borrowed. Homeowners who were still able to pay their mortgage debt felt terrible as they watched their homes prices drop. They watched their equity in their home disappear as their home prices fell like a pack of cards. As for those who could not pay their mortgage debt, their houses were foreclosed and they were left only with liabilities and high cost debt which they were unable to service.

Lesson: always recognize the difference between real and perceived wealth and never fall a victim to the wealth effect trap.

Lessons From This Commandment

1. Your own house is a bad capital asset and not an investment asset. Your house takes away money from your pocket in the

form of property tax, maintenance, society charges, utility bills and mortgage loan payments.

2. Although your house is a bad capital asset, you must still own one in order to avoid the unnecessary expense of rent.
3. Your mortgaged house is actually the bank's investment asset because it puts money into the bank's coffers in the form of mortgage loan EMIs which you pay to it.
4. The leverage factor for a home mortgage is typically the highest among all assets at 1:4. Also, house mortgage loans are probably the cheapest loans which a bank provides. In addition, the taxman gives lots of sops in the form of tax exemptions and deductions on re-payment of interest as well as capital for a house mortgage loan. Therefore, it makes sense to finance your self occupied house through a bank mortgage loan.
5. You should go in for a floating rate mortgage when there has already been a substantial hike in the central bank controlled interest rates over a period of time. On the other hand, you should settle for a fixed rate mortgage loan when there has already been a substantial fall in the central bank controlled interest rates over a period of time.
6. The best time to buy your house would be just before the peak in interest rates. That's the time property prices would have come down, cooled off from the highs, or stabilized. If you do have to sell your house due to any compulsion, you should sell it when interest rates have stayed low for a substantial period of time, liquidity conditions are easy and when money and credit are cheaply available.
7. In order to protect yourself from many of the legal financial predators, including the government and the taxman, as also for proper and smooth succession planning, it is advisable that your company owns your house and not you as an individual.
8. If you are contemplating to shift to a bigger house without any real need for it, remember that a house entails two types of costs; one in the form of property tax, maintenance, utility bills, mortgage loan payments, etc. and, two, opportunity cost — the

loss from not investing the same funds in actual investment assets.

9. It's better to get an idea of the break-even price of your house by considering different variables, such as term deposit interest rates, mortgage interest rates, rent paid on rented house, and other real estate related costs, like property tax, maintenance, etc.
10. Price of real estate will always tend to rise over the long term because the value of paper currency, i.e. money, will fall over the long term. And as more money chases the same quantity of real estate, its price will tend to rise over the long term. Further, due to inflation, the replacement cost of the house or, in other words, the construction cost, increases which will again raise the price of real estate.
11. General factors which influence the price of real estate over the long term are economic growth leading to rise in real income levels, interest rate, demographics, government policies, legislation and development of the banking system and availability of credit.
12. The factors which influence the price of your house are developments in your locality, improvements / additions done to your house, and economic activity, particularly job availability in and around your house.
13. Bear in mind that the government gives tax incentives to either buy liabilities or sell assets. Therefore, the taxman showers you with all its exemptions and deductions when you buy a house through mortgage debt.
14. Rental real estate is one of the better investment assets which month after month puts hard cash into your pocket. The trick is that it should be net cash positive after tax, i.e. the rental income should cover all the expenses like property tax, maintenance, mortgage payments, etc. on the house.
15. You can raise your rental yield if you buy commercial property, buy rental real estate in distressed sale or as a distressed asset (and then improve it), or shop for it in foreclosure auctions.

16. Indeed, there is price risk in rental real estate. However, the value of your rental real estate depends on the rent which you receive and the net positive cash flow after tax which you are able to generate. If you are able to control and increase that, you need not worry.
17. Don't underestimate the value which a good broker and property manager can bring to the table. Never try to cut on their fees and commissions; instead, try to find brokers who are themselves students of their profession and then pay them proper remuneration. They will create value for your real estate.
18. Never spend money which you don't have but imagine you do simply on the basis of an increase, or a perceived increase, in the price of an asset which you own. Always recognize the difference between real and perceived wealth and never fall a victim to the wealth effect trap.

Self-Understanding Questionnaire

This commandment opened up a very startling truth that your own house is not an investment asset but a bad capital asset. It also explained to you the importance of rental real estate as an investment asset and how to make money from it by following the net positive cash flow after tax rule. Now, honestly answer the following questions in yes or no to test your understanding of the principles explained in this commandment. The more the number of "yes" answers, the better is your understanding of this commandment.

1. Do you accept the fact that your house is not an investment asset? Yes/No?
2. Do you agree that it is not you but your company which should own your house? Yes/No?
3. Do you accept the fact that shifting to a bigger house would entail higher avoidable expense as well as opportunity loss? Yes/No?

4. Do you understand that over the long term the price of real estate might increase because of the fall in the value of paper currency due to inflation? Yes/No?
5. Do you realize that the value of your rental real estate is based on the rent which your tenant is ready to pay for it? Yes/No?
6. Do you appreciate that brokers and property managers can provide invaluable advice, service and deals to you? Yes/No?
7. Do you know about the wealth effect and how it can trap you? Yes/No?

Chapter 9

Commandment 8

Thou Shall Not Over-Invest in Speculative Items

What Is a Speculative Item?

There are lots of definitions of speculative items. My sense and thinking of a speculative item is totally different which I shall explain in the subsequent paragraphs.

Before moving forward, however, I would like to clarify one thing. This commandment is about investing in speculating items and not on wasteful spending The latter was dealt with in Commandment 4. I consider investments in speculative items as one of the biggest mistakes which investors make which is why I have devoted a whole commandment to it.

Different Types of Investments

We have already looked at the different asset classes in Commandment 1. In this section, we will consider investments based on the type of returns which one derives from the investments.

Investment for Running Income

Running income is nothing but the current income which an investment produces during its life. Since there is a continuous flow of income, hence the term running income.

Examples of running income would include dividend on shares, interest on bonds, rent on real estate, etc. These incomes are derived by the investor on a constant, i.e. runnings basis during the life of the investment. The investment need not be sold to derive running income. In fact, an important feature of running income is that the investment has to exist in order for you to derive income from it. If for any reason the investment is liquidated, then the running income from it would also stop. Remember, this is passive income as per our income categories in Commandment 2.

Investments for Asset Income

Asset income is nothing but the return from your assets. Kindly note, it is not the return on your assets but a return from your assets. Thus, while running income is derived as a return on your assets during the existence of your asset, the return from investments is a result of the asset itself being liquidated and sold, either partly or fully. Therefore, the pre-condition for asset income would be that the asset is partly or fully liquidated to earn that income. Examples of asset income would be profit on sale of equity shares, bonds, real estate, etc. Remember, this is the portfolio income which we referred to in the income categories in Commandment 2.

In any kind of investment, there will basically be these and only these two types of returns, the return on investment and the return from investments.

Speculative Items

A speculative item is an investment which only produces asset income. In other words, any investment which is not capable of producing running income would be termed as a speculative item. Accordingly, the *sine qua non* for an item to become an investment is that it should provide some kind of cash flow either in the form of dividends, interest, rent, or whatever, but there should be some regular cash payments to the owner of the investment. And nothing better than a net positive cash flow after tax — which is what I will call the ultimate investment.

The common examples of speculative items would be:

- Precious commodities like gold, silver, diamond, platinum, etc.
- Industrial commodities like iron, steel, copper, aluminum, etc.

- Derivatives — whether stocks, bonds, commodities, currencies, or on anything else.
- Currency.
- Art.
- Self occupied house property.
- Non rental real estate.
- Land.
- Club membership.

The above is just an illustrative and certainly not a comprehensive list of speculative items. As can be seen from this list, none of these items produce any kind of cash flows.

You might not be able to readily accept that some of these are speculative items. So, let's see why they are indeed so.

Commodities — Precious, Industrial and Agricultural

If you are buying precious metals like gold, silver, diamond, platinum, or industrial commodities like iron, steel, copper, aluminum in the hope of an increase in their prices, then you are investing in a speculative item. On the other hand, if you are a miner, converter, trader, or in some form or the other deal in any of these types of commodities, then you are a businessman. In the first case you are buying the commodity in the hope of a future price gain (asset income) while in the second case you are not concerned with the asset price, you are just an intermediary dealing in the asset and hence your major source of earning comes from running income or current income. Again, if you are hoarding an agricultural commodity like rice, wheat, sugar, coffee, etc., then you are investing in a speculative item. Conversely, if you are a farmer growing agricultural commodities and selling them, then you are a producer, a manufacturer, or a businessman in that commodity. Consequently, hoarding of commodities which do not yield anything would be a case of investing in speculative item.

Now let us move on to the king of all speculative items which most of us and our governments and central banks own — gold.

Gold

Although gold has been regarded as a commodity over the last four decades, for thousands of years gold was the world's purest form of money and, being nobody's liability, the indisputable store and measure of value. We may know the price of gold but what is its value? How do we determine that? We can value a commodity based on the cash flows it generates, like interest on a bond, rent on a real estate property or dividends for equities, but gold does not generate any cash flow and, in fact, it may have negative cash flow in the form of storage costs. Since there is so much investor interest in gold — and as some amount of gold might be an integral part of asset allocation as laid down by Commandment 1, — let us now try to understand what determines the true value of gold. Is gold really a speculative item? Is it an asset or a commodity? How does the turmoil in the global currency and asset markets affect gold and what might be the future course of action for gold?

Introduction

A common person may not understand the benefits of investing in stocks for long term wealth creation, or bonds for enhancing the purchasing power in a deflationary environment, or hoard cash to preserve capital in an uncertain economic world but everyone believes that he or she knows the value of gold.

Indians have traditionally been the largest consumers of gold. Importantly, most Indians believe that gold prices can only go up. Our parents have taught us to invest in gold because that is one thing which never falls and financial advisors recommend gold as a hedge against inflation. Let us see whether this is really true or simply a myth. Let us understand how to value gold and if we can't value it then how is the value of gold determined. Also, let us assess whether gold prices can fall or is it some sacred investment which can never go down. And, then, finally let us accept the fact that although some allocation to gold is desirable but it is, finally, a speculative item.

History of Gold Prices

When investors are hungry for gold, the metal has a habit of rising exponentially in a manner that has no parallel amongst metals. While base metals still have to adhere to some form of analysis along the lines of "supply less demand = inventory", gold has decades of inventory lying in the central banks of various countries which does not enter into consideration, as central banks rarely sell their inventory of gold. The last time they did that, and swapped their gold for cash, it turned out to be the wrong option. I do not believe that they will go that route in a hurry again. In fact, I believe it is that hard-learnt lesson which makes them even keener holders of gold and this has tightened up the market significantly. During the 1990s, gold mining companies used to leave their gold sales as open, i.e. they never used to hedge it and hence their profits were subject to the vagaries of gold price volatility. More recently, however, gold mining companies have, rightly, started hedging their gold sales because their primary motive is to earn money from gold mining and not speculate in gold prices.

Gold rose 2,300% over the nine-year period that ended in 1980, one of the most spectacular runs that any major financial asset class has ever recorded. While gold initially rose because the US government was unable to maintain its price which was fixed at US$ 35 an ounce in 1971, it continued climbing sharply because the gold market is tiny in the immense global financial ocean. Accordingly, a relatively small amount of investor interest was able to make gold surge as stocks and bonds languished. Today, following the long years since 1980 during which gold generally lagged other investments, the effect would be far more dramatic because the US$ 140 trillion global asset markets is so much larger. All the gold in the world is worth only US$ 7.5 trillion, yet only a small fraction of that amount is traded on financial markets. If just 1% of the global value of stocks and bonds — roughly US$ 960 billion — went into gold, the precious metal would skyrocket. The amount is eighteen times what the mining industry produces and substantially more than what is traded on gold markets during an entire year. There simply wouldn't be enough gold available at the current price.

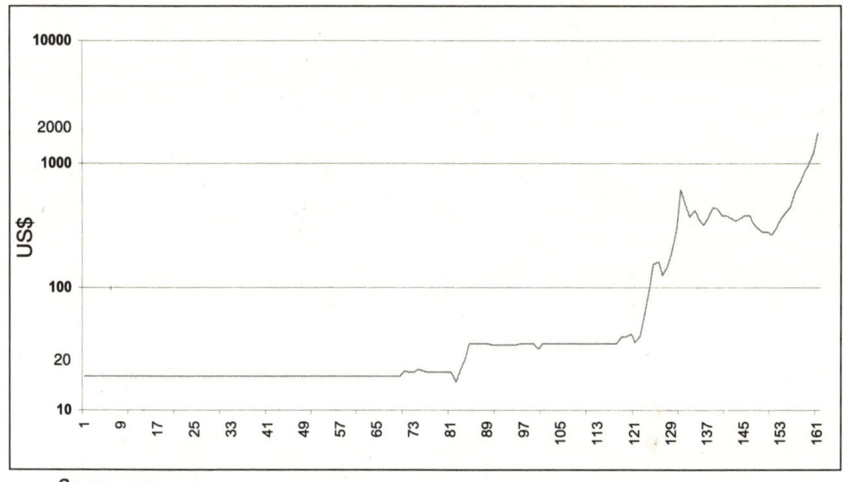

Source: nma. org

Figure 9.1: **160 year history of gold prices: 1 = the year 1850 and 161 = the year 2011**

For all the die-hard gold bugs, have a look at Figure 9.1. Gold rose from US$ 18.93 per ounce in the year 1850 to US$ 1,750 per ounce in 2011, giving a CAGR return of just 2.9%. This is hardly impressive.

Compare this with the US Dow Jones Industrial Average (DJIA). Since its inception at 41 in the year 1896, the Dow has delivered CAGR returns of 5%. This resulted in the Dow / Gold ratio which was 2.2 in the year 1896 jumping to 7.6. Now, whether this means that gold is currently under priced or that gold deserves to remain an under performer, is not easy to answer. If we compute the return from gold from the year 1971 when the US President Richard Nixon put an end to the decades-old gold peg at US$ 35 per ounce, it would surely be a source of intense irritation to the gold bugs who held on to their precious metal during the two decades that began in 1980. US DJIA went up 12-fold between 1980 to 2000 while gold gave an absolute negative return of almost 65%; yes, minus 65%. Importantly, the US DJIA has traditionally given a dividend yield of around 1.1% (running income) while running income from gold is nil — in fact, negative because of the storage and other holding costs associated with it. From 1971 till 2012, gold returned a CAGR of 9.9% as compared to US DJIA's CAGR return of 12.7% during the same period — plus the running income in the form of dividend yield on the US DJIA.

The value of any asset is the cash flow which it produces during its lifetime, reckoned at present value. Different assets produce different types of cash flows. For example, a bond (fixed deposit) yields interest, equities produce dividends, rental real estate gives rent, etc. But what cash flow does gold give — typically nothing. In fact, it has negative cash flow in the form of storage costs. Further, most assets have some use — steel is used in construction and auto industry, oil in running autos and factories, power in running machines, copper in making wires, etc., but gold has little industrial use. Besides making the "golden tooth", the industrial use of gold is practically nothing. Then what is the value of gold? Why is it so costly? Why do we pay thousands of rupees to buy few grams of it?

It's simply because we believe the value of gold will go up in future, and we will then be able to sell it at a higher price to another buyer (the greater fool theory) or, better still, we don't ever need to sell gold — it will be passed on to our children and the future generations.

In that sense, gold is a totally speculative commodity with negligible real use. Its value arises from it being treated as a safe haven — almost as an alternate currency. Its high value lies in governments and central banks (led by the US Fed) running their money printing machines continuously, relentlessly and at a brisk speed. The US dollar has lost 97% of its value against gold between the mid-1970s and 2012! Hence, it's not gold which has gone up but it's the US dollar which has gone down because of indiscriminate money printing by the US Fed. And since gold is internationally valued in terms of the US dollar, if the value of US dollar goes down, naturally the value of gold has then to go up and that is what has happened.

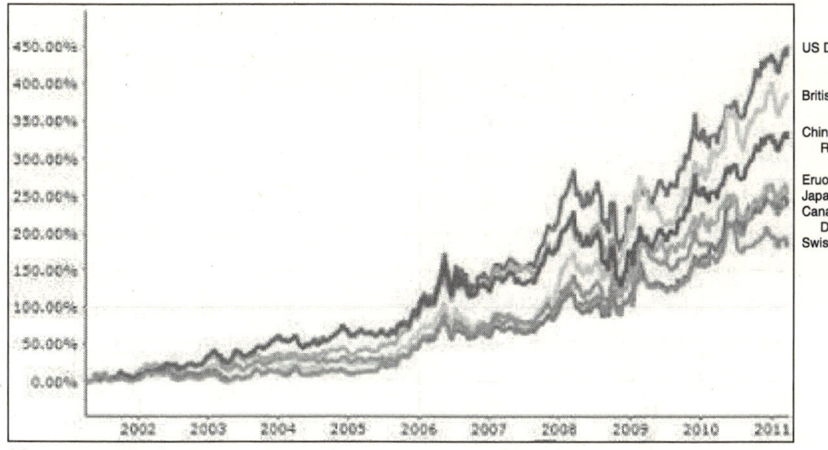

(*Source:* nma. org)

Figure 9.2: **Gold *vis-à-vis* major world currencies**

In an effort to illuminate a different aspect of the gold story, let's focus on other currencies. Let us compare the price of gold with other major international currencies over the ten-year period, 2002-12. Figure 9.2 shows the percentage gains of gold priced in US dollar and six other major currencies.

It's kind of difficult to digest, but there's a huge disparity between the US dollar's loss of gold-purchasing power (more than 450%), and the Swiss Franc's loss of gold purchasing power (less than 200%). Hence, the price of gold is nothing but a percentage of some international currency — and globally the general practice is to express it against the US dollar.

Now, has gold risen consistently over the past few decades? No, not at all. Young Indian investors would not have seen more than ten-years of gold's price history and even the older ones would not remember more than thirty years back. During this past thirty-year period, "Indian" gold prices have either been stable or climbing upward. I say "Indian" gold prices because it may shock many Indians to learn that international gold prices crashed from US $850 per ounce in 1981 to US $250 per ounce in 2001, a negative return over a long 20-year period. However, the rupee value of gold was up during the same period. Why? Is it magic? This came about simply because the Indian rupee, which was valued at ₹ 8 per US dollar in the year 1981, crashed to ₹ 45 by the year 2001. Because the Indian currency lost significant value against the US dollar, the price of gold went up in Indian rupee terms even while international gold price in US dollar terms crashed during the same period. Now, has gold given great returns over the 20-year period? Not really. Indian gold gave 8.9% CAGR over the 20-year period while the BSE Sensex gave 15.3% CAGR over the same period. In fact, over the same twenty years, simple and safe bank FDs might have given better returns than gold!

Is Gold a Hedge Against Inflation?

Many financial experts will tell you that gold is a hedge against inflation. That may, however, not necessarily be the case. The price of gold is not directly related to inflation but to "real interest rates", i.e. (nominal interest rates *minus* inflation) of US dollar denominated assets like US treasuries. When the real interest rate is down and close to the rate of inflation, gold is likely to appreciate in value. That's because the investor has to forego interest on his investments to hold gold which does not give any cash flow. Thus, real interest rates have to be low or negative to induce an investor to hold on to something which does not give any real cash flow.

Table 9.1 brings out the last 30-year history of US real interest rates, gold prices and US stock markets. It clearly highlights the fact that gold performs well when real interest rates are either very low or negative — and *vice versa*.

Table 9.1

The Time when Gold rises in Value

Period	*US Real Interest Rate*	*Gold Price*	*US S&P 500**
1973-1980	-1.15%	+32% p.a.	-7% p.a.
1981-2001	+2.7%	-3.5% p.a.	+7% p.a.
2002-2011	-0.4%	+18.5% p.a.	-3% p.a.

(*Source:* US Federal Reserve, * Excluding Dividends)

Is Gold a Hedge against Indian Rupee Depreciation?

Yes, gold is a hedge against the depreciation in the Indian rupee *vis-à-vis* the US dollar. If an investor is not sophisticated enough to trade in commodities, then holding gold gives the investor an indirect exposure to the US dollar. For example, international gold prices in US dollar terms dipped by around 20% in the year 2012 while Indian gold prices in rupee terms actually gained by almost 10% simply because the Indian rupee depreciated by nearly 25% as against the US dollar during the same period of time.

What Determines the Price of Gold

The following factors determine the price of gold in India:

1. **Value of the US Dollar:** Since gold is internationally quoted in US dollars, the weaker the US dollar, the higher the price of gold — and *vice versa.*
2. **Real Interest Rates in US Dollar-Denominated Assets:** Low or negative real interest rates result in higher gold prices — and *vice versa.*
3. **Value of Indian Rupee *vis-a-vis* US dollar:** Since Indians buy gold in Indian rupees, the weaker the Indian rupee is against the US dollar, the higher will be the price of gold — and *vice versa.*

Determinants of the Price of Gold

The US Dollar — It's Just a Currency, Not Real Money

As explained earlier in the book, the year 1971 totally changed the rules of the money game. The Nixon Shock was a series of economic measures taken by U.S. President Richard Nixon in 1971, including unilaterally canceling the direct convertibility of the United States dollar to gold. The latter step essentially ended the existing Bretton Woods system of international financial exchange. Because of this very important change, the US dollar no longer remained money — it became a currency. Nixon's action basically signified the death of money as there was a fundamental change in the nature of business transactions based on a complex, electronically managed system of valuations used for stocks, bonds, insurance policies, and other financial contracts that go beyond the simple, historic notion of money representing physical reserves. A simple view of this concept is that if everyone decides to cash out their bank accounts on a single day, there is no longer enough paper money to pay everybody.

Currently, all monetary value is ultimately measured in US dollar, the quantity of which is no longer limited by physical gold as had been required under the Bretton Woods system. Being the premier currency in virtually all of the world's central banks, the US dollar is the *de facto* foundation of the global monetary system, the metric used to weigh all other currencies, and hence the final measure of the value of everything that has a price. Nevertheless, it's just a currency and not real money. Then, too, it is a very weak currency. The US dollar being the world's currency is an exorbitant privilege since it forces other nations to absorb American liabilities and fund its deficits. The US debt has grown to more than 300% of its GDP, a level last approached when thousands of banks were collapsing in the 1930s, which makes this picture all the more striking. The US GDP is not falling today as it did in the 1930s, but its liabilities are rising at a brisk pace. Five dollars in debt are added for each dollar in American GDP.

And while US government liabilities are surging, what is happening to American consumers, who cannot raise tax money or lay off their spouses, is far more troubling. Household debt has more than doubled over the ten-year period, 2001-2011, while inflation adjusted wages have been stagnant for years. Debt payments each year are taking the largest share of American paychecks, which are already battered by sky-rocketing healthcare costs. When consumer debt keeps rising, the US Federal Reserve brushes it aside by saying that the value of the assets, primarily real estate, is growing at a faster pace. But to think that credit growth, rather than income growth, can make anyone richer is disastrous as we saw with the U.S. sub-prime crisis in 2008. The US is losing its race with debt — perhaps it's time to take a long, hard look at America's balance sheet instead of expecting that easy liquidity or QE-3 or any such other mechanism by the Federal Reserve will bail it out. The US government and its people are in a balance sheet recession and not an income statement recession which can be bailed out by printing money, easy liquidity or fiscal measures. These measures will not ignite consumers to borrow or spend. How can we expect the US consumer to continue borrowing and spending when the US unemployment figure is within kissing distance of the double-digit figure. It is perhaps this kind of recession which happened in Japan during the 1990s, or in the US itself during the 1930s. Central banks were forced to absorb trillions of deficit driven dollars in new reserves over the past few years, and have injected more liquidity into their own economies in an effort to maintain competitive currencies. Doing so has been vital — exporters to the US need their governments to maintain what has become a vendor financing system — amassing dollars and lending Americans more money so that they can continue buying attractively priced foreign products!

Approximately 60% of the "paper dollars" circulate outside the US. Also, a majority of US Treasury bonds are owned by foreigners. Today, America relies on the world's largesse more than ever before. It is the lack of alternatives which forces investors to stay with the US dollar as the reserve currency. Although the US dollar does remain a global reserve currency, but it cannot become money — which remains gold. Kindly note, gold rises when the risks inherent in holding paper currency increase, and when stocks, bonds, and other investment returns are insufficient to compensate for rising risks in the financial markets. At the time of writing, bond yields were at historical low levels with the 10-year US Treasury even venturing below 1.5% and the dividend yield on the US S&P 500 Index was more than the US 10-year Treasury yield, which is a rare occurrence. This has happened only for the second time since 1970. This would mean equity markets are demanding high yields since they see higher risks, companies are not able to deploy cash properly, implying lower valuation multiples. For all these reasons gold has been surging high and almost touched more than US $1,900 per ounce in the year 2012.

The Supply of Gold

Gold mining production peaked in the year 2001 and the average global cost of producing a refined ounce of the ever-harder-to-find precious metal doubled in just seven years after that. There were regular strikes in the South African gold, diamond and coal mines and the world's central banks constantly increased their reserves of gold as they realized that they can't hold all their assets in the ever depreciating US dollar.

Demand for Gold

Although the supply of gold has weakened, new avenues of demand have arisen, thanks mostly to gold exchange traded funds (ETFs) which allow more and more investors around the globe to buy and hold even small amounts of gold at the click of a mouse. Gold ETFs only began trading in 2004, and they are now present on several markets throughout Europe and Asia and should soon be available on all major exchanges. The growing affluence of India, the world's largest market for gold, has contributed to the increased demand. And, in 2007, Chinese citizens, the world's biggest savers, were allowed to trade gold legally for the first time.

Conclusion — Future Price of Gold

I won't even try to predict the future price of gold. As highlighted earlier, it's a speculative commodity with no real industrial usage. Instead, its price depends on the value of US dollar, the real interest rates in the US, which, in turn, depend on nominal interest rates and inflation, and the value of Indian rupee against the US dollar. So long as the US Fed continues to print money, the US dollar will remain weak; and till there is uncertainty in the global economy, the printing of money will continue. Till the US dollar remains weak, Asian central banks, like those in China, India, etc., will shift partly from US dollar-denominated securities to hard assets like gold. Till there is uncertainty around, people will move to this so-called safe haven. Until the US government and consumers move out of balance sheet recession, the prospects of gold remain bright. Till the Indian rupee remains structurally weak against the US dollar over the long term, gold prices in India would be supported in rupee terms and till the women in India keep loving gold ornaments there would be demand for gold which otherwise hardly has any real industrial use.

So the next time you think of investing in gold, weigh all these factors before doing so — and remember that while gold may go up in value like any other asset — but it is certainly not some sacred asset whose price will never fall. Like any other asset, its value will go up and also come down depending on the conditions which affect its prices.

Silver

As with gold, the supply of its poorer cousin — silver — comes from the mining industry (71%), scrap selling (21%) and government sales (8%). But there are two essential differences in silver supply that are absent with gold.

First, most of the silver mined each year is used in industrial processes. Although a part is recovered as scrap and recycled, most of the silver mined over the past one hundred years has simply gone forever. This is not the case with gold. Most of the gold ever mined and refined over thousands of years exists even today.

A second pertinent factor that is likely to constrain future supply of silver is that while the US government holds substantial gold, it has sold off all its silver. In 1970, the US government owned around 375 million ounces of silver, what was left of the US silver purchase programme initiated in the year 1933 to help the depressed mining industry at that point of time. Therefore, prices of silver are likely to be supported by falling government supply, strong demand driven in part by ETF investors, and the continual depletion of existing inventories which cannot be recovered.

Derivatives

This is another speculative item. Wikipedia defines a derivative instrument as "a contract between two parties that specifies conditions (especially the dates, resulting values of the underlying variables, and notional amounts) under which payments, or payoffs, are to be made between the parties."

Thus, a derivative is a security whose price is dependent upon, or derived from, one or more underlying assets. The derivative itself is merely a contract between two or more parties whose value is determined by fluctuations in the price of the underlying asset. The most common underlying assets include stocks, bonds, commodities, currencies, interest rates and market indexes. Most derivatives are characterized by high leverage.

Now, since a derivative instrument derives its value from another asset, it does not have any value of its own and therefore cannot produce any cash flow. Yes, you do get cash flow when you write a derivative instrument like a call or put, but the magnitude and extent of financial risk which it carries do not allow it to be classified as an investment asset. If an investment is not an asset and its value depends on some other underlying asset, and it also has a very risky high leverage factor, i.e. by paying ₹ 1 you can take position worth of say ₹ 5, it simply means that it is a speculative item.

Currency

Many people claim to invest in currencies but it's difficult to understand how somebody can *invest* in currency. A currency is simply paper money, with no backing of real assets such as gold. For example, the Reserve Act allows the U.S. to print all the paper money it needs without any real backing.

Yet many people actually "invest" in currency, a piece of paper which is continually losing its value. I certainly don't call it investment. For example, let us take the case of the US dollar where the Fed runs the biggest and the fastest money printing machine of all! Like a capital consuming monster, trillions of US dollars in annual credit-driven spending have risen over the years to absorb much of the world's savings. The US debt, which has risen faster than its GDP for the past many years, is the world's biggest asset! The US dollar comprises more than half of the reserves of the global central banks based on their faith in America's ability to control spending and to maintain the value of "I owe all of you". Over the past hundred years, doubts about their ability to pay have driven many countries, Germany, Brazil and South Korea, to name a handful, into deep and protracted recessions due to currency devaluation, a financial disaster that the US has till now fortunately been able to avoid. Over the longer term, there is a strong possibility of the US dollar collapsing and losing its value. The same might be the fate of other paper currencies. Hence, buying and holding paper currencies can't be investing, it is speculation.

Art

This is another item which many people, particularly the rich, take pride investing in. A rare piece of art from a great artist can be sold for millions of dollars in auctions. But remember that investing in art disregards the traditional yardsticks of financial analysis since it does not generate running income streams that can be discounted. It is a bet on the price appreciation of something (portfolio income) whose value after defies financial logic. In fact, like gold, art also incurs negative income in the form of storage and other associated costs. Therefore, art can certainly not be classified as an investment asset and therefore has to be a speculative item. If you want to buy art, do so for the sake of enjoying it but not because it is an investment asset. And, remember, if you wish to buy art do so out of the income generated from investment assets and not from earned income or negative leverage.

Self Occupied House / Non-Rental Real Estate / Land

All kinds of properties, whether it be a self occupied house, non-rental real estate or land, where there is no real cash flow return in the form of running income, would be classified as speculative items. We have already discussed the benefits and need for buying your own house in Commandment 7. But if you go in for buying a bigger house not required for your self occupation, or otherwise on mortgage or purchase non-rental real estate or, worse still, land, then this would not be investing but pure speculation. All these would then be termed as speculative items. In fact, most real estate takes away money from your pocket in the form of property tax, maintenance, utility bills and other innumerable expenses. Real estate does not automatically become an investment asset if it does not pass the litmus test of cash flow in the form of running income.

Club Membership

This is something which has become akin to a status symbol in today's society. Expensive clubs have sprouted in and around big cities and towns across many countries. Their membership fees runs from a few thousands to even more than a million, depending on the type of club, etc. These club memberships may help you in your social life or sometimes even to enhance your business connections. But it is not an investment asset which can be shown on the asset side of your balance sheet. It is merely an unnecessary expense. Some may argue that life membership of a club is an asset for life. But is it going to produce running income for life? If the answer is no, then it can't be considered an investment asset. In fact, clubs entail recurring unnecessary costs in the form of charges on food, games, tournaments, events, functions, etc. These events are organized in your club in order to rob you of your hard earned money. Some may argue that since the price of club membership generally keeps on rising year after year, it's an asset. The point is that even if the cost of membership has risen, can you realize any value? Can you sell your membership and get your money back? If you can't do so, then how can it be an investment asset? Just because some "bigger fool" has paid more money than what you did, does not in any way turn the club membership from an unnecessary expense or a speculative item into an investment asset. To pass the litmus test of an investment asset, the asset must produce positive cash flow in the form of running income. A club membership, on the other hand, produces negative income in the form of renewal fees, food expenses, events, tournaments, etc. Further, you can't ever realize the perceived value of the club membership because it is not a saleable commodity. A club membership is a great cash flow producing investment asset in the books of the club — not yours.

What Do You Invest For?

Now, let's ask this simple but all important question — what do you invest for — running income or asset, i.e. portfolio, income? I would advise you to always invest for running income because that gives you a continuous return without sacrificing the investment itself. On the other hand, in order to earn asset income you have to sell, partly or fully, the asset itself. It is something like the difference between the chicken and an egg. If you have a chicken, you can get an egg every day (running income). On the other hand, you can just cut the chicken and eat it (asset income). Therefore, it's always best to invest for running income. If asset income is also generated along with it, well and good; but don't invest for that. Remember a cardinal principle of investment that if you truly invest only for running income, then it's only a matter of time before asset income is also generated. That's because when you are investing for running income you would be buying "value" and that is something which invariably gets rewarded over a period of time through an increase in asset prices. When you invest for running income, you are, in effect, investing for cash flow, and are not concerned with the interim increase or decrease in the value of the asset. If you are investing for asset income then you are more concerned about increase in the value of the asset because then and only then will you earn a return on your investment as it is not yielding any running income or cash flow. The power of positive leverage is also unleashed by net cash flow positive return on investment which can come only through running income.

Should You Invest in Speculative Items At All?

The answer to this question, contrary to what you might expect after having read the earlier part of this commandment, is a definite yes. The reason is very simple and flows from Commandment 1. Nothing can beat proper asset allocation over the long term. As an individual investor, the only thing which is your friend is proper asset allocation. And speculative items do come within the ambit of asset allocation. We have also looked at business and economic cycles and have seen how different asset classes, like equities, bonds, commodities, etc. move in cycles. We have also looked at the madness of crowds and at concepts like behavior finance, crowd psychology, etc. Simply put, every dog has his day. And you have to be with the dog when its day eventually does come.

The idea of this commandment is two-fold:

1. First, to set forth the difference between an investment asset and a speculative item. You should not be investing in a speculative item confusing it with an investment asset.
2. To assess whether, when, which and how much of a speculative item should find place in your portfolio.

I have already explained the first point. Now, let us move to the second one.

Need For a Speculative Item

There is need for a speculative item in one's portfolio and it should be a part of your overall asset allocation not only because of the higher return which it is capable of producing over certain periods of time but also because it may have nil or negative correlation with the other investment assets in your portfolio.

The following are the important reasons for including speculative items in your overall asset allocation:

- Speculative items generally have nil or negative correlation with investment assets. One of the important tenets of Commandment 1 is that the various assets you hold in your portfolio should have nil or negative correlation.
- Generally speaking, returns on speculative items are positively correlated with inflation. By their very character, speculative items don't give any running income and provide only asset income. If an item is only providing asset income, i.e. capital gains, then logically its price has to go up over a period of time in order to provide you with asset income or capital gain return. And if the price of something goes up over a period of time that means it is positively correlated with inflation. In fact, many of the speculative items themselves make up the basket from which inflation is computed.

Therefore, there is a need to allocate some funds towards speculative items in your portfolio.

When to Buy a Speculative Item

Many speculative items, such as commodities, never get the same time, attention and respect of investors, advisors and media as do stocks. And, rightly so. Having said that, it makes sense to study major speculative items like commodities — be it precious metals, industrial metals or agricultural products. This will not only increase your financial knowledge and understanding, it will make you a better equity and bond investor as well. For example, if you have knowledge of the steel industry, it will not only help you know when to buy or sell steel, it will also help you in buying or selling shares and bonds of a steel company.

As discussed earlier, different asset classes like equities, bonds, commodities, etc. move in cycles. Commodities generally move in long term cycles when their demand-supply patterns change. For example, the price of gold was stable around US $35 per ounce from the year 1934 till 1971. Over this period, the cost of production and mining kept on rising but the price of gold remained unchanged. Who would be interested in setting up the extremely capital-intensive task of exploring gold at the depths of more than 3,000 meters in such a situation? Gold production therefore kept falling over this period. Meanwhile, the US had been living off trade deficits and printing money. The US economy turned shaky and so did the dollar. By the early 1960s, there wasn't enough gold in reserve to cover the nation's liabilities to other countries. Naturally, other countries, particularly the French, turned up waving their US dollar reserves and demanding gold. The then US President Nixon realized this fact and announced that the US would no longer convert dollars into gold. This was, in effect, defaulting on America's obligation to allow europeans to redeem US dollars for gold! It defies logic but governments and central banks around the world always do their utmost to support and artificially prop up prices in currencies and commodities while the sophisticated investor knows what to look out for. With gold in demand and the supply reduced by decades of artificially low prices, the smart thing to do was buy gold at US $35 per ounce. In the following decade, gold price multiplied around 24-fold — from US $35 per ounce to US $850 per ounce — while US equities as represented by the DJIA stagnated around the same levels with a lot of volatility and large interim falls. Thereafter, gold entered a big 20-year bear market, falling by almost 70% from US $850 per ounce in the year 1980 to US $250 per ounce by the year 2000 while the US DJIA advanced 14-fold — from 1,000 in the year 1980 to 14,000 in the year 2000.

This brings home the point that markets move in cycles and everything — whether an investment asset or a speculative item — has its day and you have to have some exposure to the latter to capitalize on it. Regarding the question of when to buy and sell speculative items, try to increase allocation to them during cyclical lows and reduce exposures at close to cyclical peaks. Emphasis is placed on the words "increase and reduce" simply because at all points of time there has to be proper allocation towards them in your portfolio. Since they don't offer running income, they have to be regularly added and reduced from your portfolio in order to derive the only available source of return from them, namely asset income or capital gains.

Which Speculative Item to Buy

Perhaps there is no correct answer to this. There are lots of speculative items in this world, some of which have been covered in this chapter. There may be different commodities, like precious metals, industrial commodities and agricultural goods. As with anything else in this world, the price of a speculative item also depends on its demand and supply situation. It is very difficult sitting in one part of the world to estimate what will happen to the production of coffee in Brazil or tea in Kenya or gold in South Africa or any other metals in Brazil. It would also be difficult for you to estimate the demand for various commodities from different parts of the world at different times. I am not asking you to do all that. I am just suggesting that you increase your financial knowledge by acquainting yourself with different commodities, art, etc. by regularly reading financial newspapers and journals and keeping a tab on the latest information and news by devoting some time in understanding price movements, trends, demand, supply etc. Once you do that, it would become clear as to which speculative item would be more preferable when.

And if you can't do that, then simply invest in some diversified fund which has most of the speculative items in its portfolio.

How Much of Speculative Items to Buy

Fortunately the answer to this important question is quite simple. Remember, whenever you are confused on any such point, just take solace from Commandment 1. Follow the broad guidelines below to arrive at the best allocation for yourself:

- Allocate only that much amount on speculative items which you can bear to lose, physically and emotionally, without disturbing your long term plan for achieving financial independence.
- Only allocate that amount to speculative items on which you don't require current running income simply because speculative items by their very nature do not provide you any.
- Never use leverage to buy speculative items because that will become negative leverage.
- Never put funds in speculative items through derivatives because it will become nothing but highly leveraged exposure to non-income yielding speculative items.
- Keep re-balancing and re-allocating your portfolio, particularly when the allocation to speculative items increases due to a rise in their value. Don't forget that by their very nature speculative items don't yield any income and hence money has to be made from them only in the form of asset income or capital gains. So, keep reviewing and re-balancing your portfolio to account for any significant change in the prices of speculative items, particularly a rise in their price.

To conclude, remember the title of this commandment is a "Thou shall not over-invest in speculative items". Therefore, while you should be allocating some money to speculative items following the principles laid down in this commandment, you must never over-invest in them.

Lessons From This Commandment

1. Investment assets earn two kinds of return — running income and asset income.
2. Running income is the current realized income which the asset produces during the life of the investment.

3. Asset income is the return from your assets. It is not the "return on your assets" but a "return from your assets" — the emphasis is on the words on and from. Thus, while running income is derived as a return on your assets during the existence of the asset, asset income is the return arising from the asset itself being liquidated and sold, either partly or fully.
4. Your primary object should always be to invest for running income and that is derived only from investment assets.
5. A speculative item is an investment which is capable of producing only asset income. In other words, any investment which is not capable of producing running income would be termed as a speculative item.
6. If you are buying commodities, be they precious metals or industrial or agricultural commodities, you are investing in a speculative item. On the other hand, if you are a miner, producer, converter or farmer then you are a manufacturer, businessman or an entrepreneur.
7. Some amount of speculative items are necessary in your portfolio to comply with Commandment 1 on proper asset allocation.
8. There is a need for putting some money in speculative items because they generally have zero or negative correlation with investment assets and they are positively correlated to inflation.
9. Speculative items, like other asset classes, adhere to the investment cycle principle. Therefore, you should try to increase allocation to them during their cyclical lows and reduce exposure at close to their cyclical peaks. Emphasis is placed on the words increase and reduce simply because at all time there has to be some allocation to speculative items.
10. There is no correct answer as to which speculative item to buy. You have to increase your financial knowledge by acquainting yourself with different commodities, regularly reading financial newspapers and journals, finding out their latest information and trends and devoting some time and energy in understanding them. Once you do that, it would become clear as to which speculative item would be more preferable at different times. If

you can't do that, then simply invest in some diversified fund which has most of the speculative items in its portfolio.

11. Never over-invest in speculative items.

Self-Understanding Questionnaire

This commandment introduced you to the world of speculative items and their role in your asset allocation plan. It also tried to explain which speculative items to invest in and when, and how much to invest in them. Now, honestly answer the following questions in yes or no to assess your understanding of the principles explained in this commandment. The more the number of "yes" answers, the better is your understanding of this commandment.

1. Do you agree that certain investment options are speculative items? Yes/No?
2. Do you agree that any investment can give you two sources of income — running income and asset income? Yes/No?
3. Do you appreciate that you should invest in investment assets for current running income? Yes/No?
4. Do you think that gold is a speculative item and its price can — and has, in fact — gone up and down by wide percentages for many years altogether? Yes/No?
5. Do you understand that currency or paper money can't be an investment asset and is, in fact, just a speculative item? Yes/No?
6. Do you appreciate that a non-rental real estate is a speculative item which does not yield any current running income? That, on the contrary, it takes away money from your pocket in the form of property tax, maintenance, mortgage, etc.? Yes/No?
7. Do you agree that a club membership is a speculative item offering no running income and whose value is never realizable? Yes/No?
8. Do you understand that speculative items are an integral part of a proper asset allocation? Yes/No?

—

Chapter 10

Commandment 9

Thou Shall Take Proper Financial Insurance

- How can you earn money if you have not protected yourself?
- How can you save money if you are not sure of your future protection?
- How can you invest money if you have not protected your assets?
- How can you budget for your money when you yourself don't know how much money you will be left with after fulfilling any untoward emergency?
- How can you borrow and leverage money if you have not protected your assets?

The answer to all these hows can be found in one magic word called Insurance.

Wikipedia defines insurance as "a form of risk management primarily used to hedge against the risk of a contingent, uncertain loss. Insurance is defined as the equitable transfer of the risk of a loss from one entity to another, in exchange for payment. An insurer is a company selling the insurance; the insured, or policyholder, is the person or entity buying the insurance policy. The amount to be charged for a certain amount of insurance coverage is called the "premium".

This is a typical textbook definition. However, my definitions and meanings of financial terms for those seeking financial freedom are not the typical textbook ones. If I were to follow textbook definitions then I would not be writing this book. To attain financial independence, you have to be the master of money and not its slave.

And you cannot be the master of your destiny and your money unless you protect yourself and your money.

In my view, insurance is something which makes you free.

Insurance is something which takes away the tension of your not being there. Insurance is something which allows you to do what you want to do without worrying about failure. All the other commandments in this book seek to solve your money problems during your lifetime. This commandment seeks to solve the problems even when you are no more in this world.

We are Constantly Insuring Ourselves Against Every Possible Catastrophe

Whether you are aware or not, you are constantly, right from your birth, insuring yourself against different types of catastrophes throughout your life. When you come out of your mother's womb, you instantly start breathing to insure yourself against death. You then start feeding your mother's milk to insure yourself against hunger; you go to school to insure yourself against being an illiterate; you make friends to insure yourself against being lonely; you marry to insure yourself against being unloved; you have children to insure yourself against your name dying with you; you respect your elders to ensure their blessings, you listen to your boss to insure yourself against job loss, etc. Thus, whether you know it or not, you are always insuring yourself against some untoward event or the other which you think might or could happen. The fact that you are reading this book is to insure yourself against remaining poor — to free yourself from all your money problems.

Financial Insurance

Financial insurance is integral to the goal of achieving financial freedom. Insurance is of prime importance and should be considered a part of your financial plan, especially when you are first starting out. For example, if you have no money but have three children, insurance is important in case you die, are injured, or for whatever reason are unable to complete your investment plan. Insurance is a safety net, or a hedge against financial liabilities and weak spots. Also, as you become rich and financially independent, the role of insurance and the type of insurance in your financial plan may change but the basic need and requirement will never reduce. In fact, contrary to your expectation the quantum and diversity of insurance might actually increase. Therefore, financial insurance is a very important facet of attaining financial independence.

Financial insurance is that which makes you free to concentrate on achieving financial freedom. Financial insurance would include insurance against catastrophic events, whether real, physical, psychological, emotional or perceptional which either don't allow money to come into your pocket or take away money from your pocket. Financial insurance would accordingly mean insurance against any and everything which is a hindrance between you and your money. For example, if you constantly worry about the fate of your family in case of your untoward death, then you need financial protection. If you are worried that someone will rob you of your assets, then you need financial insurance. If you are worried about an unforeseen blow to your business profits, then you need financial insurance.

Categories of Financial Insurance

Some of the major items of financial insurance include:

- Family protection insurance
- Personal insurance
- Disability protection insurance
- Loss of profit protection
- Asset protection
- Third party insurance
- Medical insurance
- Vehicle insurance.

Family Protection Insurance

You can easily imagine what dire straits your family could be in if either you or your spouse died and the source of income was suddenly removed. Family protection insurance offers a measure of financial security should the worst happen.

Family protection insurance takes the form of term life insurance to cover possibility of the untimely death of any or all of the family's breadwinners. Term life insurance can be arranged for the number of years considered most appropriate by the policy holder, e.g. till the children leave the nest, or till the date of retirement if the protection is sought for a surviving spouse. The level of cover required will, of course, depend on the particular needs and circumstances of the family in question. This is usually arrived at by striking a balance between the monthly premiums that they can afford to pay and the lump sum payout needed to enable the surviving family members to continue to enjoy the standard of living to which they are accustomed. Now, because most term life insurance policies provide for the payment of a lump sum benefit in the event of the policy holder's death, and because this sum would then need to be invested to provide a regular replacement income, some term life insurance policies are available that pay out a "regular monthly income". These are known as family income benefit policies which, in the event of the policy holder's death, make monthly, tax-free payments of benefit from the date of the claim until the end of the policy's term. However, you should steer clear of such policies as these are beneficial to the insurer and not to you. They rob you of your insurance money. From the insurer's point of view, a lower level of benefit becomes payable with each succeeding year of the insurance term. The insurance company will claim that from the beneficiary's point of view, there is the advantage of a regular income without the worry of making potentially complicated decisions about the best investments to make — and on that pretext it will rob you of your insurance policy amount. However, since you are reading this book you will know how to take your own financial decision and won't require the help of the insurance company which will rob you of your money while claiming to protect you.

Family protection insurance should not be confused with the similar sounding income payment protection insurance. The latter also provides for the payment of a regular, monthly replacement income, but does so in the event that the policy holder is incapacitated from working because of an accident, ill-health or because he or she has become involuntarily unemployed. Although this type of insurance can play an important role in protecting the income available to a family for a temporary period, it is important to bear in mind that the vast majority of such policies have a maximum payout period of no longer than twenty-four months.

Personal Insurance

This is akin to family protection; it will protect your family against your death. If you are the sole bread earner for your family, then you must take personal insurance in the form of a term policy. Remember, insurance is like charity. You are not going to get any personal benefit with something like a term policy but it is your family who is going to benefit from it. And only if you are worry free about your family in the case of your untoward death, will you be able to work efficiently towards your full potential during your life. Therefore, personal insurance in the form of term policy should be your priority.

Disability Protection Insurance

Disability, whenever and at whatever age it might occur, can disrupt your income earning capacity, particularly "earned income" because that is the income where your full time presence is required. Once you have read and understood the commandments and principles covered in this book, you would be able to create adequate source of guaranteed, passive and portfolio incomes and would no longer be totally dependent on earned income. However, if you still depend fully, or to a large extent, on earned income then any kind of accident or illness resulting in a few months of disability can severely hinder your finances. How will you pay the mortgage, utility, telephone, school fee bills, etc. in such an eventuality? Further, there would be new unavoidable and unexpected expenses in the form of doctor's fees, medical bills, hospitalization charges, etc. These could be very taxing on you and your family and can totally disrupt your current and future financial independence.

Unfortunately, many of us will need disability income protection some time or the other before we die. A study has shown that two out of five people aged 45, will be disabled for more than 90 days before they reach the age of 65. Without disability protection, such an eventuality could spell financial disaster. Disability at any age can disrupt income while medical expenses deplete your savings. Unless you have a contingency plan, the effects of even a short-term disability can be financially and emotionally devastating. Disability insurance provides a financial safety net. In the event of a disability, the benefits provided by disability insurance effectively replace a portion of your earned income. Therefore for those who are dependent fully, or to a large extent, on earned income, disability coverage can prove to be invaluable.

While choosing a disability plan, consider having enough coverage either to replace at least 60% of your annual earned income after taxes or equal to your annual expenses, whichever is higher. Take a look at Table 10.1.

Table 10.1 shows the income statement of a typical individual with different sources of income and expenses. Now, as per the above formula, the minimum disability insurance required would be higher of the following two:

1. 60% of earned income = 60% of ₹ 80 = ₹ 48
2. Annual necessary revenue and capital expenditure and unavoidable unnecessary revenue expenditure = 30 + 20 + 5 = ₹ 55 (Assuming 50% of the unnecessary revenue expenditure is unavoidable).

Table 10.1

Income Statement for Computing Disability Protection

Expenses	*Amount*	*Income*	*Amount*
Necessary revenue expenses	30	Earned income	80
Necessary capital expenditure	20	Guaranteed income	10
Extravagant expenses	10	Passive income	5
Luxury / bad capital expenditure	10	Portfolio income	5
Surplus carried to balance sheet	30		
Total	100	Total	100

In the above example, the disability insurance amount would be the higher of the two, i.e. ₹ 55. Consider extending the time between when the disability occurs and when you start receiving benefits. Choosing a 90- or 180-day waiting period instead of a 30-day waiting period can substantially lower your cost. Be sure to compare and review policy benefits carefully. Disability insurance is an affordable and indispensable option, particularly for those who have still not achieved financial freedom.

Loss of Profit Protection

Insuring your property, buildings, fixtures and fittings, stock and equipment are obviously important but so too is adequate insurance cover for loss of profits following any loss or damage at your premises. Business interruptions do happen. Apart from the direct losses that arise from, say, a fire, there are also losses that result from the interruption of a business. If damage to your business premises forces you to shut operations while repairs are made, you will still need to pay employees, mortgages, leases and other debts. These ongoing expenses can mount up quickly for a business that has reduced income — or no income at all. A policy which protects against loss of profits could act as a vital lifeline for businesses.

You should also consider having a **machinery loss of profits policy**. While a normal fire or machinery insurance policy does help you recover any material loss sustained, it does not protect you against any losses incurred due to fire or breakdown. The financial loss due to the loss of profits and the standing or fixed charges still being incurred after the loss are what get covered under the machinery loss of profits insurance. These policies generally cover against reduction in turnover and increase in cost of working.

There is another type of policy called **advance loss of profits policy**. While undertaking any project, cash flows form a vital part of the strategy. The projections are made for the revenue flow from the date of project completion / commissioning. Invariably, there may arise situations where the entire project gets delayed due to a mishap at the project site or due to an accident to the vessel carrying machinery vital to the commissioning of the plant. Both principals and contractors are being confronted with increasing financial risk exposure. As a result of the use of leverage, protecting the revenue stream with appropriate insurance is increasingly regarded as of equal, if not greater, importance than protecting the assets themselves.

Sweeping changes in the international political landscape and widespread market deregulation have made trade the driving force in our globalised economy. But expanding sales and building new customer relationships can leave balance sheets vulnerable. Economic downturns, privatization of public entities and inconvertibility or non-transfer of currency can leave your customers unable to pay what they owe you. And often by the time customer insolvency or credit loss is foreseen, it's too late to protect the company's account receivables. In most industries, accounts receivable generally make up nearly 75% of a company's current assets. And like all major balance sheet assets, they require insurance protection. The insurance which protects against this is termed as **credit insurance**.

Asset Protection

Suppose a few years ago you took a loan of ₹ 1 million for your business because you anticipated continued growth. But the economy soon fell apart, and so did your business. You can no longer pay back the loan, and the lender has filed a lawsuit both against your company and you personally, threatening to seize your home, car, and cash in the bank.

This is a common scenario for owners of small businesses, even those structured as corporations or limited liability partnerships because they are not always as well protected against determined creditors as they might think. While this probably isn't too surprising, you may be personally exposed to plenty of other circumstances beyond non-payment of loans — including non-payment to suppliers, tax liabilities, malpractice, default on equipment financing, default on mortgages, negligent acts, fraud, legal action from employees (such as from sexual harassment or wrongful discharge), and liabilities for environmental damage.

This sounds an unnerving scenario — right? Well, you can take steps now to deal with the risks by averaging in asset protection. Here are some suggestions as to what you consider doing.

Inventory Everything

Make a complete list of your assets and debts. It's a good idea to do this on a regular basis, — say, every quarter or so. Remember to think broadly. For example, do you own a vacation home or have retirement assets? Do you hold stocks in another company? These can have lots of value and may end up being taken away in litigation.

Research Exemptions and Protective Entities

A few of your assets may be exempt from creditor actions due to certain laws. These typically include your personal residence, your pension or retirement fund, and your life insurance policy. These should generally be the only ones in your name. For all other assets, consider setting up so-called protective entities, such as domestic trusts and offshore trusts. You can even layer the protection by using multiple entities. You can go even further and equity-strip the assets. This means taking loans against the assets or refinancing them — positive leverage. This makes the asset less attractive to creditors.

Avoid Personal Guarantees

A personal guarantee is when you pledge to be personally responsible for a debt. The result is that essentially you lose the protection of your company's corporate status. If you still have to give personal guarantee for, say, a bank loan for your business enterprise, then a safe approach would be to put a time limit on it (say, for one year) or to specify a particular asset as collateral.

Be Wary of the Contracts You Sign

While your company's corporate structure may provide some protection, it may not be enough if there's a tort action or claim for fraud. In such cases, you may have personal liability. That's why it's important to provide liability protection in your contracts. This includes capping damages and even disallowing certain types of damages. Also, make sure you sign contracts on behalf of your company and not in your personal name, in order to avoid the chance of the contract later being considered a personal guarantee.

Buy Insurance

While asset protection can be extremely helpful in avoiding personal liability, a creditor may still be determined to go after your assets. That's why it is important to have insurance protection. Liability insurance covers damages for personal injuries and property damages that other people cause — such as your employees.

Property insurance covers your company's assets. You may even consider an umbrella policy to cover exposure that goes beyond property insurance. As should be no surprise, carriers try to avoid paying claims. To get the best coverage, it's a good idea to have an attorney look at the policy.

For any kind of asset protection, it's smart to get the advice of a qualified attorney or tax expert. You'll likely be dealing with complicated questions. Remember that running a business is quite risky, regardless of the economic environment. Even top companies can and do fail sometimes. So, it's worthable spending some time to look at your potential liability exposures and see how asset protection will help lower your risks.

Third Party Insurance

The dictionary defines third party as a generic term for any individual who does not have a direct connection or a stake with a transaction, but who may be affected by it. In an insurance policy, first party is the insured person or the person who buys the policy while the second party is the insurance company which agrees to compensate a third party in case the insured person causes any damage to the third person. The insured person pays a premium to the insurance company who agrees to compensate the third party up to the sum insured. Therefore, third party insurance is a cover for this third party. Known as third party liability cover, it compensates for any damages made to a third party by the first party, i.e. the insured person. In other words, third party insurance is the coverage that you have on people other than those people actually on the policy.

The most popular form of third party insurance is the “motor third party liability”. It is a cover that gives you protection in case of damage by your vehicle to life or property of a third person. This is the most popular third party cover and is generally mandatory in most countries for all vehicles plying on the roads.

Medical Insurance

Medical insurance covers individuals and their families against unforeseen expenses arising from illness, injury or accidents. You may purchase auto insurance to repair your vehicle in case of an accident or homeowner's insurance to protect your property but what about protecting and repairing your health when you fall ill or meet with an unexpected accident? Medical insurance offers you such protection and this is always a smart investment. Today with medical costs rising dramatically each year, even relatively simple medical procedures can run into several thousands of rupees. In addition, the type of care available and various policy options are also becoming more complex. So, it's important to make intelligent and sensible decisions by selecting and subscribing to the best medical insurance policy available.

Vehicle Insurance

Wikipedia defines vehicle insurance (also known as auto insurance, gap insurance, car insurance, or motor insurance) as "insurance purchased for cars, trucks, motorcycles, and other road vehicles." Its primary use is to provide financial protection against physical damage and / or bodily injury resulting from traffic collisions and against liability that could also arise therefrom. Vehicle insurance is the protection you need in case you are in an accident with another car, pedestrian, or stationary object. Just as with any other insurance policy you have, you will pay a fee, or premium, that will cover you in case of this unexpected event. It is very important and also compulsory to have a vehicle insurance.

Other Important Categories of Financial Insurance

There is another category of financial insurance which you require in order to protect yourself and your wealth from money predators. This section will introduce you to those types of financial insurance which you need if you want to grow and secure your wealth. However, the sad point is that no insurance company would provide you with this category of insurance. In essence, then, you have to become your own insurance company and secure insurance for your assets all by yourself! How to do so? Read on.

Legal Insurance

There are lots of rogues around the world who know how to legally rob you of your money. Remember that there are thousands of people out their waiting for any excuse to use a lawsuit to get rich. There are people and their lawyers who specialize in these kinds of cases. And the richer and wealthier you get, the more the legal rogues will be on the prowl against you. That's why you require your own legal insurance against them.

To protect yourself from these legal rogues you need to do the following:

1. First things first; don't hold assets of much value in your personal name. Hold assets in legal entities, such as a company, a limited liability partnership, a trust, etc. This not only provides your assets the safety by separating you as an individual from your asset but also provides perpetual succession. Therefore, your asset is protected not only during your lifetime but also when you pass away from this planet.
2. Understand that sole proprietorship and unlimited liability partnership firms are bad legal entities. They are bad since not only do they put your business assets at risk but also put at risk your personal assets, if something were to go wrong with your business.
3. You should also consider taking up personal liability insurance which is nothing but a kind of risk financing to protect the purchaser from the risks of liabilities imposed by lawsuits and similar claims. It protects the insured in the event he or she is sued for claims that come within the coverage of the insurance policy.
4. To protect yourself from legal rogues and their lawyers, you need to set up your own team of lawyers to protect yourself from such an unexpected event. Don't underestimate the need for good lawyers because these are the people who protect you from

"legal rogues" and allow you to be in the business of being in the business.

Tax Insurance

This is another important insurance which you require but no insurance company in the world will offer it to you. As mentioned in Commandment 2, the taxman is the biggest legal predator of all as he legally and systematically takes away money from your pocket at all times — whether it be earning, saving, spending, investing, insuring, etc. Hence it's of paramount importance that you take a "tax insurance" to protect yourself from the taxman. Now, you would be wondering what tax insurance is and who will provide it to you. Tax insurance is something which you have to arrange yourself as nobody in the world will provide it to you. Use the following different techniques at various stages of your dealing with money in order to get a tax insurance.

1. At the Time of Earning

As mentioned earlier in the book, the government taxes income for which you work the hardest at the maximum rate while it taxes at the minimum rate such income which your money produces for you. Therefore, always strive to increase your passive and portfolio incomes.

2. At the Time of Spending

You can save tax even at the time of spending by paying it out of pre-taxed income and not out of your post-taxed income. The simple solution for this again lies in using the right legal structure, such as a company, limited liability partnership, trust, etc. Therefore, make the expenses through such legal entities and make government your partner in both income and also your expenses!

3. At the Time of Purchasing

There are different kinds of indirect taxes such as sales tax, service tax, excise duty, customs duty, etc., which government levies on you when you make purchases. However, all items purchased are not taxed equally. So, acquaint yourself with which goods and services are taxed higher and then try to purchase alternate goods or services which are taxed at a lower rate. For example, many a time the tax rate on luxury items is higher than on necessary items. So, when buying luxury goods not only do you spend a lot of money you also have to shell out an indiscriminate proportion of taxes and levies on them.

4. At the Time of Investing

The government also taxes you at the time of investing. For example, the government charges stamp duty when you invest in real estate, and securities transaction tax (STT) when you invest in equities. There is little you can do to protect yourself against these taxes but you can certainly plan your investments in such a manner that you get as much tax efficient income as possible, e.g. from equity dividends, long term capital gains, etc. so as to reduce your overall tax bill while investing.

5. At the Time of Insuring

The government does not spare you even while insuring as it collects various taxes, like service tax. Here, too, there is little protection available to you from the tax predator.

Remember that the government taxes you at every stage of the money chain — saving, spending, investing, insuring, etc. One of the simplest ways of taking tax insurance is to legally convert all your expenses to "pre-tax expense" and your taxable savings to tax free investments.

Job Protection

This is another protection which each one of us requires though we seldom realize that we need it. Even if we realize it, we don't understand how to get it and if by any chance we do understand how to get it we don't acknowledge its importance and fail to motivate ourselves to acquire it. The protection I am talking about is the protection which we require against the possibility of being unable to remain in the business in which we are today. And, mind you, business not only means pure business in the traditional sense but also any other work in which we are actively engaged and on which our financial security depends. Examples of it would include our current employment, spouse, educational qualifications, government regulations, etc. You will see weird items in this list. I will explain a couple of them for more clarity.

For example, suppose you are a housewife. Not only your love and family life but even your financial security depends on this status. Hence, God forbid, if for any reason you were to be divorced from your husband, not only would you lose your love and family but also your financial security.

Let us take another example — that of a chartered accountant. Today, all companies are required to get their annual reports and balance sheets audited and signed by a qualified practicing chartered accountant. Suppose the government were to remove this provision tomorrow, many practicing chartered accountants might simply lose their bread and butter overnight.

In simple term, competitor protection means protection for the competitive strength which you possess and on which your financial security depends. I don't have any specific answer for protection from different competitive threats that you might be facing but one suggestion is not to specialize but be a generalist. You must have heard the saying "jack of all, master of none". To your surprise I am advising you that try to be a "jack of all." Surely, you may be "master of one" but with it also try to be "jack of all". This is because the more you specialize, the more you are dependent on that singular job or industry. For example, if you only know sailing, however good a sailor you may be, you are totally dependent on the shipping industry and if for any reason that industry gets into some kind of problem and you were to lose your job, then your qualification and experience would be too specialized to find a job in another company or industry.

Love Protection

Now I will cover a very sensitive and delicate issue but the fact of the matter is that in today's modern world many people, both men and women, do get married for money. And the more the amount of money you have, the more people love you and want to get married to you. Such people are "love predators" as mentioned in Commandment 2. Many people were legally (as well as emotionally) looted by such love predators who not only ruined their lives emotionally but also financially. Many rich people had to part with almost half of their assets to such love predators. There is no insurance available against love predators. The only thing which you can do is take "love protection". What I mean by this is that you obviously do due diligence before getting married but, if possible, also have an exit plan ready in the form of a prenuptial agreement. It may be socially and emotionally uncomfortable but it's certainly financially wise to do so.

Portfolio Insurance

You invest your life's savings into different assets, like equities, bonds, real estate, commodities, art, etc. But what if the price of the asset which you buy falls? What if you bought US equities just one trading day prior to Black Monday, i.e. 19 October 1987, and lost 22.6% of your money in just a single day? You don't have any control over such events. You don't — and can't — know when the market is going to crash. Which is why you need portfolio insurance. Now, insurance companies don't sell insurance policies against paper assets, i.e. equities, bonds, etc., they do so only against physical assets.

What, then, is portfolio insurance? It is simply following Commandment 1 and having a proper asset allocation plan. That's all. Howsoever big the fall in one asset class may then be, its effect on your overall portfolio would be very limited. Don't believe it? Look at Table 10.2 which takes the above example of losing 22.6% in a single day and its effect on a well diversified asset allocated portfolio.

Table 10.2

Portfolio Insurance through Asset Allocation

Asset Class	*Before Black Monday %*	*After Black Monday %*
Equities	25.0	19.4
Bonds	25.0	25.0
Commodities	25.0	25.0
Real Estate	25.0	25.0
Total	100.0	94.4

I have taken a very simple but extreme example to bring home this point. I have assumed that your portfolio comprises four asset classes, namely, equities, bonds, commodities and real estate and you have allocated equally, i.e. 25% each, to all four of them. The first column shows the portfolio status before Black Monday while the second one shows it after the Black Monday, the day when equities lost 22.6% in a single day. Typically, equities don't lose 22.6% in a single day and this Black Monday has happened only once in the US DJIA's 116-year history. However, even with such an extreme loss of 22.6% in a single day, the total portfolio value fell by a much more muted 5.6% — from 100 to 94.4. That is what I call portfolio insurance through asset allocation — each asset class in your portfolio complements and supports the other ones, during both bull and bear markets. This again highlights the significance of Commandment 1 and the overarching importance of a proper asset allocation plan.

The above were unique but very important set of dangers against which you require "financial insurance" but which no insurance company would provide you. You have to understand the risk involved in it and take appropriate action yourself.

Insurance is Either Getting Everything Or Nothing for Something

This is a very important point which I want to drive home. In this world, nobody just gives away anything. They always want something in return. If we love somebody, we want love in return; if we respect somebody, we want respect in return, and so on. The same psychological attitude leads people to go in for insurance policies which "return" something on maturity. This is a confused approach to insurance. Always bear in mind that insurance is only insurance. It simply means that if the catastrophic event happens, then you will get the full sum assured; if it does not, you will nothing.

However, if you think that you should get something in return even if nothing untoward happens then you are making a grave financial mistake because insurers are very bad money managers. Their costs are very high and the return very poor. If a typical bond gives you, say, 10% return then an insurance policy will give you a very poor return, of around 7%, if that, which when compounded over longer term — and typically, insurance policies are for long term — is devastating for your finances.

For example, ₹ 1 lakh when compounded at 10% and 7% for 25 years turns into ₹ 1.08 million and ₹ 0.54 million , respectively. Therefore, money multiplies 10-fold over 25 years if compounded at 10% as compared to just doubling when compounded at 7%. The net result is that you end up with double the corpus over a 25-year period.

That is what happens when you take insurance to get back something; you do get something back but only half of what you deserve! That is financial stupidity. Therefore, never go in for policies like money back policies, endowment policies, guaranteed return policies, etc. because the only thing which they will guarantee is poor investment performance with high fees. Always stick only to pure term policies.

Never Confuse or Combine investment with Insurance

Many people view insurance as an investment vehicle. Insurance is not investing otherwise why would there be two different financial products at all? Never combine investments with insurance. Don't forget that insurance is always a bad investment. Think of the insurance premium as an expense. So let insurance be only insurance while investment is something totally different. You invest money for earning returns while you take insurance for providing for any untoward event. Stick to pure life insurance in the form of a term policy. This advice may be contrary to what most financial planners and experts suggest, but that's because their commission on pure term policy is the lowest. The proof that the commission is the minimum on term policy is a further indicator that even the insurance company believes it is the best product; the expenses are the minimum in it, the insurance company's earnings are the least in it and hence it does not think it appropriate to promote this product! Keep insurance separate from your investments.

What To Do With Your New-found "Wealth" — the Insurance Claim Money?

This is another important question which nobody generally thinks about. Every advisor usually advises you on which policy to take but nobody advises you on what to do with the insurance money. Suppose you are the unfortunate young widow of a man who has died and have received a reasonable sum in insurance. There will be lots of so-called financial planners and advisors running after you to sell you the next "hot" investment product with your newly found insurance "wealth". Such advisors are even worse than vultures who pounce on the remains of the dead. If you have never handled finances in your life, the situation will be a nightmare for you. Don't worry. Try and stay calm while you mentally and emotionally deal with the trauma of losing your spouse. To start with, just put the money in a money market liquid mutual fund scheme or lock it into a short term, say 3-month, bank fixed deposit. This will help you "buy" some time till you grow emotionally and mentally calmer and only then take an informed decision. Also, it will give you time to figure out if there were any liabilities of your late spouse, such as any big credit card payments or personal loans which you may have to account for. Once you have clearly understood the estate, liabilities, tax status, etc. of your spouse, then just follow Commandment 1. If your spouse had already made an asset allocation plan, then just assess, review and appraise the plan and make any necessary changes by including the insurance sum in it. Nothing can bring back your loved one but at least you can secure yourself and your children and other family members' financial security.

Lessons From This Commandment

1. It would not be possible for you to properly earn, save, invest, budget, borrow or leverage without adequate financial insurance.
2. Financial insurance simply means insurance against any and everything which is a hindrance to you and your money — whether by not allowing you to earn more money, save money,

invest money or in any form take money away from your pocket.

3. The main category of financial insurance includes family protection, personal insurance, disability protection, asset protection, loss of profit protection and medical insurance.
4. Family protection offers a measure of financial security if the worst should happen, i.e. should you or your spouse pass away unexpectedly.
5. Personal insurance is similar to family protection and will protect your family against your untimely death. If you are the sole bread earner for your family, then you absolutely need personal insurance in the form of a term policy.
6. Disability, whenever and at whatever age it might occur, can disrupt your earning capacity. Disability insurance provides a financial safety net. In the event you experience a disability, the benefits provided by disability insurance effectively replace a portion of your earned income. Therefore, disability coverage can prove to be invaluable for those who are dependent fully, or to a large extent, on earned income.
7. Insuring your property, buildings, fixtures and fittings, stock and equipment are obviously important but so too is the need for adequate cover for "loss of profits" following loss or damage of your premises and machinery. You may also require credit insurance against customer insolvency in order to protect your balance sheet.
8. You may be personally exposed to plenty of other circumstances beyond non-payment of loans — including non-payment to suppliers, tax liabilities, malpractice, default on equipment financing, default on mortgages, negligent acts, fraud, legal action from employees (such as from sexual harassment or wrongful discharge), and liabilities for environmental damage. To protect yourself from all such eventualities, you require asset protection and liability insurance.
9. You may also require third party insurance. The most popular form of third party insurance is the motor third party liability. It is a cover that gives you protection in case of damage by your vehicle to life or property of a third person.

10. You may purchase auto insurance to repair your vehicle in case of an accident, or homeowner's insurance to protect your property but what about protecting and repairing your health when you fall ill or meet with an unexpected accident. Medical insurance offers you such protection, covering individuals and their families against unforeseen expenses arising from illness, injury or accidents.
11. If you own any vehicle, whether for personal or business purpose, you would require vehicle insurance whose primary purpose is to provide financial protection against physical damage and / or bodily injury resulting from traffic collisions and against liability that could also arise there from.
12. There is also another category of financial insurance which you require in order to protect yourself and your wealth from the various money predators. This category includes legal insurance — protection against legal rogues; tax insurance — protection against the government's taxman; job protection — to be able to remain in your existing business; love protection — against the love predators; and portfolio insurance which would protect your assets against untoward large losses. These are the financial insurances which you need if you want to grow and secure your wealth. However, no insurance company provides you with such insurance and, in essence, you have to become your own insurance company and secure your assets all by yourself.
13. Don't expect something in return for your premium payments except the protection which the insurance intends to provide you with. Also, never combine investments with insurance. Don't forget that insurance is always bad investment and that investments should not provide you with insurance.
14. With regards to any money received by way of an insurance claim, first place it with a money market liquid fund or a short term bank fixed deposit and then just follow the principles of asset allocation explained in Commandment 1.

Self-Understanding Questionnaire

This commandment dealt with financial insurance. Unless you take financial insurance against different kinds of risks concerning your own self, your family members, your business, your assets and certain entities, you will not be able to achieve financial freedom. Now, honestly answer the following questions in yes or no to test your understanding of the principles explained in this commandment. The more the number of your "yes" answers, the better is your understanding of this commandment.

1. Do you believe that financial insurance is as important in achieving your financial freedom as are the other processes of saving, budgeting, spending and investing? Yes/No?
2. Do you think that financial insurance should cover you not only when you pass on from this world but even while you are still alive? Yes/No?
3. Do you concur that financial insurance not only covers live human beings but also tangible valuables like assets and also intangible valuables like business profits? Yes/No?
4. Do you realize that there are some risks to you from the legal and tax system, etc. which no insurance company will cover you against and so you have to set up such processes and systems for yourself? Yes/No?
5. Do you understand and accept that insurance is for protection and should not be confused with investments? Yes/No?
6. Are you aware of that not only is it important to take adequate policies but what you do with the claim amount is equally important as you simply cannot squander it away and defeat the whole purpose of insurance? Yes/No?

—

Chapter 11

Commandment 10

Thou Shall Learn the Rules of Money

MONEY HAS ITS OWN RULES BUT NEITHER SCHOOL EDUCATION nor a textbook will teach you these rules. You have to understand and figure them out on your own. And, remember, unless you know the rules of money, all the previous commandments will be of limited value. If you don't learn the rules of money and learn how to master money, you will always remain its slave.

Money Rule Number 1: Money is Not the Solution to the Problem of Money, Financial Knowledge is

If money is your problem, how can it be the solution? If hunger is the problem, then food is the solution. If illiteracy is the problem, then education is the solution. If loneliness is the problem, then a good friend is the solution. If unemployment is the problem, then a job becomes the solution. Therefore, the problem itself cannot be the solution.

So, if money is your problem then money itself can't be the solution. And when I refer to money being your problem, it could either be an excess or a lack of money. Yes, contrary to what most people think — it's not only lack of money but also its excess which can be a problem.

Since everybody knows, or at least everyone thinks they know, that scarcity of money is a problem, let me first touch upon the problem of excess money. If you have more money than you possibly know how to spend in your entire life and you still hanker for more, then obviously you are a very unhappy person living an extremely poor life. I am not talking of such people here. By excess money, here I mean those people who have money but don't know what to do with it; how to take care of it, how to spend it, budget it, protect it from financial predators, create positive leverage to unleash its power, invest it, grow it or insure it. Such people have money but don't have adequate knowledge about money. This can be a very dangerous situation. They may have got the money through inheritance, or by winning a lottery, or gambling. Some sports persons, movie stars and celebrities also acquire a lot of money very fast without gaining any knowledge about money.

And what, finally, is money? It's nothing but paper currency and if you don't know how to handle it, then either it will burn you or burn itself out. Then, too, money never comes alone. It brings with it all kinds of financial predators and money vultures such as the taxman, friends who you never saw before, foes pretending to be friends, relatives whom you are meeting for the first time in your life, all kinds of financial advisors — stock brokers, real estate agents, bond dealers, etc. Unless you know how to protect, budget, save, spend, leverage, invest and insure your money, it will be very difficult for you to take care of it. There is every likelihood that not only may you lose your money, you may even end up in bad debt. So, remember, that money is nothing but paper currency — similar to electric current. Just as electricity keeps flowing from one circuit to another, money keeps flowing from one person to another unless you know how to use its potential to light up your house.

Now let us address the problem of people who don't have enough money. Their problem is not so much less money but their belief that they have less money — and the fear that they will always have less money. What is money in today's modern world? Is it some precious metal like gold whose supply is limited, or real estate which cannot be expanded beyond this world, or a perishable item like fruit or vegetables which can't be stored beyond a few hours or days? No. Money is neither perishable, nor is its supply limited, nor is it the slave of any particularly individual. It is available to anybody. Money is simply an idea. That's all. If you have an idea, then no one can stop you from becoming rich — there are lots of rich people out there waiting to invest in profitable ventures. Positive leverage is easily available in today's modern banking system.

The point I want to make here is that lack of money is not the problem — the lack of knowledge about money is the problem. If you know how to protect, budget, save, spend, leverage, invest and insure your money, then nobody can stop you from becoming rich. And not only will you become rich, you will also stay wealthy. In any field, whether it be business, sports, movies, etc., it's easier to become number one but very difficult to retain the top position. Knowledge about money and its working is the only way to not only become rich but also staying wealthy for generations.

Money, therefore, cannot be the solution to any of your money problems. The solution is financial knowledge and how you deal with money.

Money Rule Number 2: Be the Master of Money

A majority of people are just slaves to money. If you become a slave to something, do you think that thing is going to solve your problems? I don't think so. If you become slave to money, then you will always think that money is scarce, which is not the case because money is so abundant that central banks can and are printing money at will. So, money is freely available. But if you become a slave to money then you will never think that you can earn enough because a slave can't take over its master. If you consider yourself a slave to money, then you will also not be able to protect yourself against the various financial predators because, by definition, a slave cannot protect its master. If you deem yourself a slave to money then how will you budget for your money because the slave does not budget for its master; it's the reverse. If you remain a slave to money then you will not be able to unleash the power of leveraging money because a slave cannot overpower its master. If you imagine yourself as slave to money then you will not be in a position to grow your money through investing because a slave can't grow beyond its master. If you are of the opinion that you are a slave to money then you would never be able to properly and adequately insure your money because a slave cannot insure its master.

Due to lack of financial education, most people spend their lives as wage slaves of their employers, tax slaves of the government, and "loan slaves" of the banks. How do you recognize whether you are a slave of money or not?

- If you look at security instead of freedom, then you are a slave to money.
- If you believe in working for somebody rather than doing your own work then you are a slave to money.
- If you believe in handing your money to an "expert" to investment rather than doing it yourself then you are a slave to money.
- If you believe in job security, medical benefits, your employer's retirement plan, government support, and such like — you are a slave of money.

If you are not a slave to money then you will not cling to job security, nor pay unnecessary taxes to the government, nor just save money to be eaten up by the monster of inflation, nor be afraid of debt. Instead, you will unleash the power of positive leverage, you will not just blindly trust fund managers, financial planners and brokers. If you are not a slave to money then you will not avoid taking financial decisions but actually wake up and take responsibility of your finances.

Money Rule 2 informs, encourages and persuades you to become a master of money. And once you imagine, think, believe and, indeed become the master of your money, you will then see how the world of money changes for you and you will automatically set off on the road to financial freedom.

Money Rule Number 3: Don't Run After Money

There is a saying which tells us never to run after three things, a train, a bus and a girl for when one goes, another one comes along (my sincere apologies to all the ladies but I am just mentioning this an example to drive home a tricky point). I will add a fourth item to this list — money. Just think. If you really want something and deserve it then do you think you should run after it? Are you going to get something by just running after it? A child may like the moon, but can it get it by running after it?

Instead, be a magnet which attracts money. Have you ever seen the sun? It's a big, powerful magnet which attracts all the other planets, including our earth, to revolve around it. You also need to turn yourself into a magnet and attract money towards yourself. By reading and learning about the principles, functioning and working of money, you can turn yourself into a financial magnet which not only attracts money but also ensures that there will always be plenty of money around you.

Money has peculiar ways. Nothing can be as simple — or as difficult — as money. It's the most peculiar thing. It's available in abundance — does anyone know the amount of money in circulation in all currencies in all the countries around the world? I don't and probably no government or central bank knows it either — but we all know that it's available in great abundance. The amount of money in circulation in all the countries across the world is perhaps many times more than any other commodity. So, where is the scarcity of money? It's only in your mind. Just free up and open up your mind and you will see the abundance of money.

Money Rule Number 4: Invest Time Before You Invest Money

What is the most important and perishable thing in this world? It is certainly not money because that can be printed and invented. It is not any other material possession. It is, in fact, time, because all other things are created by using this most precious thing of all. Everything has its own time — the earth revolves around the sun and on its own axis in a particular time period, the child grows up in a particular time period, food gets cooked in a particular time period, we all come to this world for a particular time period, etc. I have seen young people jumping into investments with hardly any experience or knowledge, thinking that there is some quick, easy and effortless formula of making money. Nothing is farther away from truth. Can anybody even imagine becoming the CEO of a big company with just six months' experience, or a star soccer player with six weeks of training and practice, or a university professor with just an under graduate degree? How, then, can a person without any experience dream of becoming rich overnight when even seasoned and experienced investors fail to do so? Therefore, my friend, before you invest money, always invest time to learn about money and its strange ways. Learn how money has been made and lost in this world before you commit your own money. Learn the simple economic principle that "one man's profit is another man's loss". Always invest time and learn about money before actually committing and investing money. By reading this book, you are indeed investing your time in learning about money.

Money Rule Number 5: Be In Control of Your Money

We imagine that we have full command and control of our money. That may not necessarily be true:

- If you are working for earned income in the form of salary then do you have control over where your money is directed by your employer? Such as into your retirement fund which you have no control over? Or, when might you receive back the money and at what rate of return?
- When you are earning guaranteed income in the form of bank interest, do you have any control as to the amount of tax which you pay?
- When you are saving money through bonds then do you recognize the risk of the monster of inflation eating through your purchasing power?
- When you invest money in assets about which you have no knowledge and no control over the income, cash flow or balance sheet, then do you understand the accompanying risk of erosion of capital?
- When you go in for money back or market related insurance policies, do you think you have control over your future protection?

If you have no control over spending money and don't know whether you really need to spend it on a particular item, do you recognize the risk that spending on items which you don't require will one day leave you with not enough money for spending on things which you actually need?

And, above all, when you don't have control over yourself and your own mind, how do you expect to have control over your money? No matter how good a car might be, if you as a driver don't have control over it, then no one would be ready to bet on it. Remember, if you are not a master of your mind, then you will become a slave of your actions.

The only way to be in control of your money is to improve your knowledge about money. Whether you invest in stocks, bonds, real estate, commodities or a business is not important. If you are a fool and don't have knowledge about money and its functioning, then in all probability you will lose money, no matter what you invest it in. Therefore, increase your financial knowledge so as to gain control over your money to achieve financial freedom.

Money Rule Number 6: Don't Work for Money; Make Your Money Work for You

Nobody can really become rich and stay wealthy by just working for money. If you keep working for money throughout your life, that's all you will end up doing throughout your life.

Suppose, you are a salaried employee. Whom do you make rich — yourself or your company? Of course, your company; you just get a salary, that's all. Typically, the overall total aggregate salaries of all the people working in a company would be less than 10% of its profits. Which means you get less than 10% while your company owners get the remaining 90%. And the irony is that you are working for money (salary) while the owner's money is working for him through investment assets in the business. Therefore you can only expect to remain poor and get poorer if you keep working for money throughout your life. Never accept a job for the salary; you might actually finish poorer at the end of it.

And don't forget one thing; if you are working for money then from January to April, i.e. for four out of twelve months you are working for the government since you pay almost one-third of your gross salary to government in taxes! You must learn to protect yourself from the different legal financial predators by playing the money game in your favor. To encapsulate, be smart with your money by making it work for you — and not *vice versa.*

Money Rule Number 7: Understand the Nature of Your Incomes and Expenses

This is a very important rule which, along with Rule 6, forms the backbone of your achieving financial freedom.

Table 11.1 shows the income statement and Table 11.2 shows the balance sheet. However, the various items don't appear here, in the traditional way. Instead, the incomes and expenses are classified based on how and from which source they are earned and how and

Table 11.1
Income Statement

Expenses	*Income*
Necessary expenses	Earned income
Necessary capital expenditure	Guaranteed income
Unnecessary (luxury) expenses	Passive income
Bad capital expenditure	Portfolio income
Wasteful capital expenditure	
Surplus going to investment assets in balance sheet (Table 11.2)	

Table 11.2
Balance Sheet

Liabilities	*Assets*
Your own money	Investment assets
Positive leverage	Necessary capital assets
Negative leverage	Bad capital assets
	Wasteful capital assets

on what items they are spent. We have already been introduced to the different items appearing in the income statement. The important points to be understood in this rule of money are the following steps:

Step 1: Convert Earned Income into Guaranteed and Passive Incomes

The first step is to convert earned income into guaranteed and passive incomes by buying investment assets. To do so, you can even take the help of positive leverage.

This is the primary tenet of income and unless you follow it you will continue to remain a slave to money, working for it and being robbed by the various legal financial predators.

Step 2: Minimize Guaranteed Income

The next step would be to minimize guaranteed income as it's against the principles of Commandment 3.

Step 3: Let Passive Income Keep Flowing and Convert Some of It into Portfolio Income

Passive income is the most efficient source of income since in this case you don't work for money; your money works for you. Further, with passive income, over time, start creating some amount of portfolio income, depending on the overall situation and in compliance with proper asset allocation as explained in Commandment 1.

Step 4: Let Your Earned Income Pay for Your Necessary Expenses

Limit your necessary expenses to the extent of only your earned income. And that's all — the purpose of earned income is only so much, and nothing more.

Step 5: Let Your Guaranteed, Passive and Portfolio Incomes Pay for Your Unnecessary Expenses and Good, Bad and Wasteful Capital Assets

This is perhaps the most important of all the points. The guaranteed, passive and portfolio incomes from your investment assets must pay for all your other expenditure — both unnecessary luxury expenses as well as the good, bad and wasteful capital assets.

Most people remain poor because they don't understand this simple rule of money. The poor can neither pay for their current expenses nor provide for their future. The middle class have liabilities which they mistake to be assets and keep throwing good money after bad by taking negative leverage to fund them their whole lives. The rich, on the other hand, have investment assets which give them income to buy even more investment assets and they can then spend without a care. The key is to convert liabilities into assets.

Money Rule Number 8: Spend Money and Grow Rich

Does this sound odd? You may think that I have gone crazy. But just sit back and consider what I have to say.

Why do you go to school? To gain knowledge and some qualification so that you can then find a good job or start some business, right? Essentially, you spend money — often a lot of money — on your education so that you can earn money in the future. Again, many companies spend millions of dollars on advertisement, publicity and sales promotion. Why? To increase their sales and profits. If you are a new investor, you would probability join some course related to investments and / or purchase some stock investment books. Why? Clearly, so that you can increase your knowledge and understanding and earn more profits through stock investing.

In all of the above cases, you are actually spending money in order to get rich. Thus, many times you have to spend money in order to get rich! The test is that the money spent should give you some kind of benefit or advantage which can then be converted into tangible wealth.

Knowing when to spend to get rich is tricky. Cutting back on the necessary spending in order to get rich is like cutting the cost on your car fuel and hoping that the car will keep running on its own. Neither the car runs without fuel nor can you become really rich unless you know how to spend money on the right things.

Money Rule Number 9: Recognize the Actual Money You are Dealing With

Seemingly very straight forward, this is not an easy rule to understand.

For example, take the case of earnings. When you are a salaried employee with a salary of ₹ 10 lakh and getting only ₹ 7 lakh in hand because of the 30% tax imposed by that legal financial predator — the taxman, then you are not earning ₹ 10 lakh but only ₹ 7 lakh which is what you actually take home and keep.

On the other hand, if you have your own company engaged in business and paying an effective rate of tax (after claiming all the permissible expenses and deductions) of 15% on ₹ 10 lakh and retaining ₹ 8,50,000, then you are earning ₹ 8,50,000. Therefore, in the first case you actually earn only ₹ 7,00,000 while in the second case you earn ₹ 8,50,000.

So, it is important to know the actual amount of money that you are earning.

Let us take the example of insurance. If you take a money back policy with a sum assured of ₹ 15,00,000 by paying ₹ 1,00,000, the real insurance component in it might be around ₹ 5,000 to ₹ 10,000. While if you subscribe to a term policy for the same sum assured, i.e. ₹ 15 lakh and pay ₹ 5,000 as premium; then the actual insurance amount is ₹ 5,000. This is because almost 90% of the premium in a money back policy is invested by the insurer in some fixed income instrument so as to give you the guaranteed money back and only a small amount goes towards insurance. In the present example, 90% of ₹ 1 lakh, i.e. ₹ 90,000 is actually "invested" in some fixed income product so as to give you a return while only ₹ 10, 000 is allocated towards the insurance component. The return which you get on the investment component is pathetically low. On the other hand, in a term policy which is pure insurance the entire premium amount goes towards your insurance. Therefore, while taking insurance you should know what is the real insurance component of your premium. And, always remember this rule while dealing with money — whether while earning, saving, budgeting, protecting, spending, investing or insuring — and clearly understand the true amount of money spent actually on each one of them.

Money Rule Number 10: Invite Good Money and Drive Out Bad Money

Let's for a moment go back almost five centuries when Sir Thomas Gresham was the financial adviser to Queen Elizabeth I of England in the sixteenth century. Gresham's Law states that when good and bad money are circulating together as legal tender, bad money tends to drive good money out of circulation.

Gresham's Law is an economic principle that states: "When a government compulsorily overvalues one type of money and undervalues another, the undervalued money will leave the country or disappear from circulation into hoards, while the overvalued money will flood into circulation." The law is commonly shortened to: "Bad money drives out good."

During the Elizabethan regime, a number of debased, depreciated, clipped and sweated (under-weight) coins from the times of the previous rulers Henry VIII and others were in circulation. Queen Elizabeth, therefore, thought of reforming the currency system. She tried to replace the bad coins of the previous regimes by issuing new, full-weighted coins. She thought that eventually the new coins (good money) would remain in circulation while the old coins (bad money) would be forced out of circulation. To her surprise, the result was exactly the opposite. As soon as the new coins made their appearance, they disappeared while old coins continued in circulation. She consulted her financial adviser Sir Thomas Gresham, in this matter. Gresham observed and explained that worn-out, debased, clipped or under-weighted sweated coins were bad money. By good money he meant full-weighted legal tender. In short, bad money is inferior coin and good money is better coin under monometallic standard (where one metal alone, generally gold or silver, is freely coined and is made full legal tender). When two such kinds of money are in circulation, it is natural for people to retain the better or new coins and pass on into circulation the comparatively old, worn-out and inferior coins. Thus, in course of time, better money would be driven out of circulation and replaced by inferior or bad money.

How the Law Operates

When both good and bad money circulate together as legal tender, good money disappears in three different ways:

1. **Hoarding:** People hoard good money and use bad money in making payments. Thus bad money remains in circulation while good money disappears owing to the hoarding.
2. **Melting:** Good new coins are melted by people when they need metal for ornaments or other art as they contain more metal compared to the depreciated old coins. Since both good coins and bad coins have the same value in circulation, people prefer to melt good coins when they want the metal instead of bad coins; thus, good money disappears, while the bad money remains in circulation.
3. **Exporting:** Good coins were exported abroad. In payments to foreign countries under the Gold Standard, national currencies were accepted in weight, and not by numbers so it was profitable to pay with the new, full-weighted coins. Old and bad coins were used for domestic transactions.

Thus, good money disappeared from circulation leaving behind only bad money to circulate. You must be wondering what relevance does all of this have today when all currency notes in circulation are just paper money. However, it remains very relevant even today for the following reasons:

1. **Hoarding:** People hold real assets like gold, silver, etc. They realize that the value of paper currency is constantly depreciating due to the constant and relentless currency printing by the central banks. In order to shield themselves from the continuous over supply of currency, people exchange depreciating currency notes for real assets like gold and silver.
2. **Melting:** People buy investment assets like stocks, real estate, businesses, etc. which are not subjected to the monster of depre-

ciation. In effect, people are just "melting" paper money and converting it into real investment assets.

3. **Exporting:** In today's fast flowing, freely trading global world, people use their ever depreciating paper money to buy good investment assets abroad. Thus, we constantly see the flush of foreign money in emerging market investment assets like equities, bonds, etc. This is nothing but the export of bad money out of one country in order to get the good money in the form of investment assets in some foreign country.

It's therefore important to learn to distinguish between good and bad money. In simple terms, assets which appreciate in value and / or produce income / cash flow are good money, while those which do not produce any income / cash flow and are subject to constant depreciation and loss in value are bad money.

If you don't know the difference between good and bad money then it might be really difficult for you to achieve financial independence as you will work the hardest, get paid less, become victim of the legal financial predators and the money which you finally get your hands on would keep losing its value because of inflation.

Money Rule Number 11: Don't Be Afraid of Money

Paradoxical? No, it is absolutely true. Unknowingly, most of us are actually afraid of money. Fearful of losing it. Fearful of not having enough of it. Fearful of not knowing how to manage it. Fearful of what to do with it, should you get enough of it — or lots of it.

If you are afraid of money, you are likely to buy a wasteful or bad capital asset mistaking it for an investment asset. If you are afraid of money you may take negative leverage thinking it to be positive. Therefore, don't be afraid of money; instead, learn all you can about it. In the end, it's not equities, bonds, commodities or real estate which will help you achieve financial freedom but the lack of any fear of money, through knowledge, which will make you rich and financially free.

Money Rule Number 12: Money is Unfair

One of the main reasons I thought of writing this book was to reveal to you the unfair rules of money which can otherwise foil your efforts towards financial freedom.

Yes, indeed, money is unfair. Why otherwise do the rich get richer and the poor grow poorer? It's painful to see educated people working for their employers all their lives for salary which is then subjected to high tax rates. Worse, they then buy a large house on mortgage and get into a bigger debt trap while their bank savings are constantly losing value to inflation. All this happens because money is unfair — those with financial education gain wealth while the financially ignorant keep losing money.

So, you must know the unfair rules of money — and use them to your advantage.

The more you work for money, the less you will earn and keep. The more you run after money, the more it will elude you. And whether we like it or not, we are all involved in this unfair game of money. The difference is how we play this unfair game. If you see money as a problem, always complain about it, always think that you don't have enough of it, then money will always remain a problem for you. Money will avoid you and never come to you — after all why should it come to you when you consider it as problem? You will always stay poor.

Even if you are well educated, have a great job and are earning a lot of money but keep buying bad capital assets with negative leverage because of your ignorance or over-confidence — then you will just have a lot of money debt and will always remain indebted to money.

On the other hand, if you learn the rules of money, respect money, are not afraid of it, and play the money game by the rules, see a world of money abundance and then make money work for you, not only will you become rich, you will stay wealthy throughout and also be able to leave money for your future generations and for charity. You will achieve true financial independence.

Money Rule Number 13: Print Your Own Money from Nothing — It's Available In Abundance

How can you print your own money when this is the prerogative of only the government? Well, you can.

Just as the governments changed the rules when the US came off the gold standard in 1971 and gave itself the power to legally print money, it also gives you the same power.

Contrary to what people think, money is one of the things which is available in abundance in this world. It can, and is, being printed at will by the governments and central banks across the world. You ask the US government to print a trillion US dollars, they will be able to do it at the speed of light by running their money printing machines overtime. However, you tell the same US government to give you an extra trillion dollars worth of gold or steel, copper, sugar or any other real commodity, they will not be able to do so because that is not in their control. Therefore, no government or central bank can provide you with real wealth, only abundant and unlimited paper wealth. And if they can do that, so can you. Only, you should know how to print your own money.

What is money? It's nothing but ideas, a thought, a creation of your own mind. If you have an open mind and are always ready to learn, you will keep getting ideas. On the other hand, if you think that money is scarce and you have to toil and work hard for it, then you will keep doing that throughout your life. I cannot teach you how to print money because you yourself have to know and use your own genius to do so. I can give you certain illustrations.

For example, I have written this book. I have to work hard and spend time once to write it. Once it's ready, then I can give rights to publish and sell my book to many publishers in many countries in many languages. If the book keeps selling in many countries, and in different languages for many years, I am, in effect, printing my own money for life. Writing the book is a skill I have and so am I doing it. In the same way, you can identify your unique gift or talent and you can do it, too.

The other misconception which a lot of people have is that a lot of money, or formal education or support, etc. are required to make money. Nothing can be farther from the truth in today's modern world where money is the most abundantly available commodity. Let us take the example of a sweeper who has little formal education. Now, how will he become rich? It's very simple — by doing the work which he knows the best. By that I don't mean that he should work overtime sweeping many houses or offices. No — that would mean working for money, which is against the rules of money. Instead, you need to use and unleash the power of money. Use the power of people. Use the power of corporations. Use the power of selling. Thus, the sweeper can gather a few of his other sweeper friends, form a group and start offering professional sweeping services, initially to smaller companies and housing societies. If they work sincerely their work will be appreciated and it will automatically create their brand name and more sweepers will be attracted to join them. Slowly but surely their sweeping business will grow and turn into "cleanliness and maintenance" business. A time will come when his business becomes so big that banks would be happy to lend him money while lawyers and accountants "will find him" to lend him their professional services. He can then convert his business into a company, win big contracts from large corporates, get loans from banks, save taxes and further invest in his own business. A day will come when his business will become so large that he will sell shares in his business to the public. This will be the ultimate money printing machine for him — selling shares in his business to the public.

So, you see, it requires neither money nor formal education to earn money — it just requires knowledge of the ten commandments and the rules of money and you are on your way to printing your own money.

Remember, you may have been born poor but there is no excuse for you to remain poor.

Money Rule Number 14: Learn How to Deal With Money Addiction

I call money a drug. And, it is the biggest and the most powerful of all drugs. People who are born rich often don't know what it is like being poor since they are always high on the drug of money. Rich children, if not given proper training and knowledge about money, are most likely to destroy their ancestral wealth. You might have heard numerous stories of how children of rich people have done so. In fact, in very rare instances does wealth continue after the third generation because future generations are not able to handle this potent drug.

Similarly, a poor person who suddenly gets a windfall gain in the form of a lottery or a large inheritance is more likely to squander away the wealth and get into debt because of the "high" of the new money. Such people will do stupid things with their newly acquired wealth, like purchasing big holiday homes, expensive cars, splurging on foreign trips, marrying someone much younger than themselves, etc. They then get deeper and deeper into debt and instead of solving their problems, money itself becomes a problem for them — a drug which they are unable to handle.

The only way to properly handle the powerful drug of money is by acquiring sound financial knowledge — the understanding of how money functions. The ten commandments of money aim to help you accomplish that job.

Lessons From This Commandment

1. Money has certain rules of its own which are unique. If you truly want to be a master of money and achieve financial freedom, then you have to learn these rules of money
2. If money is your problem, money cannot be the solution; simply because the problem itself can't be its solution. Further, the problem of money is not only its scarcity — even its excess can be a problem.

3. Never be a slave to money; be the master of your money. And once you become the master of your money, you will automatically start walking on the path of financial independence.
4. Don't run after money; instead, be a financial magnet which attracts money and ensures that it always sticks around with you.
5. Invest time before you invest money. Don't just aim at being rich without any knowledge or experience about money. Learn how money has been made and lost in this world before you commit your own money.
6. Be in control of your money. If you are not in full control of your money while dealing with it — be it while earning, saving, protecting, budgeting, investing, insuring, etc. — then it will control you and you will never be able to achieve financial independence.
7. Don't work for money; rather, make money work for you. Nobody can become really rich and stay wealthy by working for money. If you keep working for money, you would just be doing that throughout your life.
8. Understand the flow of money in your financial statements. This is very critical otherwise you will work more, earn less, pay higher amounts of tax, and let your money get eaten away by the monster of inflation, make wrong investments, buy wasteful capital assets with the help of negative leverage and never achieve financial freedom.
9. One of the important rules of money is to spend money to get rich. The truly wealthy people know when to handsomely spend on what and when to cut down. By not spending on the right thing at the right time, you might be permanently closing your doors to money.
10. Know how much you are actually earning, saving, protecting, budgeting, spending, investing and insuring. By having vague or notional figures, you are just burning away your money and life.

11. Remember that good money always drives out bad money. Therefore, you have to learn to distinguish between good and bad money. In simple terms, that which appreciates in value, and / or produces income and cash flow is good money while that which does not produce any income or cash flow and is subject to constant depreciation and loss in value is bad money. If you work hard without knowing the difference between good and bad money, then it might be really difficult for you to achieve financial freedom — you might well work the hardest, yet get paid less and your earnings will be further eaten away by the legal financial predators. Ultimately, the money which you are able to retain would keep losing its value because of inflation.
12. Don't be afraid of money. Instead, face it with courage. In the end, it's not equities, bonds, commodities, or real estate which will help you achieve financial freedom. It's your knowledge about money which will make you rich and help you always stay wealthy and financially free.
13. Money is unfair, so learn its rules in order to use them to your advantage. If you respect money and play the game of money by knowing the rules, you will see a world of abundant money and will make money work for you. That will be the stage when you will not only become rich but stay wealthy throughout and be also able to do charity and leave money for your future generations. You will achieve true financial freedom.
14. Create and print your own money. If the government can legally print notes, so, too, can you.
15. You must know how to handle the biggest of all drugs — money. Yes, it is a drug, and the lack of it or its overdose can cause serious financial and emotional damage. The only way to properly handle the powerful drug of money and not get addicted is by acquiring sound financial knowledge — the understanding of how money functions.

Self-Understanding Questionnaire

This commandment revealed the rules of money. The rules of money are very peculiar and unique. If you want to attain true financial freedom, you have to master these rules. Now, honestly answer the following questions in yes or no to test your understanding of this commandment. The more the number of "yes" answers, the better is your understanding of this commandment.

1. Do you believe that money has certain rules of its own? Yes/No?
2. Do you accept that money can't be the answer to your problems — that both lack of and excess of money can be a problem if not backed by proper understanding of the functioning and the rules of money? Yes/No?
3. Do you believe that there is no point running after money and that instead you have to invest time in learning its rules, be in control of your money and be its master? Yes/No?
4. Do you have a clear understanding of your own financial statements and the connection and money flow between the different items in it? Yes/No?
5. Do you believe that spending money in the right manner at the right time can actually make you rich? Yes/No?
6. Do you recognize the difference between what appears and what actually is the money you are earning, protecting, budgeting, saving, spending, leveraging, investing and insuring? Yes/No?
7. Do you think that money can be good as well as bad? And, that as in other facets of life, bad money actually drives out the good money? Yes/No?
8. Do you know that money is unfair and you have to get "unfair benefit" in order to achieve financial freedom? Yes/No?
9. Do you believe that money is available in abundance and can actually be created and printed at free will? Yes/No?
10. Have you ever felt the high of the drug called money? If yes, then have you taken corrective steps to come out of that high? Yes/No?

Chapter 12

Financial Freedom

Putting All the Commandments Together

NOW, YOU KNOW ALL THE TEN COMMANDMENTS OF MONEY. These commandments are not meant to be applied individually or piece meal; many of them work together. The commandments are intertwined and woven together. You have to apply one or more commandments simultaneously while dealing with different money situations. In this chapter, we will pull together all the commandments and see how they lead us to financial freedom.

The chapter describes, stage by stage, your dealings with money and explains the inter-relationship among different commandments at each stage.

Stage 1: Earning Money

This is the first stage — or at least it's supposed to be the first stage of dealing with money. It is the first principle of life that you have to give before you get — you have to love before you can expect to be loved, respect other before you can hope to get any respect, think before you speak, learn before you can expect to earn. Similarly, you have to first earn before having any right to spend. Earning is indeed the first tenet of money. However wealthy you might be, unless you know how to earn, you will not be able to stay wealthy for long. The world is full of examples of wealthy people's children who squandered away the great riches of their parents and ended up bankrupt. Even if you are born rich and may not actually need to earn money, you must know how money is earned. And then you have to apply the other principles of money, including saving, protecting, budgeting, spending, investing and insuring. So whatever your financial condition, whether you have to actually earn money or not, you have to understand how money is earned.

The different commandments taught us the best methods to earn money. They also introduced you to the concept of how much money you actually get to retain. Just earning money is not enough. You may lose it to legal financial predators, like the taxman, even before it comes to you. You now know the different types of incomes — earned income, guaranteed income, passive income and portfolio income — and how earned income is inferior because it takes up your full time and energy. If for any reason you are not around, or can't work, your earned income stops since it depends fully on you and your active time and energy in earning it. We also learnt that just like earned income, guaranteed income too is subject to the highest marginal rate of taxation. Plus, it has the great risk of losing its purchasing power and value due to the unseen monster of inflation.

The commandments further highlighted the importance of passive income and how you should always try to convert earned income into passive income. Passive income does not require your time and energy. Your money works for you and your investment assets keep producing income day after day, month after month, year after year — basically, in perpetuity — or so long as you own the investment asset. This is the lifetime income which you can and should aim to generate. Passive income finds its way to your bank account — literally — whether you are there or not. I will give my own example to prove this point. By writing this book, besides making a serious attempt to make you financially free, my other aim is to earn revenue from it. Now, if my book indeed helps lead you to the path of financial freedom, then the likelihood of it becoming a success increases. And once it becomes a bestselling book, then whether I am there or not, the book will keep selling and the royalties will keep coming. This is an example of passive income — you work once, set up an income stream, and the income then keeps flowing for life and even beyond, whether you are there or not.

This is one of the basic tenets of this book — convert your earned income into passive income.

The other important income which you should strive for is portfolio income. Once you achieve passive income, then portfolio income would automatically start flowing in over a period of time. For example, if you invest in high dividend yield stocks of good blue chip companies, then these provide you both regular passive income in the form of dividends and, over the long term, also have the potential of giving you portfolio income by way of capital gains. This is the main tenet of earning — use your earned income to buy investment assets which then start producing passive income and regular cash flows for life, plus a bonus in the form of portfolio income over a period of time.

Golden Rules of Earning

1. Earned income, which takes your full time and energy, is subject to maximum tax by the legal financial predators and is therefore by itself unlikely to make you rich and financially free. Make it your mission to convert earned income into guaranteed, passive and portfolio incomes as fast as possible.
2. Guaranteed income is also subjected to the maximum rates of tax by the biggest of all legal financial predators, i.e. the government. Try and keep guaranteed income to the minimum within the overall context of proper asset allocation.
3. Passive income is your cash flow-producing cow which will give you continuous and regular income throughout the life of an investment asset. This is the income which will help you solve your financial problems and set you on the road to financial freedom.
4. Once you put your money in the correct investment assets, over a period of time your portfolio will produce passive income for you. Passive income is your monthly cash flow, and portfolio income is your bonus on it.

Stage 2: Protecting Your Money

Once you get something valuable, what do you do with it next? Obviously you try to protect it from the predators who are out there to grab whatever they can from you. So, the next stage is to protect your money. You have to protect your money from everyone — including thieves and robbers — but the most protection is required against legal financial predators, such as the government, bankers, brokers, etc. who legally take away a big chunk of your money from your pocket. The biggest of them all is, of course, the government which legally takes away a major portion of your money even before it reaches your pocket. Just think of "tax deducted at source" — it is nothing but money taken away from you at the very source of your income, even before it reaches your pocket.

If you are not earning money from a smart and intelligent source, or if you are working for your money instead of your money working for you, then you are an easy target for the taxman. In such a case, you are also paying more than your normal share of taxes. Therefore, protect your money from the biggest legal financial predator by earning your money from the most "tax efficient" source — passive and portfolio incomes.

You also need to protect your money from other legal predators, such as bankers (at the time of leveraging), brokers (at the time of investing), etc. At the same time, give due recognition to the importance and the value created by a good banker or broker.

You can further protect your money by using the corporate structure. Let your company earn the income, then pay off all the expenses, whether revenue or capital from the pre-tax money so that you protect the maximum amount from the taxman. Remember, earning money is just the first stage — and a necessary condition — but certainly not sufficient in itself. If you don't know how to protect your money, then you would be legally robbed of large chunks of it by all the legal financial predators around.

Golden Rules of Protecting Your Money

1. Earning money is by itself not sufficient for financial freedom. If you don't know how to protect your money from the various legal financial predators, they would openly rob you of it and you will just be a silent spectator to the robbery.
2. You must earn money from the proper source in order to be able to protect it from the biggest legal financial predator of all — the government.

3. Recognize the importance of protecting your money from other major legal financial predators, such as bankers at the time of leveraging it, or brokers at the time of investing it.
4. Use the legal system to your own advantage and unleash the power of corporate structure to protect yourself from the taxman.

Stage 3: Budgeting Your Money

After protecting it, what do you think you need to do with your money? Before you do anything else, you need to have a plan for the money now left with you. You need to know how much money is going where and for what. In other words, you need to know your money budget.

You must always strive and create a surplus budget. If you are unable to do so, you would not be able to save, invest or insure properly; nor would you be able to achieve proper asset allocation. Budgeting, thus, is the backbone of your goal of achieving financial independence.

Remember that income tax reduces your gross income; interest on loans diminishes your net income, and inflation constantly nibbles away at your remaining income. Only if you are able to budget properly would you be able to convert your earned income into lifelong passive income which would also have the potential for generating future portfolio income.

Golden Rules of Budgeting

1. Earning and protecting money will not serve the purpose of creating wealth and achieving financial independence if there is no subsequent planning and budgeting.
2. Remember that budgeting for yourself *via* creation of budget surplus is nothing but "paying yourself". If you can pay others, such as the government, bankers, utility company, telephone service provider, brokers, servants, etc., then you should prioritize and first pay yourself before paying all the others.
3. You have to learn to create a surplus budget for yourself in order to convert your earned income into passive income for life

which, in future, would also have the potential of generating portfolio income.

Stage 4: Saving Your Money

Having earned money from the most efficient source, protected it from the clutches of the various legal financial predators and then paid yourself by creating a surplus budget, you have arrived at this golden stage of saving.

The next step after creating a budget surplus is to first save your money and "buy time" to arrive at a proper asset allocation for yourself before starting to invest.

However, don't forget the very important principle that saving is not investing. Never mistake saving for investment otherwise you will be in for a rude shock because you don't understand the rules of money.

In this modern age of currency, savers are losers. For this reason, you have to learn to convert your money into investment assets. Another benefit of converting money into investment assets is that you can then actually profit from inflation. When you use money to purchase assets which increase in value with inflation, you are actually benefiting from inflation!

For example, suppose you own rental real estate. Now, every time the value of money goes down because of inflation, you get an opportunity to increase your rent which, in essence, not only immediately increases your cash flow but also leads to an increase in the value of your property. Why? Because inflation causes the replacement cost of your property to go up which, in turn, leads to an increase in the price of your property. This is how you can actually benefit from inflation by playing the rules of money correctly.

To conclude, although saving might be the golden stage of your dealings with money but it is a temporary and transitory stage before you convert the paper currency money you have saved into income yielding investment assets. If you don't understand such simple concept of money, then you would be saving and holding something, i.e. paper currency or money, whose value is ever depleting against real assets such as commodities, gold, equities, real estate, etc. Therefore, just stopping at saving and not acting further would simply mean financial disaster.

Golden Rules of Saving

1. After earning money from the most efficient source, protecting it from legal financial predators and making a surplus budget for yourself, the next stage is saving. However, this is just a transitory stage before the money saved is properly allocated to investment assets, insurance, etc.
2. Before the year 1971, the rule of money was to work hard, earn money, save as much as possible, and then enjoy your retirement with the saved money. However, the rules of money were permanently altered in the year 1971 when the then US President Richard Nixon took the US off the gold standard and granted itself the license to print money. Therefore, money is the only commodity available in the world whose supply can be increased at free will as much as desired and with as much speed as the world money printing press can run.
3. Never mistake saving for investments otherwise you will be left with paper currency in your hand whose value would continuously reduce *vis-a-vis* real assets, such as commodities, gold, equities, real estate, etc.
4. Increase your odds of financial freedom by converting your savings into investment assets with proper asset allocation.

Stage 5: Spending Your Money

We now come to spending — and we all have to spend. To start with, there are some necessary expenses like utility bills, telephone bills, school fees, medical costs, etc. which cannot wait. Further, there is also some necessary capital expenditure like mortgage installment which have also to be paid on time. So, before you think about asset allocation, investing or insuring, you have to settle these necessary expenses and capital expenditure. Then there are the avoidable evils — unnecessary luxury expenses and wasteful capital expenditure. As explained earlier in the book, example of unnecessary expenses would be costly dinners, foreign travel, etc. In the same way, wasteful capital expenditure would include a new luxury car, vacation house, etc. All these expenses rob you of your wealth and ensure that you never attain financial freedom.

You should purposefully endeavor to curtail a reasonable portion of unnecessary expenses and capital expenditure and put it back into your savings kitty. Once you accomplish this, you will have much more good money to profitably invest and also insure.

Golden Rules on Spending

1. After earning money from the most efficient source, protecting it from legal financial predators, making a budget for yourself, saving it pending proper asset allocation, the next step is spending.
2. On the one hand, there are some necessary expenses and even wasteful capital expenditure which can neither be avoided nor postponed. But there are also certain wasteful luxury expenses and capital expenditure which should not only be postponed but also reduced and avoided.
3. Whatever is saved out of the wasteful revenue and capital expenses should be added back to your savings.

Stage 6: Leveraging Your Money

You have now come pretty far in your money journey. By now you know how to earn your income from the most tax-efficient source, how to protect it from legal financial predators, how to budget for yourself, then save it pending proper asset allocation and the importance of saving on wasteful revenue and capital expenses. So, what next? Apparently, investing and insuring? Indeed, you now have to invest and insure but with what and whose money. The person who invests his / her own money properly is clever but the person who invests with other's money is smart and shrewd. Remember the power of positive leverage that we discussed in Commandment 6. Accordingly, stage 6 is leveraging. This is a very important stage and one which will determine whether you become a big fish in your own pond or swim out of it and become a big fish in the vast ocean. Leverage is a multiplier. Positive leverage will help you multiply your wealth. Of course, you must know the difference between good and bad debt and avoid bad debt while using good debt to multiply your money.

Contrary to popular opinion, debt is not risky if you know how to harness the power of positive leverage. In fact, lack of proper leverage might come in the way of your achieving financial independence. Positive leverage means debt which multiplies your money by putting money into your pocket. Negative leverage, on the other hand, is debt which reduces your money by taking money away from your pocket.

You must also learn to recognize the difference between an investment asset and a liability disguised as an asset. Never use leverage to buy a liability disguised as an accounting asset because not only will it take money out of your pocket in the form of maintenance and running expenses, but also in the form of interest payments.

Leverage or debt should only be used to buy investment assets. This is called positive leverage.

To unleash the ultimate power of positive leverage, you have to aim to reach the stage of net positive cash flow after tax. Once you reach this stage, then you start making "money from nothing".

Also, you should never take on debt in order to earn portfolio income, i.e. capital gains but only for passive income, i.e. regular income in the form of rent, dividends, coupon interest, etc.

Inflation is your partner with positive leverage simply because you borrow in costlier money today and repay back your loan in cheaper money later because of inflation.

Golden Rules of Leveraging

1. Before investing and insuring, it is very important to understand leveraging, which will determine your scale and level of financial success.
2. Contrary to popular opinion, leveraging is not risky if you know how to harness the power of positive leverage.

   Positive leverage is that debt which multiplies your money. It does so by putting money into your pocket.

Negative leverage is debt which reduces your money by taking money away from your pocket.

3. To unleash the ultimate power of positive leverage, you have to aim to reach the stage of net positive cash flow after tax. Once you reach this stage, then you start making "money from nothing".
4. Remember that if you fail at this stage, then you may still attain financial freedom but your level of freedom might be very limited.

Stage 7: Investing Your Money

You have now reached the seventh stage, which is investing. This is the stage which often makes or breaks your financial success. Many of the earlier stages, such as budgeting, saving, leveraging, etc. will be wasted if you make mistakes at this stage.

The importance of Commandment 1 will be greatly felt during this stage because asset allocation is the key to successful investing.

To repeat: the only thing truly in your control is asset allocation and the good news is that 90% of the variability in a portfolio's return is due to asset allocation. All assets move in business and economic cycles of their own and while one category of assets might be in a bear market another asset class might simultaneously be in a big bull market. The broader asset groups of equities, bonds, commodities and real estate (others being art and currencies) will lead you to the gateway of long term wealth creation and sustenance.

Risk and return are inextricably entwined. As a general rule, do not expect higher return from safe investments. However, you can expect higher long term wealth creation from optimal asset allocation in investment assets whose combined risk as a portfolio is much lower than the risk of each individual investment comprising it. Portfolios behave differently from their individual constituents. The aim of optimal asset allocation is not to invest only in safe assets but to invest in a combination of safe and risky assets whose combined risk is much lower than that of the individual constituents, while the return is higher. Therefore, focus on the behavior of your portfolio, not so much its constituents. Small portions of your portfolio will often sustain serious losses but this will cause only minor damage to the whole portfolio. Thus, an all-bond portfolio is the not the least risky portfolio; in fact, the addition of a small amount of stock to an all-bond portfolio actually reduces the risk slightly while considerably improving the return. Equally, the addition of some amount of bonds to an all-stock portfolio would significantly reduce risk while only marginally bringing down the return. Keep periodically rebalancing, reviewing, changing and refining your portfolio allocation with time, and your financial goals and financial situation.

Golden Rules of Investing

1. The seventh stage — investing — will make or break your drive for financial freedom.
2. Asset allocation is the key to long term wealth creation. Further, asset allocation is the only thing in your control and the good news is that 90% of the variability of the income from the portfolio is due to asset allocation.
3. All assets have business and economic cycles of their own. While one asset might be in a bear market, another asset class might simultaneously be in a big bull market. The aim of optimal asset allocation is not to invest only in safe assets but to invest in a combination of safe and risky assets whose combined risk is much lower and the return higher than that of the individual constituents.
4. Always focus on the behavior of your portfolio and not so much on its individual constituents. Small portions of your portfolio will often sustain serious losses, but will cause only minor damage to the whole portfolio.
5. Don't ever underestimate the importance of investing because many of the other stages like budgeting, saving, leveraging, etc. will be wasted if you make major mistakes at this stage.

Stage 8: Insuring Your Money

You have now truly come very far in your money journey and are at its final stage. You are now left with only one aspect in your money journey — insuring.

Whether we are aware of it or not, and whether we accept the fact or not, but we are constantly taking insurance against something when we breathe, eat, sleep, talk, learn, make friends, marry, etc. Then why shy away from financial insurance? Insurance is of prime importance and should be considered a part of your financial plan, especially when you are first starting out. If you don't have enough money, then you need insurance to protect yourself, your spouse, children, parents and other dependents. If you are rich and have excess money, you require financial insurance all the more in order to protect your wealth from all kinds of natural disasters as well as financial predators.

Financial insurance simply means insurance against everything which is a hindrance between you and your money — whether it prevents you from earning more money, saving money, investing money, etc. The main categories of financial insurance include family protection, personal insurance, disability protection, asset protection, profit protection and medical insurance. There is also another category of financial insurance which you require in order to protect yourself and your wealth from "money predators". This category includes legal insurance — protection against legal rogues; tax insurance protection against the government taxman; job protection — protection needed to survive in the business in which you are today; love protection — against love predators; and portfolio insurance — which would protect your assets against untoward large losses. However, no insurance company will provide you with this category of insurance and, in essence, you have to become your own insurance company.

Golden Rules of Insuring

1. Insurances is the last stage in your money journey.
2. Financial insurance simply means insurance against every thing which is a hindrance between you and your money — whether

by not allowing you to earn more money, save money, invest money or in any form take money away from your pocket.

3. Financial insurance is the eighth and the final stage which will help you in holding together all the preceding seven stages.

Money Journey — Till Death and Beyond

Remember that your money journey never ends till you are on this planet; it continues till your grave — and even after that if you have failed to achieve financial independence. For example, if you leave this world with too much bad debt, or a lot of wealth without a proper succession plan. Therefore, these stages will come again and again in different and varied forms at various times in your life. Your money duties are not over when you adopt these ten commandments — in fact, they have just begun. Throughout your life you have to always keep reviewing, evaluating and refining them to suit your particular individual needs.

Chapter 13

Battling Against Yourself

HAVE YOU EVER WONDERED WHICH IS LIFE'S MOST DIFFICULT BATTLE?

No, it's not the battle to get the highest grade in exams, or to get the best bride or groom, or to get the highest paying job; nor is it the fight to earn money and achieve financial freedom.

The most difficult battle of anybody's life is the battle against oneself. This book will be incomplete if I didn't touch upon this battle — and how to win it. Because if you can't win the battle against yourself, you stand hardly any chance of attaining financial freedom.

Why Do We Battle Against Ourselves?

You were born to succeed. This is the most basic and simple law of nature. But very few people actually achieve success in their lives — and even those who do so don't reach the pinnacle of success that they could.

Therefore, while we were born to succeed, most of the time we are unable to do so. This fight between the probable and the reality constantly leaves us battling with our own selves. You might be familiar with some of the following feelings:

- You are thinking of leaving your job and staring your own business.
- You want to become a singer instead of studying medicine but are studying medicine just because your parents want you to become a doctor.
- You want to leave your family business and join politics.

- You want to leave your job and go in for higher studies.

If you have any such feelings, then you are in a constant battle with yourself. This battle leaves you tired, dissatisfied, irritated and with a persistent feeling of restlessness, resentment and discontentment.

A battle with oneself also is the biggest battle of one's life. Much of your success in life, including financial success, depends on how successful you are in this battle against your own self. Once you get on good terms with yourself, you will see how quickly others get on good terms with you. Remember, when you get yourself under control, you can be your own boss — both in money matters and in life. Swami Vivekananda rightly observed that "a person can't be defeated by others until he is defeated by his own self."

The Psychological Battleground

Our life is nothing but a psychological battleground. We are constantly dissatisfied, unhappy and in discomfort, fighting against our own selves. Often we start doing something, then think about doing something else and, finally, end up doing something totally different.

For example, take the case of stock market investing. After doing meticulous research on a stock, you conclude that its real intrinsic value is ₹ 150. Since the current market price is ₹ 100, you buy the stock. Now, for no fault of yours or that of the company — and despite all fundamental factors remaining intact — the stock falls to, say, ₹ 75. This may be due to the overall market trend or due to some rumor surrounding the stock or the sector, etc. Now what do you do? Do you panic and sell the stock at a loss? Or, do you simply hold on to the stock and, in fact, buy more of it? After all, the original premise on which you purchased the stock has not changed. This kind of decision making takes us to the realm of investor psychology. The investor enters a psychological battleground. Beating the market is difficult but beating our own selves is much more so. Beating your own self means mastering your emotions and the ability to think rationally and independently in the face of all the noise surrounding you.

In this battle against yourself, there are certain qualities which comprise your troops while certain others are the enemy. And since this is a battle against yourself, by enemy I mean those qualities which lead to your loss, which make you lose against yourself.

First let us learn the negative qualities and then how to beat them with the positive ones.

The Enemy's Troops

The following are the major negative qualities which lead to defeat in your battle against yourself and therefore comprise the enemy's troops. These qualities not only damage you physically and emotionally but also financially and are the chief reasons for people not being able to attain financial freedom or other great achievements.

Pride

This is one of the single biggest reasons which leads to the downfall of many an individual. Pride leads to downfall in one's personal, professional, spiritual and investment life.

While dealing with money, for example, if you are very proud of yourself, then you will not have the humility to seek anybody's advice even when you need it and that can be a disaster. For example, if you are very proud and think that you know everything then you may not do sufficient research or take proper advice before investing. Further, if you are too arrogant and believe that you know everything, then at the time of spending you may buy a costly product which you actually may not require. Always remember that pride is one of the biggest enemies which stalls your growth — mentally, spiritually and monetarily.

Jealousy

This is another negative trait and a part of your enemy's forces. Jealousy creates a cloud of discontent, resentment, anger and frustration around you which completely mars your vision and puts you at a substantial risk of taking wrong decisions, including poor financial decisions.

For example, if you are jealous of your neighbor because he or she has made a lot of money in some business, it may prompt you to recklessly quit your job and start some business about which you have limited or no knowledge or experience. Jealousy may make you believe that for you to succeed, somebody else has to fail — which is totally incorrect. In fact, we are all connected to one another at a higher spiritual level and no man can hope to become a permanent success unless he takes others along with him. Thus, jealousy can cloud your thinking and lead you into making serious mistakes — mentally, spiritually and monetarily.

Doubt

You might not realize it but doubt is an equally formidable enemy of yours. Doubt forces you into wrong decisions — and sometimes even paralyzes your decision making — which can be very detrimental for you financially and otherwise.

For example, you might get an excellent business proposal from one of your closest friends whom you trust. But if doubt creeps into your mind and you start wondering if he or she is somehow fooling you then it may lead to your letting go an excellent business proposal. Think before deciding but after deciding don't think — take action. Once you have done your own research and thinking, then remove all doubts from your mind — just go ahead and make your decision.

Fear

This is another flaw and we don't realize how powerful an enemy it is. Never fear taking risk in life; staying within one's comfort zone is the biggest risk of all since it's the most dangerous and uncertain place on this planet. Fear will come in the way of your success. You may recognize the difference between right and wrong but your fear will not allow you to take action. Your fear will always stop you. It will, in fact, form a web around you and will never allow you to go out and explore the world — and all the good things in it. The fears you run from actually run towards you — so never be fearful. And, remember, that every time you actually do what you fear, you take back the power that fear has stolen from you and reclaim the latent strength lying within you.

In the money world, too, fear can be a big enemy of yours.

For example, the fear of losing money may not allow you to invest in equities. Consequently, your money will keep lying idle in your bank, constantly being eaten up by the monster of inflation. Freedom and fear cannot co-exist in any person's life — a free man fears nothing. If you want true success as a human being, then move ahead fearlessly, whether in money or any other decision of life.

Worry

This is one of the biggest enemies of all and one which we hardly recognize. Some people have the constant habit of worrying constantly. Even if there is no problem, they worry so much that eventually they create some problem! Because of their worry, they are not able to enjoy the small and beautiful experiences of life.

Worry can be an equally big enemy while dealing with money. For example, the worry as to how you will pay back a loan despite having done your financial homework properly will not allow you to borrow and unleash the power of positive leverage. Therefore, throw away your worry in the waste bin and start living with confidence. Keep busy going after what you want so that you have no time to worry about what you don't want.

Ego

This is another negative quality with devastating consequences. Ego can be one of your worst enemies as it can totally cloud your vision while dealing with anything in your life, including money. Ego is worse than pride. Pride comes from something which we know or possess, ego from something which we may neither know nor possess but believe that we know or possess. A person with an oversized ego is never be able to think properly.

Self Pity

This is another lead member among the enemy's troops. Never pity yourself. Whatever is happening in your life, good or bad, is the result of many factors, some known, others not immediately knowable — your own karma. So, if you think you are getting punished, it is because of your own deeds. At the same time, don't feel embarrassed when you are rewarded, be humble and enjoy the reward because you might deserve it.

Pity can be very bad for your money as well. For example, if you jump into some money decision without proper analysis and research and then suffer due to your wrong decision, you don't need to have self pity. Instead, you must be mature enough to accept responsibility for your mistake and learn from it.

No Respect for the Most Precious Thing

This, along with the next one, is perhaps among the mightiest enemies in your battle against yourself.

It's common sense that not respecting the most precious thing you have is a big mistake. But what is your most precious thing? Some may think it's money, fame or power, or something like that. In fact, the most precious thing is the only non-renewable resource which you are continuously and uninterruptedly given. But once you lose it, you never ever get it back again — and that is time. Yes, my friend, time is the most precious thing which you have and once gone you can never ever get it back again, even with all the wealth and money in this world. So, you must have the discipline to focus your time around your priorities. Plan your time properly because failing to plan is, in fact, planning to fail. Every time you say yes to something that is unimportant, you are unknowingly saying no to something that is important. Learn to say no to the unimportant things so that you have time for the important things in life. Guard your time well. It's a completely non-renewable natural resource and once gone cannot be retrieved. Time will help you in creating money and happiness. For example, when you work for money or study for your exams or cook food — what is the common thing you are spending? It is time. Hence, time well spent is life well spent, including earning and dealing with money. Always analyze whether the time (input) you spend gives you sufficient money, happiness, health, etc. (output). For example, when you are spending time in reading this book, assess whether the time spent on reading it is yielding you enough output in the form of leading you on to the path of achieving financial freedom — if yes, read it; otherwise, leave it.

Fear of Making Mistakes

This is one of the major enemies which leads to failure for most people.

We are so afraid of making mistakes because we think that we might fail that we forget the joy of winning. However, often failure is not our fault. From early in our school days, we are conditioned to fear mistakes. A school never encourages mistakes. If a child makes some mistake in the exams, instead of encouraging and helping him find the reason for his mistake, he is labeled as a failure. However, life is full of mistakes. Some of the biggest discoveries and inventions in this world have been a result of mistakes. For example, Christopher Columbus was looking for a trade route to India when by "mistake" he ended up "discovering" America — the world's richest and most powerful country today! In the financial world, if you are afraid of mistakes, you will never be able to find a successful investment or business because their paths are full of mistakes.

Consider a mistake as an opportunity to learn something new. When you come to the boundaries of what you know — it's simply time to make a mistake and learn something new. Remember, that life is the greatest teacher of all and its method of teaching is different from traditional school teaching. In school, you are considered smart if you don't make mistakes while in life you are smart only if you make mistakes; learn from them, and move ahead. The point which we have to remember here is that when we make a mistake we have to humbly accept it instead of blaming, rationalizing, avoiding, lying, denying or justifying it. Take responsibility for the mistake and move ahead to correct it.

The things that are hardest to do are often the things that are the most worth doing. Do the things that most people don't do in order to reach the height which most people never reach. Luck is where skill meets persistence. Success lies in a masterful consistency around a few fundamentals. Change is hardest at the beginning, messiest in the middle, and best at the end. Remember that, in effect, challenges serve to introduce us to our best and most magnificent self. So never be fearful of making mistakes, in fact, make mistakes; learn from them and move ahead because the road towards ultimate success is full of minor initial failures.

There are many other enemies in your battle against yourself, foes like revenge, selfishness, possessiveness, cowardice, laziness, nagging, etc. but we will stop this discussion here because a full book can be written on this subject.

Now let's take stock of our own troops in this battle.

Your Troops

Just as there are the enemy troops, so you too have your own army. Learn who your soldiers are and make them a partner in your success.

Belief

This is perhaps the most important soldier among your troops.

There is a saying, "If you believe you can do it then you can and if you believe you cannot do it then you cannot; in both cases you are right."

Then there is the other saying that "life's battles don't always go to the stronger and faster man, but sooner or later the man who wins is the man who thinks he can."

These two sayings beautifully summarize the power of belief.

Before having any hope of succeeding, you have to first believe in your own self.

Before wanting to earn money and becoming rich, you must first believe that you can get rich. You must make hope and faith your bodyguards because misfortune rarely worries someone whose constant bodyguards are hope and faith.

Just imagine that you are a clerk in your office. Would you ever imagine — and actually believe — that you could sit in the managing director's chair? If you yourself are not able to accept that possibility, then how will others accept it? Living a positive life is not easy; but, then, neither is negative living. Given a choice, what would you select? You have to cultivate positive belief in your own self before hoping that others will believe in you.

Patience

Patience, persistence and perspiration make an unbeatable combination for success. To have the rewards that very few have, do the things that very few people are willing to do. Be in no hurry to change your finances overnight as you will not be mentally ready for it, you can't do it physically and you may not be able to bear the consequences emotionally. Howsoever strong may be your desire to achieve great wealth quickly, the world of money does not work that way. People need patience to build wealth slowly, each rupee at a time. Learn to delay gratification and you will avoid a lot of money mistakes. Patience and perseverance are key virtues not only in life but also in money matters.

Humility

This is the opposite of pride. In fact, if you are humble, a lot of your enemies such as pride, ego, jealousy, etc. will automatically vanish. Humility will open up your mind and make it receptive, will make you accept your mistakes, recognize your strengths and weaknesses — and you can then consolidate on your strengths and minimize your weaknesses. Humility is the gateway of your mind and body to your soul. Therefore, always be humble. If you are humble, then you will be able to spot those investment opportunities which otherwise you might not.

The more you worry about being applauded by others and making money, the less you'll focus on doing the real work that will generate applause and make you money. As your knowledge about money and life increases don't feel great but be grateful that God has selected you as his instrument to pass on this knowledge forward. With this knowledge, attitude and humility about money and life you are certain to obtain a fortune well beyond your highest imagination.

Asking for Help

This is a magic world. Ask and the world will do it for you. That's because all human beings are trained from childhood to do whatever is asked. In an exam, the questions are "asked" and the student has to write the correct answers. In a job interview the candidate is "asked" some questions and he has to give prompt and appropriate answers. If you love a person and want to marry him / her, then you have to "ask" by proposing to him / her. If you are ill, then you have to "ask" the doctor for medicine. Till a child does not "ask" by crying, the mother does not give him / her milk. The list can just go on and on. In short, we have all been trained and conditioned to do what is asked for. In fact, when we pray to God, we are asking him — for happiness, good health, children, good job or whatever else we pray for.

The key is to ask the right thing of the right person at the right time in the right manner — and rest assured that you will receive it.

Character

Your reputation is what people think you are, your character is that which you actually are. To double your net worth, double your self-worth because you will never exceed the height of your self-image. A person of loose character may earn money but will never get the position and respect in society — he may acquire money but will never become truly rich and wealthy. For example, a famous movie or sports star is involved in a sex scandal will not get the same love and respect from everyone which he otherwise deserved because of his skills or talent.

Never Say Die Spirit

This is a very powerful warrior among your troops. Without its support, you won't be able to win. Remember, knowledge and talent are necessary conditions for winning but by themselves they are certainly not sufficient. The characteristic which will lead you to victory would be your never say die attitude; your positive qualities of patience and perseverance. By inculcating the never say die spirit, you are announcing to the world that whatever be the circumstances, howsoever big may be the problem and however insurmountable may be the obstacle — you will never quit. And when you try continuously with patience, perseverance and a never say die attitude, you are bound to finally succeed.

Positive Attitude

There is a popular saying that your attitude determines your altitude. You must understand the importance of always having a positive attitude. You have to actively create a positive attitude. Just as absence of ill-health does not equal good health, absence of negativity alone does not make a person positive. People with positive attitudes have certain personality traits which are easily recognizable. If you want to rise high in life, including financially, then always create a positive attitude within yourself and then see how you will become a magnet and attract all the good things around.

Facing Fear Face to Face

A big obstacle between you and your success — whether financial or otherwise — is fear. Fear is that dreadful disease which always holds you back. It is that menace which prevents you from shedding a safe mediocrity and striking out for higher achievements. Fear is the invisible barrier which blocks your road towards discovering your own self. Fear blocks you from attaining your full potential. If you want to move higher in life, then you have to get out of your comfort zone and face your fears face to face — that will not only make you fearless but also put you in control of your life by handing your true self back to you.

Taking Calculated Risks

Whether you know it or not, you are continuously being subjected to different kinds of risk. For example, to love exposes you to the risk of not getting love in return, to laugh is taking the risk of being viewed as a fool, to weep is to appear sloppy, and the biggest risk of all is to live because to live is to risk dying. However, we have to constantly take some kinds of risk.

Success involves taking calculated risks. Risk-taking does not mean gambling foolishly or behaving irresponsibility. Risk-taking is relative. The concept of risk varies from person to person and is a result of education, training, experience, knowledge, judgment and wisdom. For example, for an experienced diver, a dive is a calculated risk while for a novice diving in the deep could be a suicidal risk.

Similarly, for an experienced stock market investor investing in a company after proper research and analysis would be a calculated risk. For a layman it would be financial suicide to invest in a stock on the basis of a "hot tip". Always remember, whether in life or while dealing with money take proper, calculated risks because a person who risks nothing, does nothing, has nothing, and is, in fact, nothing — the life of a person who doesn't take any risk, becomes risky

Failing Forward — Journey from Initial Failures to Final Success

This is a very important concept in life — physically, mentally, psychologically and financially.

If you know how to fail forward then you can never be a loser.

Grantland Rice mentioned that "failure isn't so bad if it doesn't attack the heart and success is all right if it doesn't go to the head."

Ken Hubbard propagated that "there is no failure except no longer trying. There is no defeat except from within, no really insurmountable barrier save our own inherent weakness of purpose."

Life is full of hits and misses. Even after doing everything necessary, you might still fail. But that does not mean that you are a failure.

Kyle Rote jr observed that "there is no doubt in my mind that there are many ways to be a winner, but there is really only one way to be a loser and that is to fail and not look beyond the failure."

The road to success is filled with many failures but if you really want to achieve success in life then you have to learn to "fail forward," i.e. moving ahead from initial failures to ultimate success. Remember the following points on your journey of failing forward:

- The major difference between those who "finally succeed" and the people who "finally fail" is that the people who finally fail don't know how to fail forward.
- People who "finally fail" view themselves as failures while the people who "finally succeed" view the situation as a failure and try to improve their odds of succeeding the next time.
- People who "finally fail" always live in their past. They are never able to get over their past failures and keep leading miserable lives.
- People who "finally succeed" embrace failures as their friends, learn from their negative experiences and then don't repeat them. This is how they increase their odds of succeeding — each time they fail, they learn and try again.
- People who "finally succeed" understand that there is little difference between success and failure — they might actually have been very close to success when they failed.
- People who "finally succeed" know that the most important moment is what they do after their failure.
- People who "finally succeed" are the people who have mastered the art of "failing forward".

This section on failing forward would be incomplete if I did not mention the name of the great scientist and inventor, Thomas Edison. He is credited with many great inventions, such as the light bulb, phonograph, movies, microphone, mimeograph, medical fluoroscope, etc. In all, he patented 1,093 inventions! However, very few people know that he also failed more than ten thousand times. And every time he failed, he used to say, "I have found one more method which will not work and that one day by failing again and again I will know all the methods which don't work — and will finally be left with the method that works."

This is called failing forward in the true sense. A typical person might have quit at the very first failure. That's why there are so many "average" people and so few Edisons.

Inspirational Success Stories of People

Here are inspirational success stories of a few people who succeeded despite of all odds — be it lack of money, education, power, physical handicaps, etc. Their stories will inspire you to succeed in whatever is your endeavor, including your struggle for financial independence.

Did you know that Sir Issac Newton, James Watt, Michelangelo, Picasso and even Albert Einstein had hardly gone to school or had difficulty in school studies but yet went on to become some of the biggest scientists and inventors?

Are you aware of the stories of people like Gillette, Henry Ford, Abraham Lincoln, Mustapha Kemal, Reza Khan, etc. who were very poor but became some of the richest and most famous personalities of their time?

Have you heard the stories of how people like Helen Keller, Annette Kellerman, Sandow, etc. became great personalities despite their handicaps?

As you know, Benjamin Bell invented the telephone but are you aware that his wife and child were deaf and dumb?

Then there is the story of Christopher Columbus who discovered America and was perhaps the greatest story of courage, patience, persistence, never say die attitude and intense belief in his own self. He lost everything, waited for decades but was finally able to obtain finance and discover America. Then there is story of a Polish girl who wanted to be a scientist but was so poor that she used to live in a garret with no windows, no gas, no electricity and no heat. She could afford only two sacks of coal for the whole winter. She could afford so little food that she often fainted from starvation! She was Madame Curie, one of the greatest women scientists the world has known and the only one to get a Nobel Prize for both physics and chemistry! My friend, there are so many stories of great people that a full book can be written on it. Just ponder, if these great personalities could succeed in spite of insurmountable difficulties and handicaps, then what is your excuse for not succeeding?

What Is Holding You Back?

Nothing in this world has the power to hold you back except you yourself.

Yes, I repeat that it is you and only you who are holding yourself back. I have given examples of great people who surmounted tremendous difficulties, whether related to money, education, physical body or something else, and finally succeeded. These people learnt the success formulas described in this chapter and applied them.

They might have failed initially but they learned to fail forward to "finally succeed". And that is what counts in life and also in the financial world. So the next time you think that something is holding you back, then think of these people who did such great things while facing seemingly insurmountable difficulties. You might then realize that your condition might actually be many times better than theirs was. And when you apply the ten commandments taught in this book with such an attitude and frame of mind, nobody can stop you from achieving financial freedom — not even you yourself.

Winners *versus* Losers

I list below certain traits and attributes found in winners and losers in similar situations:

- Winners are always a part of the answer while a loser is always a part of the problem.
- Winners always take personal responsibility for their actions while a loser always blames others when things don't work out.
- Winners look for answers in any problem while a loser searches for problems in every answer.
- Winners make commitments while losers make false promises.
- Winners are a part of the team while losers are apart from the team.
- Winners make things happen while losers let things happen.

- Winners plan to win while losers don't have any plan and, thus, in effect, plan to lose.
- Winners see the future potential while losers see the past problems.
- Winners always have a program while a loser always has an excuse.

This list of mental attitude and distinction between a winner and loser can go on. The idea of mentioning some of them is to open up your mind to recognize them so that you can assess which side of the coin you want to be on — the winning one or the losing one. I am sure you want to be on the winning side and once you are there — winning with your money will be pretty easy and automatic for you.

Steps to Become a Winner

1. Always keep questioning and you will get the answers.
2. Always have a positive mental attitude.
3. Always be humble and always be a seeker.
4. Build positive winning qualities like patience, perseverance, never-say-die spirit, self-esteem, self-respect, etc.
5. Stay away from negative influences.
6. Desire the right things and then have faith that you will get them.
7. Recognize your strengths and weaknesses — then try to consolidate your strengths and minimize your weaknesses.
8. Don't just do the things which you like but also like the things which have to be done. Doing the difficult things that you've never done awakens the talents you never knew you had.
9. Develop a continuous learning habit. Be a student of whatever you are engaged in — whether it be dealing with money, investments, your profession, or anything else.
10. Focus on achieving the goal, but at the same time enjoy the journey as well.

11. Above all, believe in yourself. If you don't believe in yourself, then how can you expect others to believe in you? Therefore, have a positive belief in yourself and your whole world will change for the better.

Conclusion

To double your net worth, double your self-worth because you will never exceed the height of your self-image. Train yourself to like the things that need to be done while developing an attitude of gratitude and building positive self-esteem no matter however dire the circumstances. Once you touch your soul, your spirit will be lifted from the darkness of hell to the brightness of heaven — where you will find abundance of life and money. Doing the difficult things that you've never done awakens the talents you never knew you had. Understand that a problem is only a problem if you choose to view it as a problem; all problems in effect are opportunities in disguise. The more you worry about being applauded by others and making money, the less you'll focus on doing the great work that will generate applause and make you money. All great thinkers are initially condemned — and eventually respected. The fears you run away from actually run towards you — so never be fearful of fear. To have the rewards that very few have, do the things that very few people are willing to do. People need patience to build wealth slowly, each rupee at a time. Sustenance and long term wealth accumulation is a boring, mechanical process. Nothing fails like success because when you are at the top of your financial life, you often stop doing the very things which made you wealthy in the first place. The things that are hardest to do are often the things that are the best ones to do. Luck is where skill meets persistence. Success lies in a masterful consistency around a few fundamentals. Don't make the mistake of ever believing that we know more about what's in our best interests than the source that created us. Move in the direction of your fear using the winds of adversity to sail the ship of your life. Learn about money, its intricacies and functioning and as your knowledge about money and life grows, feel grateful that God has selected you as His instrument to pass on this knowledge forward. With this knowledge and attitude about money and life, you are certain to experience fortune well beyond your highest imagination.

—

Chapter 14

If You Can't Give, You Won't Be Able to Receive

THIS CHAPTER, ALONG WITH CHAPTER 13, ARE THE BEDROCK and foundation of this book. These two chapters highlight the most important principles not only of money but of life as well. Remember, that finally you are a human being and you have to perform everything within the rules of this world. Nature has made certain rules which you cannot ignore. And this chapter is about a rule made by nature which applies equally to money as well.

If You Can't Give, You Will Not Be Able to Receive

Why can't I receive if I am not able to give? This is a logical question. But sometimes logic fails in this world. There is a force and a power bigger and more powerful than all of us put together — God. This book is not a religious book but I have to touch on certain realities of life because finally we have to earn money and become financially independent within this world. We have to live and breathe in this world and there are certain facts which we cannot ignore. And the fact is that the commandments and rules of money are subordinate to the rules of nature. If we have to win the money game and become financially free then we have to operate within the rules of nature.

What do you do when you invest in a bond in order to get interest or in a share in order to get dividend? First, you write a cheque for buying that bond or share, as the case may be. Then you have to wait for a certain period before you receive the interest or dividend. Therefore, in order to earn money in the form of interest or dividend, you have to first invest money to buy the bond or share. In effect, you are first giving (investing capital in the bond or share) and then receiving (interest or dividend). Or, take the example of a student appearing for his final year engineering or medical examination. He / she has to work hard and put in a lot of effort in order to secure good marks. Therefore, effectively he or she is giving time in order to receive a degree. In writing this book, I am giving my time, knowledge and experience in order to receive money, fame and, above all, fulfilling my mission of educating people about money and the attainment of financial freedom. Trying to get something without first giving is as fruitless as trying to reap without having sown. Therefore, it is a cardinal principle of nature that you have to first give in order to receive. Giving can be in any form — money, time, energy, effort, love, respect, etc. To conclude, if you can't give, you will not be able to receive and that applies to money as well.

You Owe It Back

This book has dealt with all your dealings with money, including earning, protecting, budgeting, saving, spending, leveraging, investing, insuring it, etc. but have you ever reflected on the fact that the society, the place, the country, the Universe and the people with whom you live helped you in all your dealings with money. They helped you in earning, protecting, budgeting, saving, spending, leveraging, investing and insuring it. You have learnt and earned everything by working in society. Therefore, it is your utmost duty to give something back to it. The beauty of the whole exercise is that as you strive to improve the lives of others by giving back, your own life will be lifted to its highest dimensions.

Even If You Don't Willingly Give, It Will Be Taken From You

This is another law of nature. Nothing is permanent — everything is ever changing and evolving. You are also not permanent — one day you have to move ahead from this planet. But your money will not move with you. It will stay here. Therefore, even if you don't willingly give it when you are still alive in this world, it will be forcibly taken from you when you move on from here. Therefore, take corrective action with your money while you are still alive and before it becomes too late.

Our Mission on Earth

Robin Sharma wrote in his book *The Monk Who Sold His Ferrari* that "we are not human beings having a spiritual experience. We are spiritual beings having a human experience." This statement summarizes who and what we are.

However, there is one more question. Why are we here? I don't think that anyone will dispute the fact that we are transit passengers in the journey of life on this vast planet earth. Many a time irrespective of whether you have money or not, you feel an emptiness within your heart. You may be financially well-off, rich, wealthy and completely financial independent, but you will still find some incompleteness deep within yourself. That is because you have not realized your mission on earth. So what can be your mission on earth. Each one of us has three main missions on earth:

1. Your own growth.
2. Growth of other fellow beings.
3. Proper utilization of your individual gifts and talents.

1. Your Own Growth

This is everyone's the first mission on earth. Unless you yourself grow in mind, body and spirit, how are you going to help anyone else? If you can't help yourself, then you probably can't help anybody else in this world. That is the basic principle of nature. Therefore, your first aim should be your own growth — without which you cannot hope to progress in this world — including monetarily. And remember that self-improvement has to be undertaken for right reasons and not for any ulterior or selfish motives. Select goodness for the sake of goodness itself. So, make your own true growth your first priority.

2. Growth of Other Fellow Beings

This is your second mission on earth. You have to be a selfless worker. True contentment comes from selfless service. I am writing this book to help you become financially free. The book might become a success but if my motive is simply to earn money, then I would never be truly content and happy because I would have failed in my duty towards my fellow beings. No man can get to the top without carrying others along with him. Also remember that you cannot promote yourself on another man's mistakes and weaknesses. Making other people grow through selfless service should be your second priority.

3. Proper Utilization of Your Individual Gifts and Talents

This is your third mission on earth. God has given each one of us some special gift and talent. Have you ever thought why someone is good at singing, some others at sports, and yet others in painting, writing, gardening, cooking, leadership, etc. Each one of us has some unique quality which has to be recognized and then used for the common good. In my case, it's my duty to use my gift for writing along with my knowledge to help others achieve financial freedom. Writing this book is a humble attempt from my side to fulfill my mission.

Don't Feel Great, Be Grateful

Always remember that excessive pride has been the downfall of many human beings — materially and spiritually. Therefore, never feel proud of anything, whether it be your intelligence, knowledge, talent, good looks, money or anything else. Pride will cloud your judgment and make you take wrong decisions. If you have too much pride, you will think that you are always right and not listen to others — even when they are genuinely giving you the right advice.

Whenever you accomplish something and are successful, be thankful that you have been used as an instrument of God for some higher purpose. Don't let success run riot in your mind. Each time your ego gives you a sense of invincibility, remind yourself that you are a mere human being and your life can change in a second. Albert Einstein once observed, "More the knowledge, the lesser the ego, lesser the knowledge, the more the ego." Also, always have faith in yourself because if there is anybody who is holding you back in this world, it is only one person. To find out who he / she is, just stand in front of the mirror and look into it and you will find that person. At the same time, also have faith in a higher power — his methods and thought process might not match with yours but many times we make the mistake of believing that we know more about what's in our best interest than the source that created us. So, never feel great; instead, always be grateful.

So Poor That Their Only Possession is Money

Some people live in a fool's world. They may have a lot of money and intelligence but they don't know their true worth. They have a lot of money but no true friends or companions. Such people have a lot of flatterers and false friends who flock to them only for their money; they are not true friends. Beware of the man who goes out of his way to pay you compliments which you know you don't deserve, for he is on the hunt for something you may not wish to part with. Such people are always lonely and are not able to trust anybody. They may be monetarily very rich but their mind is never content. Their ego and jealousy create more wants which, when satisfied, are replaced by further desires. Instead, be calm, humble and follow the right path. If you want to be truly rich and wealthy, then first learn to be content. No doubt, it's your right to earn money and reach the pinnacle of success. This book encourages you to become financially free but learn to be content before earning money. Then look for your higher spiritual mission. And when money finally comes to you, it will make you rich and happy. Otherwise you will become one of those poor people whose only possession is money.

Don't Just Give a Fish, Teach Fishing

There is a saying that if you give fish to somebody then his stomach is filled for one day. However, if you teach somebody fishing then his stomach is full for the whole life. Therefore, don't just give money to a needy person. If possible, teach the needy person something which will help him earn for his whole life. For example, by writing this book it's my sincere endeavor to teach the readers about money and its peculiarities so that they can achieve financial freedom. I am not giving anybody any hard cash; that will not solve my purpose of making you financially independent. In fact, it will actually make you more dependent. Whenever a money problem will arise, you will expect somebody else to come and bail you out. That is precisely what is currently happening the world over. Individuals, companies and even countries are looking for bail-outs. Money and bailouts will neither make them nor their people financially independent. Money comes and goes. If a person does not know how to earn, protect, budget, save, spend, leverage, invest or insure it, his money problem will never be solved. Therefore, instead of giving someone a fish to eat, teach him fishing. That will set him on the road to financial freedom.

Succession Planning

One another area where you need to look into is succession planning. I don't think anyone wants people to fight over the wealth they accumulated throughout their life with such hard work and dedication. When you are there in this world, you should be financially free. Similarly, when you depart from this world, your wealth should be able to serve the same purpose which it did when you were alive. Timely and proper succession planning during your life time is the way to ensure smooth, effortless and easy flow of your wealth once you leave this world. Remember, your money has to be financially independent, even when you are not around.

It's Cool to Give Back

Today many large industrialists and wealthy people are doing great charity work in different fields, including education, medical, caring for the aged, etc. Many of these people are those who have understood the ten commandments and the rules of money and have earned wealth during their own lives. By knowing the ultimate rule of "giving back" they have demonstrated that they have achieved financial freedom in the true sense. When you are rich but do not donate or do charity, then you would not be looked up to. You will be resented by the society; maybe you might lose good business deals and opportunities because of that. By giving back, you would earn laurels from employees, customers, shareholders, government and people at large. It will expand new horizons of business for you. Simply put, it is cool to give back.

What Will You Permanently Take With You?

Although you may have worked hard throughout your life earning and preserving your wealth but that is not the thing which you will take with you when you finally move on from this world. Money is certainly not a permanent thing — that's why it is called currency, i.e. it is just like electric current which moves from one point to another, from one house to another. Yes, it's very important to achieve financial freedom in you lifetime but never forget the fact that money is not permanent and you won't be able to take it with you. The only thing which you would be able to take with you would be your conscience. So, earn money, reach the pinnacle of success, attain financial independence but always aim for a clean conscience. One way of keeping your conscience clean is to ensure that your money reaches the right place after you are gone from this world. You don't want other people to quarrel over your wealth once you are no more. Therefore, do proper succession planning and do charity to the right institutions and organizations.

Afterword

I FEEL VERY PAINED AT SEEING HOW PEOPLE DEAL WITH MONEY. I am pained when I see how poor people try to make both ends meet on a day-to-day basis. I also feel greatly pained when I see middle class people working ever harder, struggling ever more, while paying huge amounts in taxes and interest, even as their money is constantly eroded by inflation and finally ending up in bigger and bigger debt. I feel equally pained when I see the rich become ever richer at the expense of the poor and the middle class. I believe that each and every one of us has the right of fulfilling our dreams, a right to education, a right to proper medical facilities, a right to a peaceful retirement — and a right to be rich and wealthy and leave our wealth for future generations and charity.

People believe that their problem is lack of money and that having lots of it will solve their financial problems. In fact, money is not the problem; the problem is lack of knowledge about money. As highlighted throughout the book, it is how you deal with money at the time of earning, protecting, budgeting, saving, spending, leveraging, investing and insuring it which determines whether money becomes a solution or a problem for you. There is no point in envying the rich. They have learnt the rules of money and applied them to their benefit. You can also do the same. As highlighted throughout the book, the one thing which is available in abundance in this world and can be increased at free will is money. Now, if money is available in such abundance, then why should it elude you. It is your right to rich, wealthy and happy. These are the thoughts which inspired me make it my personal mission to educate people on money and its peculiarities.

Personal Spiritual Mission

I said to myself that God has given me a beautiful chance of doing something wonderful — to educate people about this peculiar thing called money, to help change and refine their thinking about money and help everyone achieve financial freedom. I know that it is a very difficult task to change somebody's thinking — more so about money — but I believe that it is possible. Change is hardest at the beginning, messiest in the middle, and best at the end. With this mission in mind and with my limited knowledge about money, I embarked on the beautiful journey of money education. Money is nothing but an illusion — it comes, it goes, and it comes again. The more you run after it, the more it will elude you. So you have to reach a higher plane of understanding about money and its peculiar characteristics.

One of the things which is repeatedly tested on earth is faith — in God, parents, children, brother, sister, teacher, guru, boss, friend, etc. For example, if you ask for proof of God's existence, you will never get it; but if you sincerely believe in Him, then his existence will be made felt to you in various ways. Similarly, if you ask me for proof of whether this book will be able to solve your money problems — I regret that I am unable to give you any such proof. But if you logically, confidently and diligently follow the ten commandments and the principles of money given in this book, I am confident that your money problems will be solved and you will be transformed to a higher financial level on a permanent basis.

For me, it is my personal spiritual mission to help each and every individual in this world to achieve financial independence. That is the primary reason for writing this book. I say primary because the secondary reason is, of course, money. It will be wrong on my part if I said that I don't hope to earn money by writing this book. Earning money from writing the book is one of the reasons but that is the secondary reason — the primary being to make you achieve financial independence. If my book becomes a success then my primary personal spiritual mission of helping you achieve financial freedom was honest and correct. On the other hand, if my book is not successful then maybe I was not honest in my mission and that would be a soul searching learning experience for me.

All the Best

You have now learnt that both lack of money and excess money can be a problem if not backed and competently supported by financial and money knowledge. You must have also realized that money knowledge is not the typical textbook knowledge imparted in school. It is something which you have to learn afresh and then apply to your day-to-day dealings with money. You are now acquainted with the ten financial commandments which deal with all the aspects of money and personal finance including earning, protecting, budgeting, saving, spending, leveraging, investing, insuring, etc. They provide you with a full perspective and action plan for sustainable long term wealth creation and wealth preservation— systematic plan on how to protect, preserve and grow your wealth so that you don't just become rich but stay wealthy throughout your life and then leave it for the next generation and for charity.

Finally, in your path to achieving financial freedom, you will face many obstacles, criticisms, failures, mistakes. Don't fear them or run away from them. Instead, face your fears fearlessly and the fears will run away from you. And when you become successful and reach the top, remember that nothing fails like success. When you are at the top, it's so easy to stop doing the very things that brought you there. So adhere to the ten financial commandments and the rules of money throughout your life. That will ensure that you not only become financially free but always remain financially free. All the best!

—

Glossary for the Financially Free

Asset Allocation: The apportionment of your investment corpus to different asset classes, such as equities, bonds, real estate, commodities, art, currencies, etc.

Asset Income: The return from your assets. It is not the "return *on* your assets" but "return *from* your assets" — the emphasis is on the words on and from. The return from investments is a result of the asset itself, either partly or fully, being liquidated and sold.

Bad Capital Asset: Any thing which is classified on your asset side of the balance sheet but which actually takes away money from your pocket. Examples would include a luxury car, vacation home, etc.

Bad Capital Expenditure: Money spent on liabilities which you believe to be assets, like your self occupied house property.

Bigness Bias: Not knowing the power of small things compounding to large things over a period of time.

Buyer's Remorse: Regret at having spent money on buying things which you didn't require but got tempted into only because there was a discount available or some special-deal available.

Capital Expenditure: Any expenditure whose benefit extends for more than one year, e.g. car, furniture, etc.

Cash Fallacy: The mistake of dealing differently with money when using cash and when using credit card, cheque, etc.

Cash Flow Positive: A stage when your income from investment assets is more than the interest on your borrowings thus helping you create net positive cash flow after tax.

Common Financial Mistakes: Money mistakes which we commit at the time of earning, protecting, budgeting, saving, spending, leveraging, investing and insuring.

Debt Trap: A situation where your debt has grown to such proportions as compared to your current income and repayment capacity that you are not able to repay the debt either through your current income and / or through additional borrowings.

Decision Paralysis: The inability to take decision at the time of protecting, budgeting, saving, spending, investing, insuring or in any other dealings with money.

Earned Income: The income for which you work full time, like salary, professional income, etc. If the bulk of your time and energy are being consumed in earning a particular income, then it will come under this category.

Endowment Effect: Overvaluing what belongs to you relative to the value you would place on the same possession if it belonged to someone else.

Equity Returns: Returns from equities come from the initial dividend yield, growth in earning, and the change in valuation during your holding period.

Financial Freedom: A stage where your investment assets pay for your wasteful expenses and luxury expenditure. Simply put, the period when your guaranteed, passive and portfolio incomes from your investment assets pays for all your expenses including unnecessary revenue expenditure as well as the wasteful / bad and good capital asset.

Financial insurance: Kinds of insurance which make you free to concentrate on achieving financial independence. Financial insurance would include insurance against those catastrophic events —

whether real, physical, psychological, emotional or perceptional — which either don't allow money to come into your pocket or take away money from your pocket.

Good and Bad Money: In simple terms, the one which appreciates in value and / or produces income / cash flow is good money while the one which does not produce any income / cash flow and is subject to constant depreciation and loss in value is bad money.

Gruesome Capital Expenditure: Money spent on liabilities which you mistakenly believe to be assets. Not only do you lose money at the time of purchasing them but also end up into recurring expenses in the form of tax, maintenance, etc. Examples: vacation home, car. Simply put, money spent on buying luxury capital asset.

Guaranteed Income: Income where your investment assets work for you and for which you get a guaranteed income. This is the income which a lender to a business receives.

Income Earning Vehicle: The type of legal entity you earn your income from — individual or institutional (corporate / LLP).

Insurance: Insurance is either getting everything, or nothing, for something. Therefore, don't expect something in return for your money except the protection which insurance provides you with. Also, never combine investments with insurance. Don't forget that insurance is always bad investment and that investment should not provide you with insurance.

Investment Asset: An asset which either yields income and / or has the potential to yield capital gains which you are in a position to book within a reasonable time and at a realistic price.

Legal Financial Predators: People who legally take away money from your pocket, such as the government in the form of taxes, bankers in the form of interest, brokers in the form of commissions, etc.

Leverage: The power of multiplication: whatever you may take — money, time, effort, etc. — it's just the multiplication of it.

Loss Avoidance: Avoiding losses when they don't need to be avoided.

Market Related Investment: An investment whose price changes based on market fluctuations would be called market related investments.

Mental Accounting: Treating money differently depending on the source from which it has been received.

Negative Leverage: Debt which reduces your wealth by taking money away from your pocket. Simply put, a debt used to finance a liability mistakenly though believing to be an asset.

Non-Market Related investment: An investment whose price is not determined by market forces.

Passive Income: Income from an investment asset but where there is no guarantee or certainty either of realizing the return or of the amount of realization. For example, the income which an owner of a business receives.

Portfolio Income: Money derived from disposing of an investment asset.

Positive Leverage: Debt which multiplies your money by putting money into your pocket.

Price Fixation: A preconceived mental block to a certain price at the time of buying or selling.

Prospect Theory: A theory which explains why people behave differently when dealing with profits and losses.

Revenue Expenditure: Any expenditure whose benefit ends within a period of 12 months, e.g. utility bills, telephone bills, car maintenance, etc.

Running Income: Current income which an investment produces during its life.

Selective Thinking: Blocking your mind and not allowing all relevant information to flow into it for taking a correct decision.

Speculative Item: An investment which is able to produce only asset income. In other words, any investment which is not capable of producing running income would be termed as a speculative item.

Stages of Dealing with Money: You deal with money at different stages — earning, protecting, budgeting, saving, spending, leveraging, investing and insuring. The key to achieving financial freedom is to learn how to deal with it at the various stages.

Sunk Cost Fallacy: Throwing good money after bad money.

Surplus Budget: An excess of your income over expenses which you put aside for your own self.

Tax Insurance: The simplest way of taking tax insurance is to legally convert all your expenses into "pre tax expenses" and your taxable savings into "tax free investments".

Power of Positive Leverage: The stage of net positive cash flow after tax. Once you reach this stage, you start making "money for nothing".

Wasteful Revenue Expenditure (Expenses): Money spent on those items which you don't require and the benefits of which die out within one year, e.g., costly foreign vacations.

Wealth Effect Trap: Spending money which you don't actually have but imagine you do just on the basis of an increase — or a perceived increase — in the price of an asset which you own. Always recognize the difference between real and perceived wealth and never fall a victim to the wealth effect trap.

Course on the Journey Towards Achieving Financial Independence

I believe each and every one of us want, should and have a right to achieve financial independence in their lives. To cater to this growing need for people's financial freedom, I have designed a Course for those people who want to achieve financial independence. For achieving financial freedom expert knowledge on equities, bonds, commodities, real estate, currencies, etc. is not required. For achieving financial independence lot of hard work and becoming a "slave of money" is not warranted for. For achieving financial freedom, the understanding about money, its unique peculiarities and its functioning is required. The only thing which is available in abundant in this world is money but we see people suffering and fighting for the only thing which is available in abundant. Confused? Take the childhood example of you playing cricket or football. Now, when your ball lost — you must be worried from where will you get the money to buy the ball. However, kindly note that, ball is made up of rubber and leather, both of which, one a synthetic material while the other a natural material are available in limited quantity but the money from which we buy them is available in abundance — it is available at the free will of the Governments as they just keep printing currency as fast as their printing machines can work. Remember what is the use if we had all the paper money in the world but not the real material to manufacture it. Do you get what point I want to drive home?

What do you think — is money a problem or solution? If you don't have the answer to it then read on. If you believe that "money is the problem" or "money is the solution" then I am afraid that you are a "prisoner of money". Have you ever imagined of setting yourself on the incredible journey of your freedom from your current position as a "prisoner of money" to the attainment of "financial independence". If not, then you urgently need to. Before that, I would like to clear one misconception which might have taken roots deep inside your mind — that money will solve your problems. I regret to state that money cannot and will never be able to solve your problems. It is not money which is a problem — it is lack of knowledge about money and its functioning which is your real problem. If you are poor and think that getting too much money suddenly like winning a lottery is going to solve your problem — then you are grossly mistaken. In fact that will put you into deeper problem if you don't have knowledge about money as you will be fanatically chased by all kinds of legal and other financial predators. Therefore, both lack of and too much money can be a problem if not backed by knowledge about money. You require a course which will teach you on how to earn money from the most efficient source and then how to "handle the problem of too much money" — protecting, budgeting, saving, spending, leveraging, investing and insuring, explaining the different money mistakes which you might be susceptible to make and clearing all your doubts and misconceptions about money and wealth. In short, everybody requires a course on financial wisdom which will solve all their misconceptions about money and not only make them rich but help them stay wealthy throughout by achieving financial independence.

Are you interested in getting acquainted with:

- The best source of *Earning* Income.
- How to *Protect* it from the Financial Predators.
- How to pay yourself first via *Budget* Surplus.
- Acknowledging that *Saving* is not investing and learning to save pending Asset Allocation.
- Learning how to *Spend* to earn and save at the time of spending.
- Recognizing the difference between good and bad debt and to know how to unleash the power of *Positive Leverage.*
- Know how to *Invest* for proper asset allocation.
- Recognize the importance of *Financial Insurance.*

Hence you enroll for the financial freedom course because you want to know about money as you were never knowing before. You enroll for the financial freedom course because you want to permanently solve your money problems by achieving financial independence.

Do you want to be led on the correct financial path and open a completely new gateway in the way you think about money and all other things connected to money like protecting, budgeting, saving, spending, leveraging, investing, insuring, etc. Do you want a friend and guide who will solve your problem of lack of knowledge about money and then take you on the unbelievable journey towards your financial independence. Do you want to permanently free yourself from the problem of money?

You require a course which will free from the shackles of money problem — you require to learn the "10 Commandments for Financial Freedom". Anybody interested in learning the "10 Commandments for Financial Freedom" and permanently solving their money problem may contact me at the below mentioned email address.

Also, anybody interested in increasing his knowledge, understanding, acceptability, acquaintance, familiarity — in short mastering any of the topical subjects relating to money like equities, fixed income, mutual funds, personal finance, protecting, budgeting, leveraging and the likes then individual series of common sense articles have been developed for them. If this interests you then kindly contact me at the below mentioned email address.

I wish you all the very best on embarking on this new beginning of your money journey and great luck for achieving financial independence.

For further details contact me at: mehrabirani10@gmail.com

Visit my website: www.mehrabirani.com

Read my Blog: www.intelligentmoney.blogspot.com

Financial Freedom Game

I have developed a new novel idea — Financial Freedom Game. This will be unique set of games which will aim at imparting financial freedom to the players in the form of a real game based on my 10 Financial Commandments. There will be different games for different levels of people — basic, intermediate and expert as well as a game for the children. It will be a unique game which will first time be available in the world. The game would be available in multiple players as well as a single player format. So, there will be different sets of games. The games may vary from a very simple version wherein the individual just scrolls the board and sees how right financial decision makes him achieve financial freedom and how wrong decisions financially break him to complex ones where individuals will be put in real life situations and at every point will have to take certain financial decisions like whether to invest more money on his higher studies or business, whether to budget extra money for future or buy a car, whether to use limited available fund for important house repairs or fund a costly foreign vacation, whether to take working capital loan to expand his business or to take mortgage loan to buy a bigger luxury house, whether to invest in shares or bonds or gold, whether to hoard gold or no, whether to take positive leverage and expand business or just stay small and content, how to create positive cash flow via leverage, whether to opt for financial insurance, how to avoid the common financial mistakes, how to do proper asset allocation, etc. The game will involve important financial decisions at all points of dealing with money including at the time of earning, protecting, budgeting, saving, spending, leveraging, investing and insuring. The game will also teach the rules of money. The game will teach the whole gamut of an individual's dealing with finance, money and investments with an aim to make him financially independent. It will be a highly intelligent game wherein the player's decision at every point will ensure whether he achieves financial independence or keeps struggling with money throughout.

So you decide whether you want to keep struggling for money throughout your life or play the Financial Freedom Game and become a master of your own money. Play the most financially savvy game to achieve financial independence.

For further details contact me at: mehrabirani10@gmail.com

Visit my website: www.mehrabirani.com

Read my Blog: www.intelligentmoney.blogspot.com